THAI IMAGES
THE CULTURE OF THE PUBLIC WORLD

Niels Mulder

SILKWORM BOOKS

Some other books by Niels Mulder

Inside Thai Society: Interpretations of Everyday Life
Inside Southeast Asia: Religion. Everyday Life. Cultural Change
Inside Indonesian Society: Cultural Change in Java
Filipino Images: The Cultural Construction of the Public World

First published in 1997, reprinted in 1999 by
Silkworm Books
Suriwong Book Centre Building, 54/1 Sridonchai Road, Chiang Mai 50100, Thailand.
E-mail: silkworm@pobox.com

Cover design by T. Jittidejarak
Cover photograph copyright © 1995 by Feature Magazine
Set in 10 pt. Garamond

Printed by O.S. Printing House, Bangkok.

CONTENTS

PREFACE

Towards the end of June 1965, I arrived in Thailand. Two people met me at the airport. One was a youthful representative of the Department of Education, my sponsor. The other fellow I had met as a student in Saarbrücken. The first proposed to bring me to a hotel near the ministry, and that I would present myself there the next day. The second took me home, and gave me my first taste of Bangkok. He lived dangerously, at least as long as he was behind the wheel of his car. At the ministry they paid me part of my scholarship, arranged for my stay in a student hostel, and presented me to the Dean of the Faculty of Letters of Chulalongkorn University. There I was to receive tuition in Thai. Sulak S. introduced me to a young, bright monk at Wat Thongnaphakhun, named Uthai. With him I was to study more Thai and Buddhism. At night, I was soon fascinated by life in Sampeng, Bangkok's China town. There I met Reg. When she became my girl friend, and came to visit me at the hostel, I was kicked out. We settled in a two-storey wooden house in the Makkasan slum. It held many big spiders that preyed on the cockroaches. Reg found an old toothbrush, and cleaned her teeth. She was a poor, simple woman. She could not read nor write. I never learned so much from anybody else I met in my life. Her language, and that of the slum, my teachers at Chula refused to explain. *Maha:* Uthai did, and laughed a lot. To him and his secluded colleagues, I became a reporter from the city's underbelly. I learned polite Thai, the language of the street, how to address the monks, and more Bangkok Chinese than I was aware of. In Holland I had married. Those were confusing days. And entirely fascinating.

Well over thirty years later I still try to make sense of life in Thailand and I am still fascinated. I think I am less confused. Perhaps that is so, because now I do not enjoy the diversity of teachers I had during my first year. I have settled down, so to say, looking at a more limited range of things. These days I am concerned with the voices and opinions that arise from the urban middle classes. These are cacophonous and confusing enough. They constitute the substance of this book. I collected the materials for it in Chiangmai. I could have done so in Bangkok as well; with one exception, the written sources were all printed there. These days, however, I avoid the capital. If, during my first year, Bangkok made me happy and feel alive, it now depresses and tires me. Life there rapidly lost its charm during the early 1970s; in 1975 I chose the capital of the North.

Over the years, I made the acquaintance of many people there. The more people you know, the easier it is to get an introduction to somebody still unknown. Thus, whenever I am interested in a new subject, I can build up a network of relevant interlocutors quickly. *Acharya* Raynou Athamesara, with whom I share an interest in women's studies, was most helpful in opening the doors of the schools where I wanted to interview the teaching staff. She also introduced me to many interesting people at the Chiangmai Rajabhat Institute. Over the years, I got the run of the place at Chiangmai University. There, and at Payap University, I benefited by many interesting discussions, and probably learned most from the seminars with students and staff. Such oral exchanges are fast and efficient. Conversely, it has been difficult to solicit opinion by way of circulating the draft chapters of this book. It was Han ten Brummelhuis and Apinya Fuengfusakul who critically responded, and I enjoyed the keen reactions of *acharya* Sumalee Khumchaisakul's graduate students who even translated the text of the first chapter into Thai. However I gathered comments and opinion, I needed them, and I am grateful to all those who were so kind to abate my ignorance.

In Amsterdam, where I wrote this book, I profited from the editorial skill of Asker Mulder. For efficient publishing and the attractive format, I should acknowledge the efforts of Trasvin Jittidejarak.

Niels Mulder

Amsterdam, September 1996

NOTE ON SPELLING

Apart from names, that have been written according to established conventions or, if known, the preferences of their owners, Thai words have been rendered phonetically. Personally, I would have preferred to follow the system proposed by Mary Haas (1964) to the full. Yet, such a system is only accessible to the adepts and may cause confusion to most of the readership who will impose their pronunciation of English upon words spelled phonetically. The endlessly bedevilling problem is that English conventions are useless to transliterate Thai or to pronounce the phonetic system. I therefore propose the following compromise.

In Thai it is absolutely essential, like it is in English, to distinguish between long and short vowels. **O** is short, **oo** is long, much like in **rock** and **mote**. Writing **oo** for the long **o** entails the risk the reader will sound the **oo** of **soon**, so I decided to indicate vowel length by adding **:** to the short vowel: **o** is short, **o:** is long. The vowel **ᴬ**, phonetically **y:**, has been written as **ü:**; the ꞓ as **ô:**; the ꞟ- as **ae:**; the ꞟ-ꞓ as **oe:** (silent **e**). The **i** after a vowel is assimilated to the vowel concerned, such as in **Thai**. **Ua, üa,** and **ia** are diphthongs. Unfortunately, diacritical marks had to be omitted.

Thai distinguishes between plosive and aspirated consonants. English does not: all consonants are aspirated. To the French, all are plosive. So, in rendering Thai, **k** is plosive, **kh** aspirated. English does not have such a **k**; Thai does not have the soft one, the **g**. English shares with Thai the aspirated **c**, written **ch**. The plosive

c, therefore, stands for the sound **ty**; Thai does not have the soft **dy**, or the English **j**. Mind that Thai does not have the English **th**! The **h** in **Thai** stands for aspiration, and thus sounds like the **t** in **tea**.

Following the logic of the current spelling of **Ayutthaya**, I use **y** as the vowel substituting for the phonetic **j**. As syllable stops I avoid the **b**, **d** and **g**; only **p**, **t** and **k** occur.

INTRODUCTION

This book offers a discovery tour of modern Thai culture. To this end, it firstly explores the national social studies curriculum. This uncovers the vein of widely shared knowledge that constitutes a very important part of national culture anywhere. What we are specifically interested in is finding out how people learn to think about the social world surrounding their private experience. It is not true that school simply teaches nationalism, or civics, or morals. What we want to discover are the hidden – and sometimes explicit – assumptions that underlie the construction of the social knowledge presented. They may tell us something about a characteristic way of imagining people use to rationalize their behaviour and to perceive events in society. Since the assumptions of social construction are usually not obvious, it is worthwhile to spend considerable attention on the formal content of the curriculum and the conceptual models it contains.

Most young Thais have gone through elementary school nowadays, and the knowledge transmitted there is truly national. If they go on to junior high – and soon that too will be part of compulsory formal education – a different type of thinking is introduced, and we should be aware of its presuppositions. Later, at senior high, the teaching is more theoretical, more academically oriented, at least, that is what it intends to be. On scrutiny, it turns out to be unsystematic, and often inspired by the same ideas that guided teaching at the primary level. The extensive exposition of

1

the school curriculum offers additional insights: into dominant ideology and, probably more importantly, into teaching methods and the atmosphere of the prevailing learning process. At all levels, it still appears that Thai students are trained to memorize more than to comprehend, at least as far as social studies go.

This is, needless to say, a considerable challenge for those who teach social science at the tertiary level. My interviews with lecturers at a variety of universities and colleges convinced me that a sound social scientific approach to the study of social life is the exception rather than the rule. To understand why this is the case, the early training of the social imagination in family and at school may be quite revealing. It is simply very difficult to take an impersonal and distantiated approach to things social, and there is nothing in Thai culture that stimulates such a manner of thinking. Social life is concrete, experiential, and can thus be measured and judged in moralistic terms.

In order to counter these perceptions, to expand the social imagination of its students, and to create distance from immediate experience, the Faculty of Humanities of Chiangmai University offers an introductory course in Thai Culture and Society. The *Reader* compiled for this course demonstrates that social imagination in Thailand these days is not just circumscribed by early socialization and school teaching. Many in the younger generation have freed themselves from 'dominant' paradigms, and exercise more incisive thinking. It must be conceded, though, that such conceptualization is not readily understood by the majority of the upper and middle classes. Their minds have almost all been captured by the prevailing moral models taught at school.

The actual state of understanding is probably best revealed by the press. The third subject to be treated at length, therefore, concerns the way newspapers comment on social and political affairs. As with the schoolbooks reviewed, I thought it important to convey the tone of the presentation of news. Besides, news is made, that is, selected. Certain events are considered worthy of reporting, others are avoided – because of self-censorship, or simply because they are not valued much in the urban context

2

where newspapers are written. It therefore makes sense to offer the reader a reasoned exploration of the ways in which news is presented before offering a literal selection of newspaper reporting and comment. Put together, these two approaches yield a vivid picture of urban preoccupations and predispositions.

These are also reflected by the fourth source of social commentary presented in this book. How do contemporary novelists depict their society? How do they diagnose its condition? What are the problems they see? The images they evoke are more powerful than those offered by the daily press, for the good reason that commentary in fiction can be more interpretative and reflected, that it may attempt to go deeper or, simply, that it is a condensation of what is happening all around us. It dissects everyday life, mocks and criticizes it.

The images we look at on our discovery tour depend on the point of view of the people who present them. Some are more conventional than others, such as those we see in the distorting mirror of the school or the National Identity Office. Yet it is these that set and contain much of the prevailing social imagination. Often people simply talk that way. They feel comfortable with time-hallowed truisms that obscure the less obvious, or less desirable 'objective' condition of society. Next to such conventional opinions, we find the more incisive analyses of certain academics; the critical reflections of literary authors; the points of view of activist NGOs. All of these also influence the exchanges going on in society, and frequently they surface in editoral columns. Since such thinking is less 'acceptable', it must be deemed as pioneering, as expanding the limits of the public discourse rather than saturating it. In this book we shall review this variety of images of the public world, and consider how they are brought together in the social discourse that animates it.

An anthropological approach

This book propounds an anthropological approach to the public world. This means that it contains an investigation of how Thai people – especially those of the urban middle classes – think, and learn to think, about life outside of their circles of private association in family, community, and patronage. In this wider society surrounding private life, people tend to be anonymous to each other, and they thus mind their own business, everybody pursuing his own interests. As a public world, such wider society is perhaps best represented by the modern city, or by the country as a whole. This public world is the domain of the state and the economy, and, modernly, of an active civil society.

The question that will be highlighted in this study is how people conceive of it. What is the discourse going on in society? What is the opinion filling the public world? How is it constructed? Interestingly, even though this type of questions is entirely anthropological, only a few anthropologists have concentrated on them. This may have to do with the fact that their discipline tends to focus on communal culture, and is not much concerned with society-in-the-abstract. The study of that vast realm was left to others, such as sociologists, political scientists, economists, geographers, students of law and public administration. Naturally, all of these have contributed to the cultural study of the public world, but since they usually concentrate on modern, 'developed' western society, their findings and theories tend to be circumscribed by what is considered conventional in their own fields of inquiry.

Frequently, they take an evolutionary view of social development, considering that other societies and states will follow the example of western society: urbanization, industrialization, citizens' emancipation, democratization, and so forth.[1] To win

---

[1]   This perspective is known as modernization theory. Since the arising of postmodern consciousness, this theory is hopelessly outmoded in western academic circles, but as soon as the same people look at developments in the

favour with the developed countries, all 'Third World' governments have to establish democracy; to respect human rights; to organize according to the formers' image. To an anthropologist, such uniformity sounds naive and most implausible. It is obvious that the evolution of societies in, say, Southeast Asia, is very different from the historical experiences of others. To understand what is going on there, we need to trace the course of their social and economic development. So, while it is true that there is a wholesale transplantation of ostentatiously western institutions to the countries of Southeast Asia, we can only understand how they function if we take the environment into account in which they have to operate.[2] The study of this localization warrants an approach that takes local peculiarities seriously: while we may be on our way to a 'global village', it still seems that the different houses and their inhabitants will be recognizable as such for a long time to come. Thank goodness.

The public world

The existence of a public world should not be taken for granted. In non-complex, communally organized societies, people distinguish between insiders, those who are known and belong, versus outsiders, irrelevant others with whom one does not share common space or good. The outside world - like nature – is a field of opportunity at best, the place where one may hunt for a prize, but where one does not carry responsibility. In other words, socially there is the 'private', common domain of familial and communal bonds that is felt to be 'ours' alongside similar domains

---

Third World, the paradigm goes unquestioned. Besides, the modernization perspective seems to have taken a firm hold on the minds of policy makers and technocrats in the 'developing' countries.

2   On my approach to Southeast Asia, see Niels Mulder, *Inside Southeast Asia: Religion. Everyday Life. Cultural Change*. Amsterdam: The Pepin Press, 1996 (second revised and expanded edition). Especially relevant to the problematics of localization are the chapters 1, 4 and 8.

that are 'theirs' (and none of our business); territorially, there is the space surrounding the communal area that is nobody's and everybody's land.

Another characteristic of such non-complex societies is the low degree of institutional articulation. Political, religious, and economic establishments have not specialized yet, and most people know their way around in a shared domain of knowledge. Of course, some of them know more about certain subjects: headmen will be more adept at negotiating; midwives share medical knowledge with herbal healers; some are learned in history and lore, and may be ritual specialists, too; others still are more talented than their neighbours in making implements, such as pots, weapons, or jewellery. So, while all this stands at the beginning of functional specialization, most people share in basic skills, and all of them need to farm, fish, breed, or trade for their survival. We may conceive of this shared world as the common domain of a community in which the public and private spheres have not yet differentiated. Sometimes, in the case of Southeast Asian peasant villages, the fact that people participated in all domains of life has been seen as 'village democracy', but this, I think, is as much of an imprecision as referring to the shared world of a village as the public domain. Democracy can best be understood as a specialized institution through which 'citizens' try to regulate the – modern – public world. The question thus becomes, how does such a world come into being?

Usually, the first function to differentiate on the way to greater social complexity, is government, giving rise to the institutions of state, such as kingship, politics, public administration and, frequently, religion, necessary as a means to lend authority to the other establishments. These various institutions develop their own spheres of knowledge that become the monopoly of the specialists who run them. In this process, a cleavage develops, namely, state versus ordinary population, the two-class situation of rulers versus ruled, of a monarch and his aristocracy dominating an 'homo-geneous' populace. With the state imposing its authority, the need for its legitimation arises, and so we see the development of institutional religion as one of the tools of statecraft. It provides sacral dimensions to kingship, the blessings of the gods, and publicly staged ceremonies commanding the awe of the ordinary mass of people. The importance of the grandiose displays of state or royal power gives rise to what has been called the 'theatre state' in which pomp serves the purpose of its perpetuation.[3] The spectacle is there for all to see, it is a public exhibit, but it is not of the public. The latter consists of mere mutes, their presence at best creating the right surroundings for the show.

The state needs its subjects as its economic base, although we often see that trade, monopolized or heavily taxed, is more important to its income. Rulers need the populace for military purposes too, although the higher echelons of their armies are recruited from the nobility. The higher ranks of the clergy also tend to be from the class of the aristocrats. For these various reasons, the state holds a great interest in the maintenance of the status quo and control of the population. When trade, or other sources of important surplus production, would fall into the hands of these commoners, the state may be challenged, and lose a part of its sway. That is why rulers are suspicious of free trade. A booming economy among the ordinary people may even give these the means to appropriate the power of the state.

If the development of the state gives rise to a class of rulers, it is the expansion of the economy that spawns the middle classes. When trade and manufacture, industry and services begin to flourish, we see the growth of towns and urban groups that occupy a new space between the state-owning class and the mass of peasants. Often, the members of these new classes desire emancipation from the power of the state; they want to share in it at the very least, or even be their own masters. Because of this latent possibility, we frequently note that the state finds it expedient to leave the new economic activities in the hands of foreigners or other outsiders (Jews; Chinese; Chettiars) who pose

---

[3] Geertz, Clifford, *Negara: The Theatre State in Nineteenth-century Bali*. Princeton: Princeton University Press, 1980.

no threat to its political monopoly. Be that as it may, certain middle classes – say, of highly educated professionals – develop so much cultural power that they can exert effective pressure for their own emancipation. As the vanguard of new, more timely ideas they breach the fortress of conservatism protecting the state and its simplistic two-class ideology. The economy-based middle class of businesspeople and modern producers may also outgrow their state-imposed isolation and seek to stand on centre stage. Altogether, we see how a growing economy propels the process of professional and economic differentiation, at the same time that the economy acquires an independent status of its own: 'if it is good for the economy, it is good for us'.

We can think of the public world as the sphere of society-in-the-abstract (*Gesellschaft*) that comprises the so-called independent subsystems of state and economy alongside civil society; all these have come into being in the process of differentiation and growing complexity. This world is in the main debated and given cultural shape by the critical and participating members of the middle classes whose discourse is essential to bring it to life. They create 'public opinion', which means, in practice, the openly expressed ideas of members of the educated urban middle classes. Professionals, civil servants, teachers, priests, writers, artists, labour leaders, businesspeople, politicians and military men compose the media, write novels and plays, and teach at schools, and so spread myth, history, and other common knowledge. They propagate ideologies, nationalism, self-images, religious ideas, and suchlike.

It may, therefore, be argued that middle classes are essential to the emergence of a modern public world: a thing that cannot exist in a two-class situation of rulers and ruled. A public world of the public arises in the course of societal evolution when state, economy, and civil society assume a kind of independence from aristocratic rulers, and from everyday experience. At the same time, society will also differentiate into classes, including those of the middle stratum. From that time on, it is the institutions spawned by the state, the economy, and civil society that substantiate the

8

public world and that are the subject matter of the discourse that fills it.

In this book we shall highlight the emerging culture of this public world, with which I particularly mean the opinions and debates that animate it. Such a public world is essentially a product of modernity. Its historical arising, the shape it adopts, and the debates going on, are specific though. 'Every national society (seen as a "site" of modernity) now creates its own ways of playing with modernity'. This excerpted quote from the introductory chapter by Appadurai and Breckenridge of *Consuming Modernity* [4] stresses that modernity is nobody's monopoly any longer, and they call for a loosening of the link between the word public and the history of civil society in Europe in describing what they call 'public culture'.

I am not quite sure whether we are talking about the same thing. Sometimes they substantiate the idea of public culture in a way that approximates what I have in mind when I talk about the culture of the public world. They describe it as a zone of cultural debate between domestic life and the projects of the nation-state; the influence of transnational culture flows, or globalization, on that zone is very apparent, although not overwhelming. Public culture is also described as the realm of knowledge, history, discourse, and distinctive debates about modernity. All this comes close enough to my culture of the public world, but what I do not see is why 'the projects of the nation-state', 'formal politics', and 'print capitalism' – after all, the precursor of the present media industry – should not necessarily be related to the 'zone of cultural debate'.

I think they are right in excluding a bourgeoisie and rational communication as specifically European elements that guided the considerations of Habermas in his *The Structural Transformations of the Public Sphere: An Inquiry into a Category of Bourgeois*

---

[4]   Appadurai, Arjun and Carol A. Breckenridge, 'Public Modernity in India'. In Breckenridge, Carol A. (ed), *Consuming Modernity. Public Culture in a South Asian World*. Minneapolis/London: University of Minnesota Press, 1995, pp. 1-20.

Society.[5] I also deem it felicitous to emphasize the diversity of public cultures arising, and that globalization does not mean homogenization, such as in the Frankfurter School's mass culture scenario. Yet, interestingly, the authors seem to subscribe to Habermas's idea that, in our time, the public merely consumes its culture, instead of critically participating in it. This is obvious from the contents of *Consuming Modernity*: sports, television, cinema, travel, radio, and museums.

In what follows, these specific carriers of messages – together with the advertising, fashion, lifestyle and recreation industries – will largely go unmentioned, not because they do not belong to the public world, or influence ideas circulating there, but because I choose to concentrate on debate and opinion making. It is precisely in the latter two that we cannot exclude 'the projects of the nation-state' such as, for instance, indoctrination through the national school system. The inputs from state and economy are very important in shaping the ongoing debate that fills the public world.

What we should be aware of at the outset is the peculiarity of the subject of our investigation. The culture that animates the Thai public world has specific origins; it only came into being in the twentieth century. We may note a few 'universals', such as its urban setting; the presence of middle classes; their desire for emancipation and power-sharing; and the importance of a developing economy. In the Thai case, global cultural flows, often carried home by students and travellers, have been very important all along. But whereas there is much that is cosmopolitan about contemporary Thai middle-class culture, it remains strongly influenced by older ideas, in the setting of which modernity has had to be accommodated. This will be very notable when we examine the debates going on in the public world, especially on the subjects of democracy, human rights, and the rule of law. We

---

[5]   Habermas, Jürgen, *The Structural Transformation of the Public Sphere: An Inquiry into a Category of Bourgeois Society.* Cambridge, Mass.: MIT Press, 1989 (German original 1962).

shall then be reminded of the foreign origin of such ideas, and the distortions they undergo in the process of their domestication in the Thai milieu. Be this as it may, in this study we are interested in tracing the origins of Thai middle classes, and the worlds of ideas they produce and in which they operate.

The Thai public world

If we begin by scrutinizing the evolution of the Thai public world in the illustrious city of Sukhothai, it is not because I subscribe to the popular periodization of Thai history. We would like to know about the earlier history of the Thai ancestors. To begin history with the description of a fully fledged kingdom, the ruins of which still attest to its power and cultural glory, is highly unsatisfactory. Yet, in view of what follows, it is convenient for the reader if we present our historical considerations more or less within the framework propagated at school. There, Thailand all of a sudden appears on the stage of history as a state.

Even a cursory look at the ruins of Sukhothai reveals the grandeur of a premodern royal polity centring on a city. The many temples – in Thai Buddhist and Khmer Brahmin style – demonstrate the link between royal power and religion. From what we know, it is clear that institutional religion was – as it still is – an instrument of statecraft, needed for blessing and legitimation. We may surmise that Sukhothai assumed the characteristics of a theatre state. Yet, its early power was such that there was more to it than self-aggrandizement through ritual and pomp. The early state – personified by the king – must have been rich. The monuments still certify this. Money was also needed for military campaigns that ranged in all directions, extending its sway over most of the territory we now know as Thailand. To have such income, more was needed than could be squeezed from the peasantry in produce and labour, and trade must have been a mainstay of the political economy. This can be testified, among others, by the finds of Sawankaloke pottery throughout most of Southeast Asia.

Next to trade, crafts and industry, religious studies flourished, and gave the realm the reputation of a centre of Buddhism. This did not necessarily affect the population at large who most likely maintained their atavistic, ancestor-centred religious practices. But to some of its members, Buddhist learning was available, especially if they moved to the towns. There, religious specialists thrived. It is fair to say that Sukhothai, among other centres, was a cradle of urban-based Thai civilization that focused on statecraft, with its adjuncts of Buddhism and Brahmanism; ceremonies and arts; and control over agricultural production and commercial communications. Seen from the point of the totality of its social formation, we may note that the state – and with it, institutional religion – had differentiated itself from the lifeworld of the ordinary denizens. It needed them for their produce, labour, and military levies, yet, the impingement of the state on the lives of its subject population was probably slight when compared to the later developments in Ayutthaya when the burden of servitude was as much as six months a year; when forest produce, next to rice, constituted the tax base; and when all but the king were excluded from overseas trade.

During the rise and prosperity of Ayutthaya, the ordinary people remained in their villages, surviving on a subsistence basis. The state flourished as an international centre of commerce where traders from all over East Asia, and later from Europe, found it profitable to transact. Many of the craftspeople living there were foreigners too, mostly of Chinese extraction. One could say that two economies coexisted: that of the peasantry, and that of the state. The owners of the state, that is, the king and nobility, jealously guarded their privileged status: imports and exports were their monopoly and, as long as they kept trade flowing, they fared well. In this situation, it is not appropriate to consider the economy to have differentiated from the lifeworld of the people or even from those who directed the state. On the one hand, we see a peasant economy, inclusive of a way of life, and on the other an economy that is part and parcel of statecraft. This situation changed dramatically when foreign pressure pried the Thai market open and brought an end to the royal monopolies.

In the second half of the nineteenth century, parts of the economy began to differentiate from peasant subsistence and the direct influence of the state. Yet, the peasants of the central plain, where rice was then cultivated for export purposes, hardly benefited by these developments. They remained under the thumb of aristocrats who profited from their labour, and grew prosperous. The industrial and trading activities surrounding the crop fell largely into Chinese hands, while western enterprises also acquired an important purchase on the commercial and extraction components of the economy. So, what we do not see emerging are a robust peasantry and a bourgeoisie. The first traces of a native Thai middle class need to be looked for elsewhere. It got its chance of arising when the combined threats of western imperial aggression and obstinate, unruly local grandees forced the king to reorganize the realm. In what is known as the administrative reforms of the last two decades of the century, the monarch succeeded in centralizing and professionalizing the government apparatus while overcoming most of the influence of the locally powerful. The implementation of a salaried bureaucracy and a standing army necessitated the modern schooling of those destined to staff them. This resulted in the sending abroad of young, promising commoners to seek the needed skills.

Their group – and the outlandish ideas they carried home – had grown influential enough to successfully challenge royal dominion and to demand a constitution. The coup of June 1932 brought these new people to the fore; influenced by Europe, where they had studied, their ideas were optimistic, ranging from humanism, socialism, and democracy, to enlightened socialist and fascist state guidance. The common point of all these is the belief that society is constructable, that it can be made a better, more civilized place. Among the new politicians, statist ideas predominated. If they thought about the ordinary people at all, these were to follow their well-intentioned plans, whether this concerned state-led agrarian reform, or as employees of the publicly owned companies that were to free the Thai economy from foreign domination. It is therefore fair to say that the new middle class was carried – like the previous dispensation – by the state, and its members thought accordingly which is, in a sense, a remarkable continuity with the earlier period. It stood in opposition to the foreign owners of the mainly commercial economy: European and American trading houses and, above all, local Chinese. Even the latter – although local – stood apart from Thai society still, and were not considered to constitute its middle class.

At the time of the putsch of 1932, other, equally optimistic modern ideas had begun to circulate. In that very year, Buddhadasa Bhikkhu, son of a Chinese immigrant, established the Suan Mokha forest retreat from where he would propagate his individual-centred interpretation of Buddhism for more than fifty years to come. He stated that persons can grow wise, and liberate themselves. Others were more impressed by the social conditioning of people, such as apparent from contemporary novels. Yet, Sri Burapha and Seni Sawwaphong – who would write their great social-critical works after World War II – saw a way out: to them it did not matter so much whether 'all men are born equal', but whether they would enjoy equal chances to better themselves. Consequently, it was the very hierarchical and compartmentalized structure of the Thai social edifice that raised their ire. Only when these structural barriers were dismantled, would the Thais and their society be able to develop to their full potential.

It is fair to consider this variety of early intellectuals of common descent as people who participated critically in the events of their days. To most, democracy, and having a constitution, were good things. Soon, though, they were faced by a long string of military potentates that stifled the further evolution of civil society, and many dissenters suffered for their ideas in jail and in exile. The fact that progressive ideas were produced all the time, in spite of repression, demonstrates their inexorability, although their spread was not great. They were stimulated by the advent of

14

'development', set in motion by the policies of Field Marshal Sarit Thanarat in the late 1950s. This meant the welcoming of foreign investors. A short while later, the big American friend became more visible because of his voracious appetite for 'commies', a taste which the Thai military shared. The Communist Party of Thailand started its armed resistance, and the brilliant Cit Phumisak became one of the first victims of the army's effort at repression. Irritating Americans displaying their manliness through Thai women; military arrogance; suppression of democracy; rising levels of awareness, all of these led to the events of October 1973 that forced the Tyrannical Trio into exile. For three years, Thailand became an open society like never before, engendering endless debates about its destined course. These stimulated the political cleavage between left and right to emerge.

The student generation that spearheaded these developments consisted of the younger members of the early middle classes. Their parents, on the average born in the 1920s, had lived through the momentous events of 1932 and into the periods of optimism, fascism, nationalism, then developmentalism. Many of them were civil servants, some were independent professionals, and many again were successful Chinese or their descendants who, by sending their progeny through Thai schools, were rapidly on their way to full assimilation in urban Thai society. As middle-class people, all of them needed more breathing room in order to open out. This aspiration was expressed by their student children. Basically, they were heir to the earlier spirit of optimism. They avidly read the works of Sri Burapha, Seni Sawwaphong, Buddhadasa Bhikkhu, Cit Phumisak, and other socially committed writers. Translations of Mao Tse Tung and fellow communist gurus flooded the market. Their generation would bring about a better, a more equitable society. What they did not know yet was that they were destined to be the last ones inspired by such idealism. In October 1976, many of them were forced underground and into the jungle. When they re-emerged some four years later, the new optimism centred on rapid economic growth, not on social reconstruction.

Since the very beginning of planned economic development, growth had been steady and significant. This, in turn, created novel professional and business opportunities, and the middle classes evolved in pace with the changing and expanding economy. A fine indicator of the social sea change going on is the rising demand for higher education. Throughout the 1960s, we see a rapid increase in the number of students enrolled at the tertiary level, rising from 15,000 early in the decade to 55,000 by 1970. From then on, growth becomes explosive, with almost 600,000 persons studying at college and university in the year 1990. To this we should add a much smaller, though very consequential elite group studying abroad, estimated at some 8,000 during the mid-1990s.

From steady economic expansion to the boom of the late 1980s and early 1990s, the economy has impelled Thai society into the future, leaving its 'old' moorings in a patrimonial 'bureaucratic polity' that lorded it over a mainly agricultural society behind. This comparatively recent past almost seems irrelevant, especially in the urban setting that has lost the cultural connexion with its rural hinterland. The new generation, being trained to staff the new economy – industry; services; tourism; transportation; construction – also seems to have lost its touch with a more high-minded past, if there ever was such a relationship. These people attained their majority in a period of consumer culture, growing up with television rather than with books. They are not interested in social reconstruction, but at best in the construction of condominiums, shopping malls, and urban transportation systems. They are not politicized such as the students of the early 1970s were. Cynical about politics, and motivated mainly to live up to their chosen lifestyles, they are far removed from being critically participating citizens; politically seen, they are kibitzers at best. Even if Black May brought them onto the streets in 1992, their protests were less programmatic than directed at military arrogance and the loss of democratic space.

The public world they live in looks more like a market dominated by business and commercial interests than like a civil society filled with the critical discourse of a committed public. Of course, public opinion plays its rather passive part; in general, it seems to be satisfied with being cynical regarding politics, and unable to influence the wheeling and dealing of the influentials. This need not be so. As we shall see, there is considerable stir in the field of opinion making (chapter 5), but on the whole society seems to be dragged along by the same dynamics of the economy that also appear to overwhelm the state. The openness of communicative globalization leaves some with the hung-over feeling of being lost in a stream of fleeting signals and symbols. They react by trying to get a grip on life again by joining moralistic, esoteric, or luck-enhancing sects that are a far cry from Buddhadasa Bhikkhu's optimistic rationalism. They appear apathetic when compared to the more activist-inclined exponents of civil society who pry into political-economic decision making ... but can the latter change anything?

It is not appropriate here to propose a scenario for the future. The last observations seem to indicate the point where – urban – Thai society has arrived in the late 1990s. Its middle classes send a variety of signals, some of which will be presented in the substantive chapters of this book. They will be reconsidered in the consolidating chapter and summarized in the conclusion.

Organization of the study

The first chapter traces how and what contemporary Thai school children are taught about wider society, that is, the public world beyond their early, essentially private familial-communal experiences. At school certain images of the individual, history and society are impressed upon their minds in a process of teaching that has sometimes been called 'legitimate symbolic violence'.[6] This is thought to be warranted because students need to be prepared to participate in wider social life. School texts serving this

---

[6] According to Bourdieu and Passeron, all pedagogic action aiming at the

purpose are therefore a very important part of the culture of the nation-state, reflective of the 'dominant mentality', at least as seen and interpreted by government and bureaucracy. In order to convey their gist as accurately as possible, it has been attempted – as it has in the presentation of all the texts analysed in this book – to capture their tone and atmosphere too.

The chapter begins by introducing the highly original elementary social studies curriculum. Subsequently, the main texts currently in use are scrutinized in order to identify the principles of social construction and ethics; these imply a particular view of the individual. The ensuing image of society is reinforced by projecting it into history. As a consequence, social studies present a national ideology that integrates history, society and people. These manipulations result in certain images of history and society that are analysed in depth, then commented upon. The chapter can also be read as a critique of Thai educational practice.

A similar procedure is followed in the second chapter, that reviews and analyses the images of history and society such as presented at junior high school. The tone that is set in the early chapters of the ministerial series in use, is very different from what the students have learnt during their earlier school experiences. By declaring the economy to be the basic ingredient of social life, changes in the latter are explained by the dynamics of the former. This gives good occasion to dwell at length on the merits and negative consequences of economy-driven social change, and the extensive treatment of present-day social problems lends some interesting insights, not only in Thai societal developments, but also in the principles of social construction. If, at primary school, society, nation and country were presented as a moral construct, we shall note that this cultural-ethical scheme is smuggled in again

---

reproduction of culture may be called legitimate symbolic violence. The force of this violence derives from the prevailing relationships of power that the pedagogic action conceals. Bourdieu, P. and J. C. Passeron, *Reproduction in Education, Society and Culture*. London, etc.: Sage Publications, 1977, pp. 13-5, 24-5.

– in spite of the proclaimed primacy of the economy – until it all but pervades the interpretation. Needless to observe that the presentation of history, much like it was the case in grade school, strongly reinforces the moralistic – and hence, somewhat timeless – presentation.

There is more to the frozen image of history than pervasive moralism. The way it is presented has much to do with a persistent projection of the present into the past that serves the current requirements of the state and its national ideology. The periodization that constrains it, as well as the repetitious inventories of the mandatory ministerial format, lend the image of history a certain woodenness, and deny the view of history as a continuous unfolding that should lead to an understanding of the present.

Besides their discussion of social problems, and the moralistic mode in which they do this, the struggle of the authors to explain what democracy is all about makes for very interesting reading. How to explain the idea of equality in the Thai setting? How to explain human rights? After all, the latter are guaranteed in the latest Constitution, but to bring them to life, to make them imaginable, is no sinecure in the prevailing social context. Because the authors do not consider the Thai way of life and the ideas that inform it, their elaborations about 'the democratic system of government headed by the king' go astray. They are much clearer in explaining that Thai democratic subjectship means the execution of tasks and duties. In other words, one of the deeper interests of the chapter is with all that remains unsaid, but is yet very recognizable.

Some relief is offered though when, in the third year, the Thai practice of democracy is factually described. Again, cultural setting is neglected, but the critique of vote-buying, personalism, abuse of elected office and suchlike, is refreshing. Another interesting aspect of the school texts discussed is their very simplistic approach to religion in general and Buddhism in particular. Values, ethics, laws, and religion itself are reified: they become causes of happiness and peace, of prosperity and well-being.

The third chapter, about the senior high school social studies curriculum, has been subtitled 'impairing sound reasoning'. This is because of the so-called conceptual approach in which things social are presented; it merely leads to confusion. This needs some explanation, and therefore considerable attention is given to the ways in which concepts are explained. Although not concerned with Thai history any longer, senior high school does impart a generous portion of knowledge about Thai society, but again, it is more concerned with truisms and twaddle than with the objectification of the world the students live in. What connects the higher grades with the previous school experience is a generous dose of moralism, national propaganda, and an emphasis on social problems. Again, the simplistic remedies suggested are interesting as a key to basic social conceptualization, at least, as exhibited by the authors. The elaborate presentation of what democracy is supposed to be, again offers fascinating reading. What students should practically or intellectually do with it remains, graciously, unquestioned. Yet the struggle with the concept is, in itself, revealing of its bad fit with Thai social practice.

It is of much interest to be attentive to the things left unsaid about Thai life; because of them, an idealized self-concept arises that seems to live a life of its own. Contradictions in the texts, for instance, about the reasons for important decisions, or the democratic inclinations of kings, keep the reader on his toes – and probably confuse students and teachers further. As the main finding of the chapter we may probably posit that the absence of a theoretical approach to the subject matter prevents the authors from drawing firm lines through the evolution of Thai society that, moreover, never seems to reach the present. This means that its current condition remains nebulous, in spite of the attention given to democracy, social problems, government and politics, and economic development.

The fourth chapter takes us out of school and into Chiangmai University. Conscious of the quality of social studies at school, the faculty at the Department of Humanities designed an introductory course aimed at rectifying the impaired social reasoning. This is a formidable task, and we have no means to evaluate the results. It is clear, though, that there are certain critics within Thai society who can analyse in a scientific manner, and the *Reader* [7] the faculty compiled for the course contains some of the best insights formulated in the country. It has been composed to introduce the aspiring students to modern social thought about Thai society and culture, to offer alternatives to historically fantastic, ethical-moralistic, uncritical nationalistic, or simply apologetic and nostalgic opinions. It does not shy away from offering certain more traditionally oriented chapters, though. It is up to the teachers to guide the students through such and other refreshingly iconoclastic readings. This fourth chapter, therefore, comes as a kind of shock after the dulling of the senses school teaching caused, and hopefully refreshes the students concerned as well as the readers of this book.

In a way, the fifth chapter, about the press, can be compared to the fourth. It offers themes, and a striptease. It not only provides a great contrast with school knowledge, but fills in the details of *phra* Prayut Payutto's general sketch of the condition of Thai society that I supplemented to the discussion of the *Reader*. It is not a nice image. Because the chapter traces more than the plain reporting about life in Thailand, it can amply comment on social and political conditions by quoting from the editorial columns written to hold up a mirror to the Thai public. It is, like the fourth chapter, the antidote to school wisdom, and one can only wonder why the school spends so little attention to all that is happening in its surroundings. After all, the students in the higher grades read the newspaper too, and those among them who have reached the age of eighteen are even entitled to vote.

Of all the chapters, the fifth is probably the richest in commentary about Thai public life. It presents a vast quantity of interpretative detail about the ongoing debates. The quality of

---

[7] Kanika Lekbunyasin (ed), *Bot a:n wicha: sangkhom lae: watthanatham thai* (*Reader on the Subject of Thai Society and Culture*). Chiangmai University: Faculty of Humanities, 1991.

these exchanges is a fine indicator of the level of maturity of urban civil society. The chapter, therefore, concentrates on ideas about the value of freedom of expression; on emerging public opinion as such; ideas about the press; and, most relevantly, the discussion about human rights. Some other matters of dispute are noted and discussed too, such as the practice of politics. By its very nature, this subject touches upon all sorts of economic and environmental issues, and highlights the plunder of public resources by the temporary grandees of the land: politics is business; more than that, it is big business. As the press acts as a self-styled watchdog against the excesses of the instruments of state, politicians, and businessmen, its reaction against these mirrors public awareness and opinion.

The sixth chapter contains brief discussions of five novels, four of which are explicitly social-critical; the remaining one being satirical. The purpose of the exercise is to discover the images of Thai society the authors want to convey. Some of these images are very recognizable, especially to urban readers, while others may reflect a state of affairs the newspaper also writes about, such as crime, with which the reader may have no first hand experience. Again, similar to our schoolbook analysis, we are interested to see how the authors construct their images, and what their hidden or expressly stated assumptions are.

There is a pervasive touch of anxiety that colours the social critical works, yet the authors also express hopes and try to point a way out of the less than satisfactory condition of Thai society. In this 'Botan' is more optimistic than Wimon Sainimnuan. 'Botan' sees the possibility of reconstruction, not so much social reconstitution, but the possibility of a new Thai individual emerging from outdated practice that has lost its use in the current process of social transformation. This is not to say that she is not aware of the tremendous force of inertia caused by prevailing conservatism and fear of change. Her perception of these becomes very clear from the allocation of characters in her novels, and the fact that in the relatively optimistic one, only two of them survive the onslaught of social pressure and ingrained routine. Anyway, reconstituted individuals who can stand on their own feet and make their own decisions, who do not shy away from carrying responsibility, are the hope for the future. As we shall see, in agreement with the venerable Prayut Payutto whom we met in the fourth chapter, Wimon does not share in 'Botan's subdued optimism. Like the monk, he blames the basic human condition for the mess contemporary people find themselves in. Of course, he too grants that wisdom would be the key to liberation from the fetters of material existence, but who wants to be wise in a society where everybody desires to be rich?

The seventh chapter contains a discussion of an official image presented to foreigners. Such as can be expected, the National Identity Office is not about saying negative things about the country and its people, and yet the book it published, *Thailand in the 90s*,[8] is full of surprises, ranging from a rather slipshod presentation to a certain naivety founded on taking things for granted that need explaining to an English-reading public. The way history has been narrated is quite satisfactory, although it stops short from clarifying the recent past, and thus does not really allow us to proceed into the 1990s. Naturally, the monarchy has been given pride of place, but the other pillars of Thai society, to wit, religion and the nation, have not been convincingly depicted. What is said about Buddhism and its importance in the life of the people, is highly stereotypical and fails to reach any depth. The introduction to the nation, heavily relying on outdated foreign ethnographic literature about life in the countryside, dwells in the past and raises questions rather than giving answers. In spite of all this, going over the text with a fine-tooth comb is quite revealing, were it only because it brings to light the refusal to reflect on 'national identity'; the hiding behind standard images; and the subjects considered to be matters of course. These critical observations have been elaborated in the final pages of the

---

[8]   *Thailand in the 90s*. Bangkok: National Identity Office of the Prime Minister, 1991.

chapter, with the aim to explain the things the book implies but fails to elucidate.

The last substantive chapter, the eighth, concerns an analysis of the main players in the public world. They, that is, the state, the economy, and civil society, at once constitute the public world and shape, or construct it by creating public opinion. Such opinion is not a rigid thing. It is an ongoing discourse in which the voices of the constituent partners can be heard. Besides, these 'partners' are not homogeneous in themselves. 'The state' sends moralistic messages that are contradicted by the practice of politics and the exercise of power. Besides, the state is in fact represented by a plethora of institutions that all send their – often conflicting – signals. Such can also be said of the impulses economic institutions give to opinion making. While normally devoid of direct moral content, they are full of advice on how to be in the world, how to dress, what to buy, and may even suggest that using a certain detergent makes one a good citizen because you will then refrain from further damaging the environment.

The great catalyst of all these impulses and messages is civil society itself. This is not a homegeneous entity either. Not only do individual people have their differences of opinion, they may also have opposed interests, and often these interests differentiate them into groups that represent a variety of opinions. This, of course, does not prevent people classified that way from having different priorities, one possibly stressing his own economic advancement, another prioritizing a healthy environment, and others still set on a novel religious style of life. In other words, the public discourse may, at times, be rather cacophonous because of the great diversity of sounds that can be heard. In a study of this kind it is not possible to consider them all, and in the eighth chapter we can only listen to the apparently dominant voices in their interplay. A persistent one among these, often colouring the social discourse, does not even belong to the public world proper. It is the strong influence of lifeworldly thinking on the public discourse, and this is given pride of place in the considerations.

The structure of life in the private domain at home produces a number of givens, say, the hierarchical order of relationships, that are imposed on the public world, and that influence the way it is seen and opined about. They meet in the practical construction of the public world in which the exercise of power is the crucial good. As long as such power is morally legitimate, it can be accepted in the terms the lifeworld provides. Most often, though, power is indifferent to moral constraints, and this very opposition fuels much of the discussions that bring the public world to life. The tone of these debates has changed over time, in tandem with the evolution of political and economic circumstances. It is these dynamics, reflected in the atmosphere of the discourse, that will be described in the last pages of the chapter.

In the Conclusions some of the points raised throughout the book will be considered in their consequences for the further development of the ongoing discourse about the public world. The current practice of formal school education will be assessed as to the contribution it makes to train people for participation in public affairs. Another issue that is highlighted is the tendency to shy away from the critical analysis of things Thai, a weakness for which more than the experience of a narrow-minded formal curriculum appears to be responsible. Next to these, we will also reflect on the development of urban culture and how this affects the question of the legitimacy of the exercise of power. By questioning the identities of the social discussion partners, we find that the public discourse still lacks inputs from the population at large and its diversity of interests. Yet, by being aware of the vigour of the growth of public awareness, there is reason for some optimism, the onslaught of consumer culture notwithstanding.

As to the format, the following still needs to be observed. All references have been listed in full detail in either the footnotes or the main body of the text. The authors concerned also appear in the Index of names. The main newspaper sources have been abbreviated: *TN* refers to *The Nation*, *BP* to *Bangkok Post*, and *SP* to *The Sunday Post*.

Chapter 1

INDIVIDUAL, SOCIETY AND HISTORY ACCORDING TO GRADE SCHOOL TEXTS

S ome fundamental thinking about the public world is introduced at school. It is there that some basic skills, such as the three R's, and images of the individual, society, and history are transmitted. We shall examine the latter inasmuch as they are contained in those books aiming to prepare the student for participation in wider social life. Such school texts are a very important part of the culture of the nation-state, reflective of the 'dominant mentality', at least as seen and interpreted by government and bureaucracy. It may thus be expected that the Department of Education exercises strict control over textbook content and considerable influence over the actual presentation of the curriculum. It formulates the purposes of primary education as follows.

> Primary education is that basic education that aims at developing the student in such a way that he can promote the quality of life at the same time that he is useful to society in the sense of fulfilling his role and duties as a good member of the populace according to the democratic system of government headed by the King by giving the student basic knowledge and skills to sustain life while being abreast of change, to maintain good physical and psychological health, and to be able to work and seek livelihood in a peaceful manner.

In organizing education according to the present curriculum, the following qualities must be instilled in the student:

1. to acquire basic learning skills that should cover the abilities of reading, writing, and arithmetic;

2. to have knowledge and understanding of the own person, the natural environment, and social change;

3. to be able to take care of personal and familial health and hygiene;

4. to be able to analyze the reasons of, and to suggest solutions for, personal and familial problems in a fashion the logic of which is inspired by skill in scientific reasoning;

5. to be proud of being Thai; to have the qualities of not being egoistic, of not taking advantage of others, and of being able to peacefully coexist with others;

6. to love reading and to be always thirsty for knowledge;

7. to have basic knowledge and skills for working, to love work, and to be able to cooperate with others;

8. to have knowledge and understanding of social conditions and the societal change affecting home and community, to be able to behave according to role and duty as a good member of family and community while all the time taking care of and promoting the environment, religion, arts, and culture in the community around the home.[1]

---

[1] Kowit Prawanlaphruek (ed), E:kkasa:n naenam laksu:t chabap prapprung phô: sô: 2533 (Document Introducing the Revised Curriculum of 1990). Bangkok: Educational Technique Bureau, Ministry of Education, 1990.

The texts[2]

In primary school, social studies comprise three subject areas: (1) to form character and disposition (*sô:lô:nô:*); (2) to prepare for the experience of life (*sô:pô:chô:*); and (3) to introduce the basics of work and profession (*kô:pô:ô:*). Each of these courses encompasses a variety of subjects: the first bringing together moral education, arts, physical education, music and drama, scouting and youth red cross; the second combines health education, man and environment, our country and its neighbours, plus economics and remunerative work; the last introduces work in and around the house, practical agricultural activities, and manual skills.

---

[2] *Klum sô:lô:nô:* (*sô:lô:nô:* Grouping)

Somsak Sinturawet *et al.*, *Nangsü: rian klum sa:ngsoem laksananisai* (*Studybook of the Grouping Concerned with the Formation of Character and Disposition*). Bangkok: Watthana Phanich (Books *1* (1992), *2* (1992), *3* (1993), *4* (1994), *6* (1990).

Bunsong Cirawut *et al.*, *Cariyasüksa:* (*Ethics*). Bangkok: Watthana Phanich (Book *5* (1991)).

Klum sô:pô:chô: (*sô:pô:chô:* Grouping)

Educational Technique Bureau, Department of Education, *Nangsü:rian sa:ngsoem prasopka:nchi:wit* (*Studybook Preparing for the Experience of Life*). Bangkok: Book Development Centre of the Educational Technique Bureau of the Department of Education. (Books *1* (1991), *2* (1991), *3* (1991), *4* (1978), *5* (1978)).

ibid.. Bangkok: Sales Organization of the Khurusapha. (Books *6. Muat sukkhapha:p ka:i lae cit* (*Section Physical and Mental Health*, 1992), *6. Muat manut kap singwae:tlô:m* (Section People and Environment, 1992), *6. Muat ba:nmüang khô:ng raw lae prathe:tphüanba:n* (*Section Our Country and Its Neighbours*, 1991), *6. Muat setthakit lae ka:nthamma:ha:kin* (*Section Economy and Work*, 1993).

Klum kô:phô:ô: (*kô:phô:ô:* Grouping)

Sanguan Ongsikun *et al.*, *Klum ka:nnga:n lae phü:ntha:n a:chi:p* (*Grouping Concerning the Basics of Work and Profession*). Bangkok: Khurusapha. (Book *2* (1990)).

Saci Suthat na Ayutthaya *et al.*, *ibid.* (Book *4* (1991), *6* (1991)).

These three clusters are tied together by endlessly repeated moral exhortations and by considerable overlap in subject matter. How important they are held to be becomes clear from the school time devoted to them: in the first two grades we see an equal division of teaching hours between the three R's and the social subjects; in the third and fourth grades only thirty-five per cent of time is devoted to the 'hard' subjects; in the last two classes, even three quarters of available time goes toward 'the preparation to enter society'. This is warranted by the fact that most Thai children do not go to school beyond the sixth grade, and so they had better train to be useful and moral members of their communities and the nation.

How to be useful and moral was laid down in the policy of 1977, and implemented in the official curriculum of 2521/1978. In the wake of the counter-revolution of 1976 and as a reaction to the 'fall' of Vietnam to communism, this policy was informed by the idea that the instilling of certain religious and nationalistic values would promote the stability of the country. Henceforward, the school should serve the purposes of state and nation-building. In order to illustrate how the school is to accomplish this mission, much care has been taken to preserve the tone of the texts.

The course on character and disposition aims at personality formation by way of teaching the mastery of one's physical appearance, accomplished expression through artistic skills, and right values. Next to mastery of the body, physical education should foster sportsmanship; the abilities to lead and to follow; and team spirit. Dramatic expression, especially dancing, alongside the training of respectful greeting (*wai*) and paying obeisance (*kra:p*) are supposed to lead to graceful and polite movement. Scouting and red cross activities aim at discipline, cooperation and skills. Altogether, the emphasis on physical activities should lead to correct, self-confident movement and the ability to present oneself elegantly and in a dignified manner, so contributing to individuality and personality (*bukkhalikapha:p*) formation. This training is combined with the teaching of values that are anchored in family, school, and religion (Buddhism).

The course is basically about moral education, the combination of conduct, bearing and morals hinting at an aesthetical conception of ethics. The idea of morality it offers is simplistic, black and white. This either-or approach, in which persons are portrayed as either good or bad, may have to do with the philosophy behind the teaching of Buddhist principles, precepts and proverbs. The core idea is to develop insight, to realize why certain conduct is to be recommended; having acquired such wisdom withholds a person from doing unwise, stupid things. In other words, a wise person, one who is filled with knowledge and right reasoning (*mi: he:tphon*), is a righteous person. To such a person it is clear what is right and what is wrong, or stupid. So, what I surmise to be the deeper motive behind the teaching of morals in black and white is that it approaches morality by way of insight, or wisdom, while supposing that people are capable of learning and, ultimately, of grasping truth. Ethics, then, becomes more than a demonstration of social refinement and smoothness; what moral education fuses are 'the good, the true, and the beautiful'.

The course that focuses on the experience of life may be expected to deal with concrete situations. It introduces the human body, health and the dangers that threaten it because of bad habits, dirt, carelessness, poor hygiene, drug addiction, and contagious diseases. Then the environment expands to home, house and family: to keep these in order, people should know their mutually different places and unequal obligations. If everyone is dutiful, home, then school, then community, will be in desirable functional order. This is reason enough to repeat the values of the ethics course. In the family setting people should help each other and cooperate, exercise self-denial and endurance (self-restraint and tolerance; *ô:tthon*), be diligent, perseverant and economical. The school adds to these the values of orderly behaviour, respect for the rules, self-discipline, and gathering knowledge; similarly to what was taught about the family, pupils are exhorted to care for the reputation of their alma mater, too. Together these characteristics make for the 'good person' (*khon di:*) that community and nation require to function happily (*mi: suk*) and smoothly (*sangop suk*).

Starting in the first grade, the physical environment is introduced with all kinds of maps; with the ecology of plants, animals and humans, while emphasizing green consciousness; with boring lists of natural resources, regional products and administrative organization; with physics (gravity, magnetism, sound, electricity, and so on), chemistry (molecules, chemical reactions), all the way up to the solar system. The stress on usefulness and the polluting effects of productive activity lead to inform about elementary economics. This is elaborated on in sketches of occupations and professional ethics (*khunnatham*).

The private, natural and physical environments are complemented by their ideological setting in nation, its history and government, civics and religion. This procedure offers a splendid opportunity to inject generous doses of moral and behavioural recommendations. Communication in all senses, from letters to satellites, is discussed too, the most interesting aspect of this being the exhortation not to just consume news, but to be critical of it. Added to all these are scattered facts about nearby countries.

The course about work and profession aims at practical activities. Its first part is very repetitious throughout the six years, endlessly instructing how to clean the house and do the dishes, never failing to emphasize that the members of the household have the responsibility to care for the home, and that the execution of the duties involved enhances the family's happiness: the place where we live should be clean, orderly and beautiful. So should our clothing be, that we carefully select to match with the season and occasion. In this part of the course, the fun is probably in the cooking lessons, while care for textiles and babies, sewing, and food conservation are also taught. Agricultural activities, the second part, consists mainly of caring for plants and observing their growth, mixing earth and manure, and grafting techniques, while going into immense detail regarding the tools involved. Finally, manual skills covers the making of a wide array of mostly decorative, useful and playful things. This also serves to instil

31

ecomomy in the use of materials, an enhanced perception of usefulness, and the value of meticulousness, while contributing to the survival of Thai decorative forms.

Principles of social construction

In the lowest grades some basic assumptions about social life are quite explicitly stated. According to *sô:lô:nô: 1*,

> The family is a part of society. Everybody of us is a member of a family, and that is why we are part of society, too. Society will be peaceful and quiet if everybody is a morally good person who is possessed by responsibility, diligence and perseverance, the will to sacrifice, and knows how to help while not exploiting others. Yet, the fact that people will possess all of these qualities must have its basis in the morally good family. A good family is a family of which all members know their individual roles and duties, have responsibility, while knowing to sacrifice their self-interest for the interest of the majority (192).

Community leaders and parents are then presented as exemplary persons, while it is further argued that persons who just follow their whims and wishes cause competition and strife, quarrels and disorder, to the point that neither family nor society can enjoy peace and happiness. The key to the latter is the willingness to self-effacement/self-sacrifice/give in (*sia sala*). It is also stated that the family is the smallest unit of society (192-3).

From these assumptions two semi-contradictory principles stand out: (1) good order and disorder both stem from individual behaviour, yet, (2) the individual is primarily considered to be an integral part of a family, or group. The solution, then, is to emphasize moral principles: the good of the family follows from the good qualities of its members, the good of society follows from its being composed of good families. How to bring this about is elaborated upon in the second grade (2:211). First it is explained that family members are unequal, were it only for the sake of age, and that people should behave towards each other through conduct befitting their mutually unequal positions (*tha:na*). These positions must be respected. This hierarchical foundation of order further requires cooperation, politeness, honesty, clemency, kindness and sympathy, or concern, among family members, who must also give in to each other, mutually knowing to forgive errors and bad habits. Their respective duties entail different tasks that must be executed meticulously so that the result will be profitable for all. Moreover, family members must help each other in accomplishing their respective tasks.

It is realistically acknowledged that obstacles occur. No family happiness will result from jealousy, quarrels, drinking liquor, smoking, drugs, extravagant spending, rowdiness, gambling, staying out late, stealing, disinterest in work, and so on. Since we already know that such bad behaviour stems from individual dispositions, or from bad families and friends as such, the pupils are again exhorted to behave as good family members first of all (211).

Two stories in clear black and white help to illustrate that family happiness follows from moral behaviour. As soon as bad parental habits (gambling, liquor) are overcome, poverty will turn into relative prosperity, orderliness and happiness. In other words, the reason for being poor is with the poor themselves: they do not work, are not diligent and perseverant, and have bad habits (211-2). The other story is about a rich family that goes to ruin because of the extravagant spending habits of the individual members that follow from their tendency to live according to their personal whims and wishes. This is contrasted with the economical habits of a simple, solidary family that consequently rises high in terms of money, prestige, and happiness (224-6).

A wider social environment is offered by the school itself. If the moral ways of the inner core of life lead to the family's wholesomeness, the moral ways of the school lead to discipline, because a place where many people mingle together needs order, conventions, rules, and enforceable regulations. If everybody behaves according to these, the school will be a peaceful, hence a good place, as opposed to the chaos that results from everybody following his own inclinations. Disciplined people are morally good; they are considerate people loved by others and are welcome company, quite unlike the unruly types, who are shunned. Thus pupils had better respect the rules that are conducive to good order, thus creating feelings of responsibility and discipline (*1*:199-200; *2*:245-6). Instrumental to such desirable traits are: (1) respect for and obedience to the teacher; (2) diligence and perseverance; and (3) to know how to control oneself (250).

At this point it is prudent to inform the reader that we have just surveyed a very small selection of pages. Yet it is remarkable how often certain key words, such as diligence and perseverance, self-denial and endurance, obligation and discipline, are mentioned. The same values will be overused throughout the texts up to the point of becoming mantras, and although I shall try to avoid too much repetition, we may still quote from the section 'The qualities of the Thai child the nation desires' (*1*:207). Predictably, they are the above, to which an interesting pair is added, namely, to be docile and tractable (*wa: nô:n sô:n nga:i*), and to be self-dependent. [Later on, both will be claimed to constitute Buddhist wisdom, which makes their interpretation very interesting (257; *3*:255-6)]. As always, the rewards of demonstrating these qualities are specified: such persons will be admired, praised, loved, accepted; people will seek their company, social life will be peaceful, and they will experience the satisfaction of all this being thus (*1*:207-8).

Since self-dependence is a core Buddhist value, it is instructive to see how it is interpreted. According to the books, it means to be able to look after oneself (dress, clean, wash, homework, intellectual effort) and not to request others' help or to become their problem as long as a person has not tried to solve his own (212-3).

34

Because family and school are thought to be essential to produce moral people – and thus a good society – they are at the core of the social teachings in the lower grades. It hardly comes as a surprise, then, that the first sets of Buddhist teachings to be explained are those that reinforce these primary institutions.

The family, here the parents, comes first. Father and mother are the sources of the highest goodness (*phrakhun*) for their children, always, and in *sô:pô:chô: 6, Health*: 105-8, it is made absolutely explicit that all children are loved by their parents, even if they express it in an awkward way. Because of this children are under the absolute obligation to please their parents (*tham hai phô: mae: plü:ncai*) in order to demonstrate their gratefulness and to reciprocate the boon of love and goodness received. The unequal reciprocation of the child consists of respectful and obedient behaviour, helping in the tasks around the house, being honourable and upright so as not to upset the good name of the family, and later, of caring for the parents in sickness and old age, then making merit for them after death (*Health*::106-71; *sô:lô:nô: 1*:221-8; *2*:255-6).

The goodness of teachers runs second to that of parents. They impart the knowledge the pupils need to lead a moral life and refrain from all bad conduct. Besides, their wholehearted teaching stimulates understanding and the will to seek learning. The pupil reciprocates this goodness by demonstrating sincere respect, obedience, helpfulness, politeness in discussion, and by following the rules of the school (*1*:240-1; *2*:257).

Next to parents and teachers whose goodness (*bunkhun*) is one of a superior quality, people should mind and reciprocate the goodness of elders, patrons, and all those who assisted or supported us or our families (257). In short, receiving goodness obliges, and so we are also obliged to the country's three basic institutions, Nation, Religion, and King. The land upon which we depend and the sacrifices of our ancestors oblige us to Nation; because of its hold on the mind of the people while urging to do good, religion is important for national unity: If all members of the nation love and compromise with one another, the nation will be secure and nobody will be successful in assailing us, and so we are obliged to Religion; all the kings have been greatly important for the country, having only the benefit of the nation in mind, which obliges us to King (258).

The principle of gratitude and obligation (*khwa:mkattanyu: katawe:thi:*) is so central to the social construction under investigation that it is repeated over and over again through the years and the diverse texts. It makes it possible to locate some primary values in that part of experience where hierarchy comes naturally: children depend on parents and teachers, they are little whereas adults are big. This hierarchical and obliging model is then enlarged to encompass 'the three basic institutions', Nation-Religion-King, so projecting a familial model into the public world or, in other words, the public world becomes personalized and privatized, subjected to the same moral rules that pertained to being a child in a hierarchically structured familial world. This manipulation is made more authoritative by declaring the gratefulness and obligations to the Three Institutions to be part of the Buddhist teachings (258).

We should also note the reasoning that the Three Institutions are interrelated in the sense that ancestors, religion and king all serve as nation-builders, which in turn obliges the populace. Normally, however, the importance of religion is related to wholesome social life, to a peaceful society composed of righteous individuals. Later we shall see that the contrast in meaning between Nation and society does not exist in the minds of the text-writers as they consistently conflate the notions of 'the Thais', nation, country, state, society, nation-state, public (*suan ruam*), and populace (*phonlamüang*), and so fit it all seamlessly into the national ideology.

Religion and the concept of ethics

Religion teaches us how to be good, a thing that we all want, because if we are good, everybody will love us. For instance, the

Buddha taught people to be tractable, or docile (*wa: nô:n sô:n nga:i*), also to be diligent and perseverant (*1*:257). Religion teaches order and self-discipline, to stick to the precepts, to be honest, to come on time [*sic*], and so on, which results in refraining from doing bad things, not because of fear of punishment, but willingly, following the laws, rules and regulations of society too (*3*:185). In other words, people who are religiously good will also be tractable subjects (*phonlamüang di:*) who, because of this, contribute to the country's prosperity, stability and peacefulness (186). Thanks to religion, people can know what is right and wrong and thus, how to achieve a quiet existence together (*2*:255). We can rely on religion; it bolsters society and nation, creates order and happiness. There are so many problems, so much suffering and unrest in the world these days because people do not follow the tenets of their religion (*4*:140). From this it would seem that save for having religion, there is no other way of knowing how to be good and create an orderly society; religion is the treasury of moral knowledge.

Religion, as a guide to a desirable or ethical way of life, is conceived of less as an attitude (for instance, 'do not do unto others what you do not want to have done unto yourself'; 'love thy neighbour') than as rules for right living. These rules need to be known, and must therefore be taught and learned (hence the importance of those who teach: the Buddha, the monks (*Sangha*), parents, and school teachers). Through repetition the rules, precepts and advices are drilled in, until they become precious possessions (*sombat*) of the individual. So, outside knowledge, contained in religion, becomes, through a learning process, personal property, and it is widely thought that to be without such education results in hardheadedness, self-willedness, and obnoxious behaviour. Such lack of manners, or knowledge of religion, is thought about as the savagery that is due to the absence of civilization (*pa: thüan*).

This thinking about ethics as outside, formal rules that become an individual possession that then results in an orderly life for self and society, reifies ethics and makes it very tangible. Knowledge of it is put into the individual (*sai tua*) which explains the repetitious, or drill-like teaching method that results in the observable fact that most Thais can classify the world in 'good' and 'not good', in a simple black-and-white model that is divorced from the experience of everyday life. Yet the school seems to like it and places the burden of social melioration on individual shoulders while acknowledging that not all is well.

When the teacher had finished explaining, Wibun asked: 'Sir, they say that present-day people have almost no ethics, no right reasoning, and no sense of justice. Do you agree, Sir?'

'I think I have to agree, although it is not so that this applies to everybody. In wider society we shall inevitably find that good and bad people mix. At present the number of people has risen while the level of material prosperity has gone up much less; mentality and ethical behaviour seem to be deteriorating. So, people compete for resources; they almost never enter the temple, and every day they grow more distant from religion, unlike in earlier days. In a variety of ways, clever people try to take advantage of those who are ignorant or in a lower position. Sometimes they do not use their common sense, just following their emotions. People who have power, influence, or go against the law, do think themselves to be worthy people. This is why society is confused. If we assist each other in totally eradicating that type of people by not praising and admiring them, and by not electing them to parliament, we will be able to construct righteousness in social life' (*sô:pô:chô:* 5:83-4).

For the rest the books are quiet about social reconstruction, and because the idea of eradicating the rascals may run counter to what is practicable, the course on character and disposition continues with explaining Buddhist principles, sayings, precepts and recommendations. All classes are supposed to exercise some meditation, too, and to be instructed about how to follow suit in religious ritual.

The emphasis on gratefulness and reciprocity stands out, so reinforcing the idea of the social nature of the human being. It is, therefore, not surprising that the idea of self-dependency is not pursued beyond the third grade where it still stresses self-reliance in the execution of tasks and duties plus the benefit of being diligent, and suchlike. Besides, other people cannot really help us, although they will admire the person who succeeds all by himself. The reasoning is so crooked as to defy logic, basically pointing out that children should not make a nuisance of themselves, and so we are taken back to Thai culture rather than to Buddhist wisdom (*sô:lô:nô: 3*:255-6).

The fact that it is Thai culture that is being presented is also clear from the disparity in interpretation. According to orthodoxy, the saying 'Man depends upon himself' (*ton pen thi: phüng hae:ng ton*) is an exhortation to exercise and use the own judgment and not to believe people because they are older, in authority, or presumably wiser. People should certainly not place their faith in the spirits and the gods. It is obvious, though, that the orthodox view disagrees with the way Thai society is supposed to function. Thus, by interpreting Buddhism to fit in with the Thai ethos, a picture emerges that seamlessly integrates Buddhism in the construction of wider society, at the same time that it leaves all other types of Thai worship beyond view and discussion, even though there is an occasional [unintentional?] mention of them, for instance 247-8; *sô:pô:chô: 5*:83-4; and 6, *People*.114-7.

The reverence for spirits, gods, and *saksit* power; the potency of ritual and merit-making, of amulets, Buddha images and shrines; similarly, the admiration for powerful persons or those who are smart; magic, horoscopy, spirit possession and worship, fortune telling and the seeking of blessings, auspicious ritual, Buddha's life stories, nirwana, popular cults, the next life, the significance of dreams, and soul-binding (*tham khwan*); all these and many more manifestations of common Thai life and the experience of the pupils are conspicuous in their absence. At the same time,

Buddhism is presented as endorsing hierarchical society with its gratefulness, obligation, obedience, rote learning, desire for disciplined subjects, and stability. In brief, an interesting mixture of Buddhadasa Bhikkhu's self-reliant intellectual interpretations and the requirements of the state.

Society as a construct of ethical rules
(*sô:lô:nô 5; sô:pô:chô: 5* and *6*)

In the fifth grade, occasion is taken to summarize and spell out all the moral rules that have been presented earlier. In a neat bureaucratic fashion, responsibility is specified in six clusters of duties, namely, the obligations to oneself, to the family, to the school class and fellows, to the school, to the community, and to the nation-state. All these are then specified in sets of four to seven rules to stick to, for example the duties to the nation-state being: (1) to respect the law; (2) to pay taxes; (3) to assist the officials in maintaining national stability; (4) to be loyal to and to defend Nation-Religion-King; (5) to preserve national independence, Thai arts and culture, and to let the good of the nation prevail over self-interest (*sô:lô:nô: 5*.1-9).

The Thai subject is then urged to maintain discipline and to come on time. He should see to it that order and high standards are maintained in his group (school); also that all behave as 'good people' so as to assure the contented condition of quiet order and the avoidance of upset; all the while seriously following the rules of good order so that they may be internalized as self-discipline. As always the negative effects of contrary behaviour are then discussed (15-9).

Follow the musts and benefits of good manners. Although it is specified that politeness has an inner and an outer aspect, it is especially elegance, courtesy and order that are stressed. As a result, all the postures of greeting and paying obeisance need to be scrupulously repeated. Added to this are the demonstrations of how to behave at the table: it is specified in eleven clauses;

appropriate sleeping and toilet manners are mentioned in four; about dressing it is observed that clothing should befit sex, age, and colour of the skin, while one should not dress up in front of others; in public one should give up one's seat to weaker people, and men should be polite to women; how to speak suavely is set out in seven points (23-33).

A functional view of social life is discussed in the next chapter; people are not alone in this world, depend on and need to assist each other, which is a good occasion to introduce the notions of self- and public interest. The latter can be given shape in cooperative effort, but also in the exercise of the different professions and occupations that complement each other. Extreme self-interest – egoism (khwa:m hen kae: tua) – is then illustrated by traffic behaviour and littering which equate with disrespect for the common good and a disturbance of smooth social life. It is related to the common tendencies to care about one's own business only, and to be irritated by the intrusive attention of others (37-44).

Follows an attractive explanation of the benefit of meditation that is, not surprisingly, at a level beyond the understanding of fifth graders (48-53). Then the advantages of diligence and perseverance are once again demonstrated by success stories. Interestingly, a case is being made that there is no absolute separation between male and female tasks, and that there is no harm in men sharing in the work at home. Systematic and careful work practices then serve to illustrate the four Buddhist causes of accomplishment (56-63). In the texts the words diligence and perseverance are used a thousand times and almost always coupled with patience-tolerance-self-restraint-self-denial. There is no cause for wonder that the next lesson is about these useful qualities with emphasis on the idea of self-control (66-70). Lessons follow on honesty; on reason and justice, and how these are interconnected; on being economical; on cooperation, self-sacrifice, forgiveness, mutual assistance, listening to each other, and sympathy (73-104).

At that time we have reached the central pillar of school indoctrination again, 'Good people know/possess gratefulness and

41

obligation'. As if the subject matter were new, the book indefatigably reasserts the superior qualities of parents and teachers, to which the obligations to home, school, and the Three Institutions are added; appended is a section on natural resources, apparently substituting for the traditional gratefulness due to Mother Earth, Mother Rice and Mother Water. More Buddhist values follow: kindness and sympathy (*me:tta: karuna:*); and to be contented with what one is and has (*khwa:mphô:cai*), not desiring what is others' (113-25).

The lesson on dangerous drugs necessarily feeds on 'realism'. It begins with smoking with which boys prove their masculinity to each other. Like other drugs, it helps to suppress feelings of anxiety that may arise from parents who quarrel, from mothers who gamble, and fathers who get drunk or come home late because of their visiting mistresses. Then, cigarettes may be substituted for more powerful stuff, until jail and death follow. Causes are enumerated, such as associating with the wrong people; family, physical and emotional problems; extravagance; and lack of education and guidance. The consequences of drug use are illustrated by the physical appearance of junkies; their antisocial and undesirable manners; their dirty environment; and the destruction of good society, inclusive of national stability (128-33). This ruin of awareness is contrasted with the values of right-mindedness and good sense (*sati*), thoughtfulness, conscience, shame, and the fear of doing bad things (138-43); the ruin of the body is set off against sportsmanship (149-53).

This brings us back to Nation-Religion-King and national stability. All these are interrelated. Nation means the people and the country, united under one government. Without such a nation, Religion and King cannot exist. Without religion people will be without moral direction and will lack their human quality (*khwa:mpenmanut*); they will exploit each other, be in trouble, and there will be no stability. Finally the nation will come to its end, and so will the institution of kingship. The importance of King, therefore, is that it ties the hearts and minds of the Thai people together at the same time that He is the nation-builder, the saviour of independence, and the exemplary religious leader. Without King, people will be divided, and no Nation can exist; without a stable nation, Religion cannot exist either. The Three Institutions are interdependent, and we can rely on them. Because of their goodness to us, we must be grateful to them and fulfil our duties. Our foremost obligations are: to be moral people; to follow the religious teachings; and to be loyal subjects (157-61).

At this point, it is politic to bolster the feeling of being Thai through a short exposition about culture. It is defined as the goodness, the beauty, and the truth in human life that has been handed down to us over the ages in order to serve as a guide for life. Added is a short discussion about customs and traditions, and art. Put into a historic perspective, it is conceded that, although the Thai had a culture of their own, all kinds of foreign influences left their traces (Indian, Khmer, Mon, western), and exercise their influence in the present process of cultural change. In spite of these, Thai identity is rooted in its culture, which is advanced enough to protect us from being culturally overwhelmed by others. The latter, in their turn, will even admire the Thais because of this. That is why we should care for and live according to our culture. Royal history is then used to illustrate the virtues of courage and moral self-confidence. A few pages about change (natural catastrophies; manufactured pollution; death; accidents) subsequently conclude the book.

Moral messages are inserted into all the texts, especially those that prepare for the experience of life. So, while the latter give specific information about the geographical, historical, social and physical environments, including the human body, the more socially oriented pages stress obligation, listening to others, cooperation, giving in to majority opinion, exerting oneself for the good of all, trust in elders (phu:yai), such as leaders and civil servants, respect for the law, at the same time that considerable importance is attached to the formal administrative organization of the country and its bureaucracy. In addition, personal qualities are highlighted. In the section Health for the sixth grade, pupils are even invited to rate each others' visible personality characteristics, from how a person dresses to his posture, from his manners *vis-à-vis phu:yai* to his helpfulness, from being meticulous to showing resolution and public spirit (6, *Health*: 31). The issue is apparently so important that, a few pages further on, the evaluation exercise is repeated (55).

The overall picture is projected from the point of view of mutual complementarity, emphasizing the need of being conscious of duty and of exercising oneself to be good, resulting in a functionally consistent, hierarchically ordered, and morally supported social construct that basically grounds in the concrete experience of the family.

The presentation of history

In the lower grades the mention of national symbols and days offered the opportunity to introduce the component elements of Nation-Religion-King; as of the fourth they are placed in a historical perspective. The first question raised is about the origin of the Thai people (*cha:t*), yet no definitive answer is given. They are supposed to have migrated to the country while gradually establishing their lordship over the resident populations, whom they largely absorbed. History really begins with Sukhothai and its great warrior-kings. Admiration for power, conquest and success in war is balanced with the royal promotion of the Buddhist religion and the propagation of its precepts and ethics to the people; in *phraya* Lithai's days (fourteenth century), Sukhothai could really be described as the centre of Buddhist religion. What is emphasized is that all the kings were always busy building prosperity for the Thai people while governing in a fatherly manner so that the population could live in abundant and happy circumstances; they were also perenially concerned with the promotion of the well-being of the Buddhist religion. We are not enlightened, however, about original Thai religion, the history of Buddhism in Thailand, or the people and their circumstances other than the information that all able-bodied men must be soldiers in time of war (*sô:pô:chô:* 4:149-53).

The next chapter introduces famous kings, such as Naresuan, Narai, Watchirawut and the present sovereign. In the presentation, King Naresuan (sixteenth century) demonstrates the qualities of leadership, courage, and self-sacrifice in the liberation and defence of the country and people, building the stability that enables the populace to live happily. This supreme goodness (*phramaha: karuna: thikhun*) places people under the obligation to take good care of country and nation, now and into the future (154-65).

King Narai (seventeenth century) is pictured as the clever manipulator of foreign relations, playing off the commercial demands of the Dutch by opening diplomatic ties with France. In manoeuvring in the contested area of trade, he was able to get the best of all worlds, even introducing western forms of art and governance. As an important centre of commerce, the country did very well economically and enjoyed a good measure of stability; the people benefited by this. To counter French Catholic pressure, the monarch intensely promoted the Buddhist religion, the Thai language and culture. Because he was sucessful in so many endeavours, he has since become known as His Majesty King Narai the Great (184-5).

The above two rulers give a foretaste of the Ayutthayan period, a subject matter that is properly discussed in the fifth grade. Because the other two great kings mentioned belong to the twentieth century, I think it better to focus on them when they actually arrive on the scene of history. The point to make here is that 'Our country has had ruling kings since a long time. All our kings have promoted the prosperity of the realm, have been the leaders in defending and protecting the country, fighting the country's enemies while caring for the peacefulness and happiness of the population who so inherited a realm in which and of which to live. This is why all Thais should remind themselves of the superior goodness of the Thai king and support each other in taking care of the country, making it prosperous and peaceful, now and into the future' (184-5).

The discussion of Ayutthaya begins with the assertion that kings and ancestors were united in fighting for the country, overcoming all obstacles while building prosperity and strength, a benefit we should more than gratefully remember (5:161). Yet, the fatherly ruler of Sukhothai had to give way to the absolute king because of the increasing size of the realm and its population; as a result, the distance between monarch and population became larger, the king becoming exalted like a god (*the:wara:t, caw chi:wit, the:wacaw*) (163).

> That the kings of the Ayutthayan period were very powerful, is true, but there was also the tradition of the king being held in check by the Ten Dhammas of the king and their firm belief in the Buddhist teachings. Because of these the king administered people and realm in such a way that people could live peacefully and happily. From time immemorial, the Thai kings have loved and have been worried about the populace as a father about his children. As a leader the king has promoted the good and prosperity of the country so that the populace could always enjoy peacefulness and happiness. That is why we worship the institution of King forever (164).

These theses are then illustrated by the royal trading monopolies and taxes that all benefited the people (164-6).

Relations of trade with western countries and the belligerent ones with Burma precede a discussion of the forms of government and administrative organization; an analysis of the Burmese assaults on Ayutthaya follows in which the reasons for the success of the second attack (1767) seem to contradict the ideological messages with which the pupil has been bombarded. Anyway, true patriots still existed, and we should be grateful for their self-sacrifice and courage in fighting the invaders (178-80); we are especially indebted to *phraya* Tak for restoring our independence. It was the latter who subdued the other princes of the realm – each desirous for primacy or independence – and who succeeded in rebuilding and enlarging the dynastic realm, encompassing Laos,

Cambodia, Chiangmai, and half of Malaysia. No wonder that the period of King Taksin was characterized by warfare without end and that religion and culture were relatively neglected. He was on the throne until 1782 when the Bangkok or Ratanakosindra period begins (181-90).

In the sixth grade that era is to be discussed, and the founder of the current dynasty is the first to receive the spotlight. Since he was also the king who made Bangkok the new capital, while being supportive of religion and culture, he has given goodness to all Thais and is, therefore, remembered on the sixth of April every year (6, *Country*: 2-7; 6, *People*: 108-10).

Regardless of the own desires, during the fourth reign the country is forced to begin to participate in the wide world dominated by aggressive colonial powers, and so the Bowring Treaty (1855) receives considerable attention. Politically, the monarch manages to maintain the country's independence (which expressly places the population under a debt of gratitude to the king), but economically it becomes partly subjected to the demands of the British and the open market, the crown losing its trading monopolies, and customs duties being curtailed. The economy, though, swings up and prospers while western science and culture stream in. Altogether this results in the birth of an ongoing process of political, administrative, social, cultural and economic change (6, *Country*: 8-12).

These changes become very visible during the fifth reign (1868-1910) when all sorts of modernities are introduced, from piped water to hospitals, from formal education to railroads, from electricity to postal services. Very important are the administrative reforms and the diplomatic activities to keep British, and especially French, colonial aggression at bay; whereas the country had to cede some territory, it maintained its independence. The account highlights the emancipation of the slaves in 1905 and the gratitude of those so liberated; the king's openness to the problems of the people which changed their attitude from fear to love; and interestingly, a preoccupation with foreign opinion. The slaves were emancipated because the institution of slavery was indicative of being behind the times and of lacking in civilization. Because some white foreigners held a low opinion of Thai customs, the king decreed that people must dress properly. At the same time, foreign relations and the modernization efforts gave the country prestige in the eyes of the major powers. The supreme goodness of the king did more than just oblige the populace; he earned their love, and so he is remembered as The Beloved Great King (13-21).

His successor, both known by his official name and as The Learned Great King, receives more attention than any of the other rulers (esp. 4:176-85; 6, Country: 22-33; 6, People: 122-5). Politically and administratively, he basically followed in his father's footsteps, but he is equally credited with farsightedness, for instance, because of joining in the First World War on the side of the Allies. This resulted in the double benefit of showing the world that Thailand was a civilized country, and brought it in a very favourable bargaining position after the war when the country could rectify the unequal treaties with the various western countries. He founded the Wild Tiger Corps (defence volunteers), the Boy Scouts, and introduced compulsory education. He designed the Thai flag, coined the slogan of the national ideology, namely, Nation-Religion-King, and should be considered as the father of nationalism and love of country; he is also credited as a democrat but, alas, the people were not yet prepared for popular government. He changed the calendar to the present system; introduced the first Thai coins; and the use of family names, all of which demonstrated to the world that 'we are civilized'. He exemplified a very high level of culture and education, being an accomplished dramatist, poet, columnist and essayist with a very impressive literary production. All these things bear witness to his foresight and learning, and are evidence of the boon of goodness he bestowed on us, the people, who should gratefully remember him.

The history text then gives some attention to the heroic deeds of a few commoners in the Thonburi and early Ratanakosindra periods (6, Country: 34-42), to the literary composer Sunthornpu (43-9), phraya Ratsadanupradit as an exemplary regional leader

(50-4), and a selection of historical, mainly religious, sites (55-68). This appears to be a convenient interruption of the chronology that allows for the introduction of 'Our King' (sô:pô:chô: 4:186-96) and 'The Institution of King and the Democratic System of Government' (6, Country: 101-9 and 110-4). The accounts focus on the king's interest in the welfare of villagers and other suffering people (Red Cross; wounded soldiers); the royal development programmes in the hills and mountains; agriculture, artificial rain, water projects and school building. This goodness can be reciprocated by being good people. This last exhortation is occasion enough to summarize the moral lessons that emphasize obedience to parents and diligence in school that both result in a righteous people of the land who hold firmly to religion and worship the superior goodness of the king; all this will result in a prosperous nation (4:195).

The material of the sixth grade adds to this the king's important role as the patron of religion; the good luck of the Thai people of having a centre of unity in the monarch; the function of the king as a cherished, protective guardian (mingkhwan) of the people; the unifying role that enables the people to feel that they are one family (6, Country: 106-7). The chapter also dwells on the constitutional position of the ruler who is in a 'sacred' position (thi: sakka:ra) and who exercises sovereign power in the name of the people. As a result of goodness and position, the Thai people should demonstrate their loyalty by showing their respect, by fulfilling their obligations, and by living according to the royal teachings that emphasize honesty and justice, emotional self-mastery, patience and self-restraint, abstaining from what is bad while devoting oneself to the common good. Follow an incomprehensible, formalistic scheme of the three branches of government that should elucidate 'democracy', and an even more complex one about the system of justice, that are both surely beyond the power of any teacher to explain properly (110-4).

At that moment we go back to the founding of democracy and why Constitution Day is considered to be a royal day (126-8). In the discussion of the seventh reign reasons need to be given for the coup d'état of the People's Party of 24 June 1932. They are, that the foreign educated Thais had come into contact with European democracy; the inspiration of the example set by the Chinese, Japanese, and Turkish revolutions; the economic crisis; the role of the press in leading the public to detest the government; absolute monarchy was behind the times; while the people felt that the privileged under absolute rule had very much power which increased the distance between the – two – classes of people. The king had anticipated all this, and was, as a matter of principle, in favour of instituting democracy. He was, however, held back by the grandees of the realm who believed that the populace was not ripe for it. So, basically, he was a modern monarch and a democrat, allowing the people to participate in government. His good intentions were pre-empted by the coup, yet, on the tenth of December that year, he gracefully bestowed a constitution upon the Thai people (115-21). For quite a few years, the event was celebrated country-wide and on a big scale; nowadays we have done away with that extravagance while gratefully remembering the superior goodness of the seventh king (6, *People*: 126-8).

National ideology integrating history, society and people

The image of history

The image of history the schoolbooks project is that of royal history: without King, there is no Thailand, and there would be no Nation. As a consequence, there is no place for ordinary people in this view, and chronological history stops short in 2475/1932, or in 1935 at the latest, when the seventh king stepped down from the throne. Since 1932, Thailand has democracy, which means that people participate in government somehow by way of exercising their right to vote. Yet, as an historical and structural phenomenon, it remains suspended in the air, and so the better part of the twentieth century remains without actors: this period is denied as history. It is presided over by the present king who is represented as a father of the people, as one who takes their problems to heart. His wisdom and kindness offer relief from misery and natural adversity. Such as it is reiterated of all kings, this places the history- and face-less commoners in a dependent relationship of gratefulness and obligation. Without King, there is no Nation; without their leader, the Thais are nobody.

The people appears as an undifferentiated whole. There is no social structure, and it is only incidentally that the reader learns about slavery and a class of privileged lords and masters. On the whole, though, Nation is an anonymous mass, alternately equated with the Thais (*khon thai; cha:w thai*), the country and nation (*prathe:t; prathe:tcha:t; cha:tha:nmüang*), the people (*pracha: chon; ra:tsadon; phonlamüang*), society (*sangkhom*), state (*rat*), and the common interest (*prayo:t suanruam; sa:tha:rana prayo:t*). This populace is the recipient of exalted goodness and, therefore, under the obligation of being good themselves. How to be good is taught by the fountain-head of moral guidance, namely, Religion. In practice this means the statist interpretation, which might explain why the Buddha is said to have instructed that people must be tractable, solve their own problems ('independence'), be obedient to the government, come on time, and feel grateful and indebted to Nation-Religion-King. Besides, the people is presented as a homogeneous mass which is child-like relative to its leaders; thus the populace is clearly in need of the moral guidance of monarchs, elders, officials and monks lest they stray aimlessly in the wilderness.

Nation is the most dependent of the Three Institutions; it is at the bottom of the pile, just like in the European Middle Ages when the estate of the Nobility tried to lord it over those of Religion and People. But whereas in the western situation the Church was a most formidable opponent of kaisers and kings (with all of them losing much of their power when emancipated urban middle classes – People/Nation – emerged during Renaissance and Reformation), there is no doubt that in Thailand, Religion has always been under royal patronage, and that Nation is considered to be a dependent creation of kingship.

So, looking at the three 'estates' that compose the national ideology, it would almost seem as if they all fuse in 'King', that is, in a unitary nation that is defined by morality more than by borders, law, political economy, or body politic. Altogether, this projects a static and eternal image, leaving no room for the analysis of social and economic structures, or for change, let alone for the emergence and emancipation of the commoners as middle classes, or their demands on 'the system', such as education; a constitution; democracy; free enterprise; control over government and bureaucracy. Especially in relation to the recent past, say, since the Bowring Treaty, the dynamics of Thai history and society become incomprehensible because they are not historically and sociologically presented but cast in a moral mould that blurs all distinctions.

Society as a moral construct

The moralizing image of society offered in school is rather simplistic: you either belong to it, or not at all. The task of the school is to reproduce morally good people who are determined by a rather simple-minded set of values. In the family, people are taught to be diligent and perseverant, tolerant and to exercise self-restraint, to be helpful and economical, possessed by responsibility and a sense of duty, while giving way to others. As children, they must also be obedient. Such are the qualities of morally good people.

To this, primary school adds the values of discipline, self-mastery, (moral) knowledge, and sound reasoning. People who demonstrate these values will qualify as good humans. Being good is a safeguard against individual loss of face and also promotes the reputation of the group; if everybody behaves accordingly, family, school, community and society will be peaceful and free of trouble.

In a black-and-white fashion, 'good' is constantly contrasted with 'bad'. Good leads to the rewards of acceptance, love, admiration, and contentment; bad to negative experiences, upset, loss of love and goods, yea, even to ill health and death. Basically the choice is with individuals, but morally seen it is not a choice at all, because people are obliged to be good since they are members of families and schools, that is, children of parents and pupils of teachers. This entails that they must reciprocate the goodness received, and this is achieved by being good.

Because of the steady emphasis on goodness received, gratefulness and obligation to reciprocate appear as the cardinal principles of the social construct. As this obligation also applies to increasingly vaguer and more distant entities, such as community, country-and-people, and the Three Institutions, moral ties are extended to include all and sundry within the kingdom's borders. That totality is presented as a homogeneous collectivity of people which is embedded in its indebtedness to the supreme goodness of King. In this view there is no place for structural oppositions (e.g., rich–poor; privilege–rightlessness), let alone for conflict. By stressing the good while rejecting the undesirable, the moral model offered in school does not deal with society in any real sense, but depicts a utopian community.

This projection of what is basically a theory of the moral, functionally integrated, solidary family into wider society, naturally extends familial duties to the nation-state. Hence, its subjects are required to be usefully occupied, not just taking care of themselves, but also contributing to the common welfare. Together with this, the functional representation of tasks and duties – all work is honourable and useful, whether as a doctor, police officer, or street-sweeper – makes it possible to present society as a seamlessly integrated, structureless whole, in which differences in prestige, power, position and life chances, are nullified.

Seen from the perspective of the moral family, this is irrelevant: if something is good for daddy – for instance, to earn himself a pile of money – it must be good for the children as well, and so in wider society the (corporate) boss cannot go wrong. Also, in terms of giving moral guidance, father has the final word, and his authoritarianism cannot but be for the benefit of his dependents. Thus teachers, headmen, commanders, or prime ministers obviously speak rightfully, and should be trusted. As patrons they can only have the good of all in mind.

It should be clear that this conception has the potential of terrorizing the individual subjects of a state: they have functionally integrated obligations that construct the whole, thus contributing to its well-being. They should, therefore, shut up and do their work, which equates with fulfilling their moral task and duty, with being good people, and so it does not come as a surprise that the word role-and-duty is commonplace throughout the texts whereas 'right' only occurs in connexion with voting.

Consequences of the moralistic view

A moral theory that is basicaly a theory of a solidary family unit, is a poor means to grasp social complexity, and if it is still used to introduce the nation-state and the roles of the members of the populace, it introduces ideology. In doing so, social life remains opaque, and its changing nature becomes inexplicable. In the end, there is little to hold on to but a possible sense of nationalism. Because the theory used compels the authors to be extremely selective, it is of interest to look at all the things and everyday experiences that they fail to explain.

The cognitive way ethics is taught and repeated makes it appear that morality equates with a certain knowledge that enables people to classify almost all actions as either 'good' or 'not good', but since this labelling is done outside of real-life contexts, it remains a purely academic exercise that has little to do with everyday experience. Moreover, in real life the opposition good versus bad does not exist, both elements mingle and mix, in persons as well as situations.

Ethics is also made the principle of social construction. If all people are good, so will society be. It is never considered that individuals are social products whose perceptions and behavioural choices may be conditioned by circumstances and context. An undisciplined, egoistic driver may be the nicest family father all the same. Social conditioning is only mentioned in passing: good families are essential to create good people; good schools discipline them; and if you associate with morally good people, you will be morally good, and if you associate with smokers, drinkers and drug addicts, you are bound to follow their negative ways. But for the rest the burden of responsibility for good society is conveniently placed on individual shoulders and the personal knowledge of right and wrong.

In itself, this makes it understandable that the application of a moral model makes the scrutiny of society superfluous. While it is recognized that not all is well, and even that there is a lot of danger threatening human existence (bad health; traffic; pollution; fire), the remedy is not in social reconstruction, but in individual awareness. Small cause for wonder that power, politics, social diversity, the economy, et cetera, remain out of sight, and that in the image chosen there is no place for commoners other than to figure as supers and mutes. Ordinary people are implied as grateful and duty conscious family members, and their history is denied. Social structures do not exist; the formal *sakdina*-ranking of people in Ayutthaya is not even mentioned; where the slaves and the masters came from remains a mystery; and there is no need for history beyond 1932.

That there are many problems in society, and that especially the people in the countryside suffer, is avowed, but why that is so is not worthwhile dwelling on, since education, royal projects, unity among the people, and cooperatives will alleviate it all (*sô:pô:chô:* 4:222-31; 5:242-55). There is no army, no coups, no functioning or malfunctioning democracy; no economic change, politics, new middle classes, or urbanization; no real-life situations other than statements about them without context or explanation. In short, it is impossible to understand the contents of a newspaper if we go by what the school teaches. The only way out is the conclusion – after reading the press – that wider society is made up of power-hungry politicians who are given to personal greed, that it is full of abuses and rotten to the core, and that it fits with what the student has learned to be the negative side of the ethical model. Causes for undesirability must, of course, be sought in the morals of the perpetrators of bad deeds who – if being taught and aware – will be redeemed and accepted as desirable subjects. Yet, politicians are self-serving; the police are only in it for the money; and the poor are lazy. Why the good, hard-working peasants suffer so much remains enigmatic; they need education, probably.

The teaching of religion is equally selective. It is taught as an ethical system that additionally gives some advice on how to restore inner health by way of meditation. In the books, religion is presented as precepts, wise advice and proverbs, and of the traditionally important merit making there only remains prostrating oneself in the correct manner and the early morning offering of food to the monks. A few grandmothers going to the temple and listening to the preaching also figure. The influence of Buddhism à la Buddhadasa Bhikkhu is clear: religion is an ethical/wise edifice of precepts and insights, and all other things practised in its name should be banned. Since the venerable monk opined that the Thai practice of merit making was no better than 'raising chickens to feed the eggs to the dogs',[3] all merit-making practices and ceremonies have been left out of the texts; in that vein, all official, however obscure, Buddhist Days have been mentioned, but the very popular *kathin* celebrations have been left out.

Death ritual, house-warmings and weddings do not occur – other than a village headman explaining the benefit of registering one's marriage officially (this is done under the inviting title 'The Law, Duties and Responsibilities of the Populace'; *sô:pô:chô:* 5:191-

---

[3]   Buddhadasa Bhikkhu, *Khwa:mlongphit khô:ng sangkhom nai rüang ka:nthambun* (*The Misguidedness of the People Concerning Merit Making*). Bangkok: Organization for the Revival of the Buddhist Religion, 1973, pp. 27-33.

5). Unnecessary to observe that spirit shrines, guardians and *the:wada:* (deities) go unmentioned – as if a pupil would ever enter a school or a temple where they were not abundantly present; *sing saksit* (holy objects), amulets, and other everyday manifestations of the religious are only grudgingly acknowledged as being sacred to 'certain groups of [old-fashioned?] people' (*sô:lô:nô: 3*:247-8), but beyond showing respect there is no mention of the appropriate behaviour *vis-à-vis* such important spiritually charged things and places. The existential dimension of power, secular or spiritual, has been censored out; there is no seeking of blessing or auspiciousness; ancestors and deceased parents have no need for merit or ceremony, and the consoling effect of communal ritual and merit making have no place. Religion is for the intellectually and ethically mature only.

Needless to say that democracy is no more than a word that seems to imply voting and a constitution; since there have been fifteen of the latter in sixty years, it is probably beyond the power of any teacher to elucidate why they are held to be important. Even so, schoolmasters do not need to worry: constitutions do not stand in need of explanation. The books instruct about a good populace: tractable, and willing to accept the wisdom of officials (*kha:ra:chaka:n*), headmen and *kamnan* (subdistrict heads); they are not concerned with citizens or what the notion of citizenship may imply.

Whether desirable or not, to teach about society according to a moral theory does not explain the pupil's life situation or the society she lives in. This is not to say that individuals should not try to improve both of them, but to do that the teaching about them should have a measure of realism, and not paint a world that is filled with devils and saints only.

In designing a real society, one could depart from the symbolic representations that pervade the practice of Thai everyday life. In such an endeavour the understanding of *phrakhun*, of goodness and wisdom that dominate the school narratives will soon need to be balanced by the overwhelming importance of *phrade:t*, of power, whether in its spiritual forms or simply as money, influence, hierarchical position, and prestige.[4] By excluding this dimension of life, and the conflicts – of interest, of 'face' – that it entails, one excludes ninety percent of the world the students need to find their way in. When seventy-five per cent of school time is used to explain ten per cent of experience only, an irrelevant outsider might raise his eyebrows and, perhaps, find some questions to ask.

Comments

It is clear that the books – at least in the opinion of this author – do not hand down the elementary tools a pupil needs to understand the news, to read the newspaper, or to make sense of his experience beyond family life. Not all of this is necessarily due to the objective content of the books, though, because teachers can attempt to put things in perspective and make them applicable. Yet, if they also have to fulfil curriculum requirements they are in for a hard time.

Even supposing that the books offer a guide to go by, one wonders about the teaching method. The first thing that strikes the reader of the books is the extreme repetitiveness in the presentation of the subject matter. Sometimes one gets the impression that certain clusters of 'values', say, to-be-diligent-and-perseverant-patient-and-tolerant-devotion (*khayan manphian ô:tthon siasala*) have been printed on every single page so that they begin to sound, and probably function, as mantras rather than as knowledge, at best stimulating boredom rather than the will to act in a certain way. Such is not only the case with 'values'. Other sets of knowledge, such as sweeping and cleaning the house, receiving guests, greeting and paying obeisance, the goodness of

---

[4]   Niels Mulder, *Inside Thai Society. Interpretations of Everyday Life.* Bangkok: Editions Duang Kamol, 1994 (4th revised edition); Amsterdam: The Pepin Press, 1996 (5th revised and updated edition), chs. 2, 3 and 4.

parents, teachers, rulers, and so on, hygiene, food conservation, grafting, certain religious teachings, and so forth, are not only repeated within courses, but generously overlap with what is offered in the other two clusters of social materials.

Since all of it is given an ethical slant – for instance, to clean the house is a kind of obligation that demonstrates one's responsibility for the well-being of the home and the happiness of the family while expressing gratefulness to parents by showing that one is a good child – repetition may serve the ambition of creating people who are 'good', that is, untainted by the contingencies of this world. Because such aims are well beyond what ordinary people can hope to achieve, the ideals need to be repeated lest they are lost sight of. The pupil remains nothing but to commit the lessons to memory, and to admire, love, and accept those who are always inquisitive and perseverant, enduring and independent, at least, such is the often repeated message about the teacher's darling students. I know nothing about Thai psychology, but it does seem unusual that school children will love, accept, and admire the most successful child of the class. Besides, by always confronting the students with what is unattainable anyway, their will to achieve that which is within their means may be impaired.

Apart from repetition, overlap, and a black-and-white presentation that is far divorced from real life and experience, memorization and rote learning are certainly encouraged by the relative difficulty of the material presented. On the ethical side, the pupils are confronted with standards higher than they can ever hope to achieve; intellectually, they are supposed to develop understanding of Buddhist teachings that are beyond the grasp of most members of the monkhood, and of theories of physics that their own teacher probably does not understand. In the third grade, the dhamma about the connection between justice and right reasoning is introduced, not only in an obdurate technical language that it shares with other Buddhist teachings, but also as if such thinking could be readily understood (sô:lô:nô: 3:207-8).

In the parallel course about life's experiences it is taken for granted that children, or Thai people in general, can read maps, that they inherently understand physical geography, that they are interested in the formal structure of government and economic geography, that percentages, averages, export crops, balances of trade, and soil conditions make sense to them, all at the same time that theories about energy, heat, electricity, sound and magnetism are introduced. More physics, chemical reactions, gravity, tides, even locks and water power, plus the solar system follow in the fourth grade.

Besides these intellectual hurdles, the teaching of religious precepts and principles seems to be impossible without referring back to its Pali sources, and so the text concerned is littered with difficult words. The monarchy-centred treatment of history is no better, since the deeds of kings can only be described in language befitting royalty. The teachings about the human body confront the pupil, from the first grade onward, with anatomical cross-sections and other complex representations of all the organs, save the reproductive ones, although giving birth, family planning and sterilization are mentioned and taken for granted. In discussing the environment, physics, chemistry and the universe, carbon dioxide and molecules, asteroids and diodes, comets and the movement of the stars, and the like, are taken as understood, so that the only way out of the confusion is more rote learning, a mere committing to memory of things that may be forgotten after the next test or examination.

Altogether, it would seem that school knowledge has little to do with explaining the world the student lives in. He does learn the extreme importance of presenting himself in the right, polite manner, which, in the Thai setting, is useful knowledge. He should also behave respectfully towards holy objects, such as the shrines of guardian spirits and gods in which certain people place their trust [the way it is phrased almost excludes the possibility that the Buddhistically enlightened school children would put their trust in anything besides what is propagated by the Sublime Life Mission Foundation]. It is probably also considered practical to go by the book, by formalities, and please not to think. The books are also realistic in emphasizing the exalted position of *phu:yai* who should be followed and trusted, and the counter examples that should not be imitated, such as drug addicts, smokers, gamblers, gossips, polluters, reckless drivers, and other representatives of the ways of the world.

For the rest, though, it seems as if school knowledge occupies a separate segment of reality that needs to be mastered in order to acquire diplomas rather than that it functions to get an intellectual grip on the world, or to be able to evaluate what is happening there. The worlds of power, pretence and expediency are located beyond the school yard, and must be learned through experience.

The contrast between formal school knowledge and practical life may be enhanced by the very emphasis the school places on order, discipline, obligation, duty, and excellence. By trying to force students into the moulds of obedient subjects of the state, self-controlled Buddhists, and tractable children in relation to parents and seniors, Thai schooling may stifle spontaneity, motivation, and initiative so much that pupils will unwind as soon as they are on their own and engage in all the kinds of horseplay they can think of. It seems that the school offers no moral guidance beyond its walls, leaving its students to the confusion of their own emotions, in that way stimulating the reputed tendency to Thai 'individualism'.

I still wonder what this type of education is about, what its philosophy and purposes are. By forgetting that religion, and a modern school education for that matter, in a 'democratic' and rapidly changing country, should be more than just in the service of producing an obedient and tractable populace, it is sad to see that the school does so little in preparing its pupils for active participation in public life. Often the school seems to provide blinders rather than critical knowledge. The individual-centered approach to ethics provides the means of glossing over the structural causes and systematic problems of corruption, exploitation and social injustice, thus making the ideology propagated at school very much a tool in the service of the rich and powerful. Besides, the stress on primordial loyalties (to family, school, Nation-Religion-King) distract from building up a sound and practicable identification with the public interest, or the common good of a modern nation-state. That common weal seems to be left beyond the view of the people, to be run and exploited by the economy and its managers, and the state with its politicians, soldiers and officials.

From the analysis and this commentary it may be clear that the fulfilment of the purposes of this curriculum, as stated at the beginning of this essay, may be doubted, at least if we go by the formal content of the social course material. To this author, the discrepancy between stated purpose and actual content is so serious as to lead to doubt about the pupil's capacity to come to grips with social life if he were to go by school knowledge alone.

Conclusion

The intention of this exercise was to investigate the images of individual, society and history, as they are presented in the formal texts in use in Thai grade schools. The individual was seen as a basic moral agent whose actions determine the condition of society. To act morally, though, that individual was in need of the guidance and moral knowledge that enabled him to be conscious of self, social place, and obligations. Because of moral knowledge, the individual became increasingly social, that is, a responsible part of a group.

The dilemma between being a 'basic agent' and a group member was solved by depicting the individual as part of a family. She cannot be conceived of without others. By presenting her as a dependent child, (moral) hierarchy could be introduced, and so the person could be placed and socially defined. The moral, functionally differentiated, hierarchically ordered, and solidary family then became the model in which to think about nation, country, state, society, population, and public interest, all more or less fusing in the institution of King. Because of the solidarity requirement, inner differentiation was negated, at best referred to as complementary and functional, all the time stressing the moral duties of the component people, society thus becoming an aggregate of faceless individuals committed to a moral way of life. The resulting image of society, therefore, became utopian, in contrast to a realistically depicted one.

All this was integrated in the image of history. The emerging picture was ingeniously constructed along the lines of the nationalistic ideology of state with, again, the king fusing its component parts. History became moral history in which historicity, particularly for most of the present century, increasingly had to give way to mythology about the perennial continuity and integrity of the Three Institutions.

In summary, what has to pass for a course in social studies that has as its stated aim to prepare students to deal with the problems of life in a changing environment, is no more, and no less, than a course in moral education and state endorsed nationalism. It is the latter two that lend their colours to the overall image.

Chapter 2

THAI LIFE SEEN FROM THE VANTAGE POINT OF JUNIOR HIGH SCHOOL

The principles of social construction:

first semester

The first thing one notices when consulting official textbooks for junior high[1] is the apparent lack of continuity with the materials used for social studies at the primary level. If the elementary curriculum stands out for its ideological and moralistic content, with a steady stress on gratitude and obligation, then the secondary course impresses by its matter-of-factness and bold statements. At least, so it appears at first sight in the chapter dealing with economic change in Thai society.

Change is the normal condition of society, a sound statement that is illustrated by the ill-chosen simile that humans are born, age, and die. The reason for social change, though, cannot be explained in terms of the process of aging, but is to be found in the dynamics of the economy that are said to constitute the basis for the other changes in society. This is formulated in the idea that everybody's life is related to production and consumption of

---

[1]   Educational Technique Department, Ministry of Education, *Nangsü: rian sangkhomsüksa: prathe:t khô:ng raw* (*Social Studies Textbook Our Country*) 1, 2, 3, 4. Bangkok: Khurusapha:. Books *101* (1992), *102* (1992), *204* (1992), *306* (1993).

goods. In modern life, these activities are connected by the important activity of trade.

This thesis is illustrated in historical terms by a certain view on the evolution of the Thai economy that will often be repeated throughout the course. The olden times, including the early Bangkok period, are characterized by subsistence production in which people basically depend on their own efforts. This mode of production came to an end when the Bowring Treaty opened the country up to foreign trade and terminated the royal monopolies.

The most immediate effect was the spectacular increase in the production, trade and export of the formerly strictly controlled strategic commodity of rice. In time, the opening up also resulted in the exploitation of the northern forests, foreign investment in tin mining, and in the building of railroads that in turn stimulated the expansion of rice farming. In other words, in the first seventy years following the Treaty, the economy changed to a money-dependent market economy fuelled by export of rice, teak, tin and rubber. The middlemen in this economy were mostly Chinese.

Although economic change did not affect the country in a uniform manner, a new mode of production impacted on the country since the reign of Marshal Sarit Thanarat (1957-63)[2] who introduced the five-year economic development plan along the lines of the Americans and Europeans [sic] (101:90). Such planning is thought to remedy the poverty of underdeveloped countries, and is supported by the USA. The first five-year plan of 1960 stressed provision of infrastructure; education to develop human resources; encouragement of foreign investment; and promotion of international trade.

Over the past thirty years, the results of this planning have greatly affected the country. In agriculture, the forces of nature have been replaced by the wonders of technology that increase

---

[2]   Erroneously, the ministerial text suggests 2502-8 (1959-65) to be the Sarit period (101:90). About the marshal and his policies, see Thak Chaloemtiarana, *Thailand: The Politics of Despotic Paternalism*. Bangkok: Thai Khadi Institute, 1979.

production, and enable it to closely follow market demand. This resulted in new export crops, at the same time that industrial production for export was evolving to the present level, with petrochemical complexes along the southern seaboard. The impressive statistics of speedy economic progress are subsequently demonstrated in relative and absolute figures. Such development brings rapid urbanization in its wake. Before Bowring, towns merely had an administrative function; to this was added a remarkable commercial activity; nowadays many cities are host to industry, too. These developments affect life in the countryside; many of its present and former inhabitants are now working in factories, in trade, or in the service sector. In other words, economic change has a strong influence on social life.

How all this changed politics, government, and demography is then explained through modern Thai history. It places the Bowring Treaty in the context of western imperialism which, in its turn, is driven by economic forces, such as trade, quest for raw materials, industrialization, and search for markets. In reponse to foreign pressure, the Thai king concerned himself with guiding the country into modernity by carrying through basic administrative reform. Slavery was abolished. The subsequent efficiency resulted in – institutional – change in the country's financial, agricultural, communication, and educational systems which, in their turn, influenced the economy. For instance, the emancipation of the slaves resulted in free labour and its migration, while poll tax substituted for corvée (statute labour). These measures gave rise to an increase in personal freedom and an active labour market. Another example is provided by the construction of railways between 1916 and 1925 that increased production of and trade in rice.

The relationship between policy making, the bureaucracy, and economic development becomes even clearer in the thirty years past. All the governments since 1960 have had economic development as their policy, and the country's administration should serve this aim. Dams, power-houses and roads need to be constructed; schooling is now available in every village. These, and rural development projects, affect the countryside. Such activities increasingly involve the private sector, and stimulate rapid progress. This is also reflected in the country's demography. From less than five million inhabitants in 1850, population grew to over twenty-six million in 1960, then on to fifty-six million in 1989. This resulted in a rather high population density and necessitated a more effective use of land.

Economic change is not necessarily for the better only; it has negative effects too, and touches on the conditions of life of the population. Economic development first of all means material progress, such as a higher level of well-being and an increasing standard of living: nutrition improves; life gets more comfortable; people have more spending money; health services improve; certain diseases disappear, and life expectancy increases. Schooling is now provided up to the sixth grade, and soon it will be available up to the ninth. Yet, negative things also occur. The environment suffers badly, and the balance of nature has been severely disturbed, causing all sorts of problems. Industrial pollution, deteriorating quality of air, and the suffocating urban environment, all result in a lower quality of life and worsening mental well-being. These give rise to psychological problems; crime; a general relaxation of moral standards; new types of illnesses: cardiovascular diseases, cancer and AIDS. Be this as it may, the negative impact of economic change can be softened, or even overcome, if government and population cooperate in a reasonable manner, such as will be pointed out later, in the chapter 'Our Lovely Land' (155-64).

Apart from this note of optimism, the reasoning about the economy, its changes and impact, is basically sound, although, perhaps, a little over the heads of students fresh from elementary school. The last page and a half, however, remind of their earlier school experience when they appear to offer a solution, under the title 'Harmonizing Ourselves and Our Livelihood with Changing Conditions'. To do that requires some original thinking about how to bring our lives in line with the law and morality, because the old ways are invalid now. Our working habits have to become more efficient. Land is limited, and we must find more effective methods of working it. Increased efficiency will also drive ruralites to learn new, modern occupations.

There is more to this than adapting one's profession to the times. To have a satisfactory life, people will have to increase their knowledge, about hygiene, family planning, drugs, and AIDS. We must adjust our psyche, and build a firm foundation for our mind by studying religious truth in order to avoid becoming slaves of materialism while forgetting about ethics. We need to understand the tensions and anger induced by urban living, and avoid the problems of industrial society in Europe and America [Japan, or Asian Tigers, apparently fall beyond the horizon], such as broken homes and families, psychological problems, and loneliness of the elderly. If we understand the causes and effects of the advance of materialism, we can find a way out. Each and every one of us can help the other by executing our duty to maintain ourselves through the pursuit of right livelihood.

We can also defend ourselves against the problem of poisoning the environment by not littering public places; releasing waste in surface water; letting exhaust fumes and chemicals freely escape into the atmosphere; and by avoiding the lavish spraying of pesticides. We should face the problems of rapid urbanization through a way of living that fits with the urban environment, such as sticking to its laws and regulations concerning traffic, building and construction, and environment. We should also be modest in our use of public utilities and services. Adjusting ourselves to industrial and urban living is really very important. With these last observations, we are back at the elementary school wisdom that the good order of society depends on individual awareness and morality. As we shall see in the following, the enthusiasm for economic conditioning with which the chapter started will gradually diminish as other causes of social dynamics are propounded.

This is readily apparent in the next chapter, which focuses on societal and cultural change. In summary, this chapter hopes to show the interrelatedness of social, cultural, and economic change;

to consider the desirability of the changes concerned; to demonstrate how such changes affect personal life; and to suggest how individuals must adjust in order to harmonize themselves with the changing social environment in order to be able to live smoothly and happily in present-day society. Here it should again be noted that the emphasis is on adapting oneself – not on discussion, on new ideas, a programmatic approach, developing a vision, or simply protest. Such social-critical musings are known as 'fighting society'. As we shall see, this basic thinking in terms of adjustment, harmony, and smoothness/happiness will resurface every time the subject of democracy is broached.

First, however, a discussion of societal and cultural change is offered. Following upon the bold assertion about the primacy of the economy in social dynamics of the previous chapter, the warning is sounded that it is very difficult to distinguish causes from effects. So, whereas it has been demonstrated that economic change has its influence on urban life, population growth, lifestyles, and government, such social changes in turn resulted in higher levels of education, scientific and technological knowledge, communication systems, and so on, that induced economic progress.

Be this as it may, many changes must be positively rated, while others have a negative impact. (1) Let's dwell on urbanization. In contrast with the countryside, people in town hold a great diversity of occupations; they also have to live in limited space. They have to race against the clock, and free time is scarce. As a result, helping each other and cooperation diminish. All people seemingly work in isolation from each other, and thus they have less warmth than ruralites. (2) Family life is also different from the earlier days when the Thais lived in extended families. Family planning and urban living have reduced the size of our families, which also contributes to geographical mobility. (3) Idealization of the past, and other tricks to create pictures in clear black and white, surface in the comments about the absence of intimacy and closeness of present-day Thais, even among those in the countryside. Especially in town, relationships have become businesslike. (4) Whatever the content of interpersonal relations, people have more dealings with the state and its bureaucracy. Economic development planning emphasizes cooperation among people in the villages and in town, and civil servants help people to organize in order to help themselves. This mentality, shared by government and people, contributes greatly to the development of the country [?, *sic*] (103).

(5) Public services in the fields of health, education, safety, public utilities, communications, and media have become widely available. Health care and education contribute to physical well-being and increase the quality of human resources, both fuelling rapid development of the country. Although crime rates are still high, our police and civil servants are very concerned about public safety; their efforts are reassuring. The government is additionally preoccupied with supplying utilities, such as safe water, electricity, efficient communication and information services, and transportation networks, all of which result in a better quality of life.

(6) All this gives rise to an informed population and a thirst for news; mass media are flourishing, and many sorts of information and knowledge are spreading rapidly, giving people the chance to be up-to-date in their decision making. This results in expanding markets and an ever faster pace of economic development. (7) Although cultural development was neglected in the earlier plans, people are now very interested in that matter. This is so because many have begun to worry about the speedy adoption of western ways, and insisted that the government should take the lead in spreading Thai culture and traditions. In the recent past these efforts resulted in increasing the pride of Thai people in their own country and nation. (8) Western cultural penetration also stimulated interest in reviving original values, ethics and religion. Nowadays, Thai values are widely accepted. Yet, the young generation is still interested in the universal values of consumerism and materialism. For this reason the educational system and institutional religion will have to cooperate more to propagate Thai values. Many people hope that the promotion of Thai values will cause a change for the better.

(9) Because of financial constraints, the restoration and preservation of our heritage of old sites and objects has been neglected, and many persons do not mind at all. Several among them even prey on these historical places, considering them their private property. Nowadays, though, government and mass media stress the importance of preservation, and money is being made available, hopefully resulting in convincing the populace of the importance of conservation and restoration.

The evolution of consciousness regarding our old heritage must be deemed a positive cultural development, just like the other eight changes discussed so far. Some of them are induced by the economy, and conversely, social and cultural developments stimulate economic progress. When the student understands these dynamics, he will be able to support those changes that lead to positive development of our nation and country.

Whether the burden of individual responsibility for such macro-processes as economic and social dynamics really will help guide the country on its desired course, may best remain undiscussed, but it befits the occasion to raise the awareness of undesirable consequences of change. (1) First to receive the spotlight is the jammed traffic. People who grow more prosperous buy cars, but those who cannot afford them take to the road as well, albeit by bus. There are so many vehicles in the towns that they simply stop moving. The stalled traffic keeps its engines running, poisoning the air, and wasting petrol which means, wasting foreign exchange and disturbing the balance of trade. As if this were not enough, to be caught in the urban gridlock is also bad for nerves and mental health, leads to bad-temperedness and scolding; this, and the bad air, are detrimental to physical well-being.

(2) Accidents have become a major cause of death these days, and most of them occur on roads. The victims tend to be young; this taxes the strength of the nation. Others are disabled, which means economic and social loss; if we look at this waste of resources, we note a considerable drain on the life and money of the people. Still, defending ourselves against the accidents is not

so easy, because we are ill-adjusted to rapid social change. The best thing to do, therefore, is to instruct people how to deal with the situation.

(3) Consequences of population growth, migration from the countryside, and rapid urbanization are the spread of slums. The migrants there have little education or professional skills, and thus they can earn only little money. Living tightly packed together results in deteriorating health. Besides, slum conditions are the source of criminality, prostitution, and drug abuse. Impoverished, without education, and in bad health, the people concerned can neither help themselves nor their communities. The spread of slums is a changing circumstance that is dangerous to society, yet difficult to solve. The government must see to it that the people concerned have better housing, better income and, above all, better education.

(4) Drugs are a global problem that has penetrated Thai society over the past twenty years. Their sale and abuse are on the increase here too, often targeting the youthful, the very strength of the nation. Apart from the ruinous effects on health, the demand for drugs leads to all kinds of crime. It constitutes a problem that is particularly hard to solve. (5) A frightening problem is the poisoning of the environment. Next to this, we find the destruction of our natural resources; cutting down forest means drought and flood, erosion and vanishing natural species. Garbage and waste degenerate the quality of water and sea, killing marine life in the process. Dirt along our beaches makes them unattractive to tourists, and their staying away negatively affects our national income. Apart from dirty water and air, pollution in cities includes excessive noise with all its detrimental effects on mental health. Still, such degenerated circumstances are purely manufactured, and threaten to make life in towns insufferable if nothing is done about it in the shortest period of time. It is especially individuals and NGOs who campaign for a solution to these problems.

The reader may feel a little uneasy with this list of undesirable aspects of rapid change because they are insufficiently related to causes, and also their interconnectedness remains vague. This apprehension is even more justified when considering the last cause of discomfort with modernity, namely (6) changing values. The dynamics of economy, society and culture have caused lifestyles of Thai people to change: some foundations of morality and good manners are abandoned, and new values have taken their place. Protest has been sounded that the heartfelt values of the past have been substituted by – imported – materialism, which in its turn induces change in behaviour among the youth. Their drive for unlimited consumption has been criticized; they do not respect those who are older; they are not interested in basic – and beautiful – ethics; practise free sex; dress awfully; do not control their body movements; and so on. The rapidly changing values of the new generation make the senior one – which constitutes the foundation of the nation – worry. All *phu:yai* fear that Thailand's progress is merely materialistic, and thus only superficial. All those who wish the best for our country hope that more spiritual values will arise. Value change means an important change in culture that affects morality, ethical standards, and the civilizing principle of society. For this reason, well-meaning people are deeply anxious about these developments. It is this consciousness of the negative aspects of rapid change that makes us realize the problems. This understanding, in turn, helps us to defend ourselves against them, and ultimately, to solve them.

The chapter about the demographic evolution of Thai society aims to bring the relationships between population, economy and society to mind, while inviting the students to consider the importance of their actions: 'All members of society should behave themselves in a way that demonstrates their responsibility for themselves, their family and society, so as to help each other in solving and preventing demographic problems'. Apart from this personal approach, the chapter is technically sound – and of little direct interest to our present discussion – although not consistent in seeking structural solutions to structural problems. It is observed, for instance, that the aging of the population results in a great number of old people: a group that is ill-understood, and not well cared for by the young generation. Consequently, our youth had better sympathize with and understand the elderly. It is thus suggested that this moral, or sympathetic approach can solve the problem.

The above consisted of a brief discussion of the second section of the book, the first, about geography, not being immediately relevant to our purposes. This is also the case with the third section about the physical environment, aspects of which we already reviewed in the foregoing. Of importance, though, are details that slant the analysis to individual reponsibility and morality. Later this trick will often be repeated, and it is good to be aware of the a-sociological content of sentences such as, 'The problems of the environment are problems of society or problems of every single individual. They must help each other to solve such problems' (135). It does not come as a surprise that the introduction to the section states that, because the rapidly changing environment affects our way of life, it is the duty of every individual to take part in the care for, and the promotion of, the quality of the environment (136).

Frequently, recourse is taken to a simple black-and-white approach to explain the characteristics of the present, for instance through glorifying the past, when water was clean, fish abundant, and rice grew without the benefit of chemicals. To be part of life in those days was a pleasure of peace and happiness. Degeneration set in with the advance of progress: the comforts of the car are accompanied by sound and stench, and so forth. Ultimately, it all leads to the ecological disasters of drought, flood, erosion, and even global warming. In the final analysis, population pressure, inappropriate technology, rapid economic expansion, and wasteful consumerism are identified as the main culprits.

Ecological awareness is tightly connected with individual measures to preserve, or at least to minimize damage to the environment. 'The degeneration of the environment is, on the one hand, to be blamed on inadequate knowledge or ignorance and negligence. On the other, it originates from passion and prejudices (kilesa) or the unlimited desires of people who are never satisfied and who accordingly strive to become very rich and wealthy which results in converting natural resources to serve human covetousness. Thus, at least in one way, the destruction of natural resources is related to the problem of the human mind' (160-1). Because of this, discipline, right conduct, and moral principles become important factors in considering the solution of environmental problems.

The premiss at the beginning of the discussion, namely, the supremacy of economic factors to explain other changes, has been forgotten. Capitalism and obsessive economic expansion are simplified to cupidity, and thus a seamless transition has been created to elaborate on religion and customs, which comprises the last section of the book.

In the introduction to the chapters concerned it is asserted, 'the mind is the master, the body is the servant', and that a person's moral condition depends on his spirit. Just as the body needs material sustenance, so the mind needs spiritual food; it is religion and wisdom – Dhamma – that conditions the mental health and energy that can stimulate individual progress and contentment. For personal and social progress, therefore, it is important to understand how to live accordingly. It is also of interest to observe religious ritual faithfully and wholeheartedly. Thailand enjoys peaceful happiness because its people put their faith in religion.

This last statement appears to fly in the face of the facts – at least as they are presented in the very book under study. Next to this, the student may wonder about the contradiction between what he learned in elementary school with what he is presented with here, namely, the importance of ritual and ceremony that, in his previous education, was strictly circumscribed to paying obeisance and making offerings to monks. We shall come back to this later. First there are many other confusing inconsistencies and weird metaphors to observe.

It is asserted that the message of the Buddha was revolutionary. He lived in a society that was dominated by Brahmanism, a religion that held firmly to the caste system in which birth and life were thought to be conditioned by predestined fate from which there was no escape. Whereas the three higher castes enjoyed education and a good social position, the lowly members of the Sudra caste had no opportunity to study and could not make any personal progress. They were poor, suffered, and were ignorant. We can imagine them as the basis of society; they compare to the sand on which the social edifice was built. As a result, Indian society of those days was unstable and did not generate conditions for progress.

This lack of progress, therefore, roots in the caste system and its faith in fate. The key to development is to change these, and to instil better beliefs. Because the Buddha was a minor prince, and thus did not have the political means to achieve this, he had to find another method to free the people from suffering. He found this in the middle way, that is, The Noble Eightfold Path. The revolutionary aspect of this method is that the following of the Path is open to all, that people are basically equal in opportunity, certainly so if they have access to education. Good manners are not the privilege of aristocrats and the highly born – they can be learnt, which is also the importance of the Discipline of Monks: all are equal by observing the same rules. It is their serious practice – or comparable lay discipline – that conditions individual 'fate' (karma). Doing good results in good, doing bad results in bad; everybody is to reap the results of his own actions; it is not birth – and thus fate – that defines one's circumstances, but the individual actions that condition personal karma.

Propagating the message of active responsibility for individual karma versus predestination and fate was especially the task of the disciple-monks who paid a personal sacrifice in order to improve society. Their message concerned social progress and individual equality. The idea of equality also included women. Their position became elevated almost to the level of men, which is exemplified by the many nuns (bhikkhuni) and their spiritual progress. The fact, however, that they were dependent on men for their protection from rape made the Buddha decide to restrict their numbers, so as not to become an obstacle to the practice of the monks.

76

The chapter concludes with the observation that the Buddhist doctrine does not rely on foolish faith (*sattha: thi: ngomnga:i*) but on the understanding of experience, and that it is especially satisfactory to intellectuals in this age of scientific progress. In the summary, the importance of learning and equality are stressed once more, to the point that the spreading of the Buddhist message 'made the people of India feel that they were brothers and sisters, that they were real friends' (176).

Before commenting on the implied improbabilities of the last paragraph, it is better to analyse the chapter on the Buddhist teachings and ceremonies first. It opens with the observation that the human being is a noble animal in the sense that he is capable of culture, of reason and progress, particularly of developing humane moral principles. In Buddhism, these are basically contained in the Five Precepts; their practice depends on the continuous exercise of self-knowledge and awareness. Follow the Four Noble Truths about life. Explaining first that life is not a free ride, but that we are born to live with problems, and even if these are minor, that we have to live in systems of imposed authority, rules and discipline. Besides, nobody escapes from the basic causes of suffering: birth, disease, old age and death. The Truths explain the human condition as Suffering, which must have Causes. Suffering can be defeated by overcoming the craving that is its fundamental Cause. The following of The Noble Eightfold Path achieves this, so putting an end to the problems of life.

It is most interesting to see how this train of thought is then transferred to the more mundane aspects of the human condition, namely, the desire (craving?) for happiness and success. To fulfil these depends on one's own efforts, and the Four Ways to Success, if seriously practised, serve as the unfailing guide. Follow the Four Ways of Progress, because everybody hopes for progress in life, and this desire can be fulfilled by the practice of the Four Ways. The student is then admonished to be close to his high-minded teachers, to pay deep attention to their teachings, and to consider them carefully. When he then realizes their beauty and seriously applies them to his condition, he cannot fail but to succeed in school and to enjoy the appreciation of his mentors. A third recipe for success and progress is given in the Four Benefits to be Reached in this Life. By practising these insights, a humble birth, poverty, and bad luck can be overcome, and turn into their opposites. After all, the Buddha taught that happiness originates from (1) having wealth; (2) knowing how to use it; (3) not being in debt; and (4) honest effort. If one really sticks to the Four Benefits, poverty and lowly position can be overcome, and a person may even grow very rich and enjoy high prestige.

It may be that students and teachers take all that is printed by the Ministry for granted, but I am highly confused by these observations. Why does the Buddha's insight that existence is suffering, and that this is caused by craving and desire, result in all kinds of recipes to fulfil the desire and craving for money, position and honour? How did the Buddha succeed in abolishing caste and inequality in contemporary India? How come Indian society has not crumbled because of its caste system and its oppression of the poor who constitute, is it not, the unstable feet of society? How come that the thought of equality fails to take root in Buddhist Thailand – where happiness and peace reign because of religion – at the same time that the country's stability seems to be anchored in hierarchy? Besides, almost all Thais seem to hold the wrong values, since their own efforts lead to the success of very few people only – or is it possible that there are structural constraints, too?

Let me stop voicing my disgruntlement and come back to realism. Whereas the grade-school curriculum has faithfully been designed according to the insights of the venerable Buddhadasa Bhikkhu – who declared that the practice of Thai merit making is utterly useless – the present text, at least, squarely acknowledges the importance of merit-making rituals in Thai life. Besides, the text avows, rituals, even of uncivilized mountain people, indicate the progress, culture and civilization of the people concerned. They are useful, mark purpose, and serve as a calendar organizing life; they should be admired.

Apart from death ritual, all merit making aims at happiness and progress, auspiciousness and peace. That is why we make merit on the occasions of anniversaries, house-warmings, marriage, and so on. Death ritual aims at annihilating negative forces, or rather, turning them into positive, beneficial influences. The purpose of merit making is to abate greed and egoism, while fostering sacrifice, friendliness, cooperation. It also promotes Buddhism by caring for the monks whose study and propagation of the Teachings help us understand how to be good. It also helps the poor [how?], while part of the results of our good deeds is sent to benefit the ancestors and the recently deceased which, by the way, is a manner to express our gratefulness to them. Upon this introduction follow the fine points and details of organizing merit-making rituals, the symbolism involved, the meaning of the holy thread (sa:i sin), and the tasks of the organizer of the ritual. Then, after explaining the spreading of merit to all living beings, it is elucidated that the generosity of dedicating merit to others even increases the merit obtained by the giver! In any case, to make merit equates with acting within the moral precepts.

This is important to understand in relation to meditation. Its practice without the precepts also results in psychic power, but of a destructive variety, fuelling cheating, corruption, and social unrest that largely go unpunished because of the cleverness and guile of the perpetrators. It is, therefore, important to live within the bounds of the precepts, and to reinforce resulting goodness by meditation that will result in a calm, good, regular, and merit-making life, a life that spreads happiness, peace, and stability

During the lessons about the importance of ceremonies, it is emphasized that people should follow them faithfully and wholeheartedly – despite the intellectual basis of faith, extolled in the first chapter about Buddhism. Rituals are a means to ensure, even to extort blessing and prosperity. In religious terms, they may only constitute the bark around the wood and its core, but without the bark that serves to feed the rest, the tree cannot prosper, which is the reason why Buddhists must understand the meaning and importance of the rituals. And on this umpteenth limping metaphor, I had better leave the two final chapters about Brahmanistic and Christian principles undiscussed.

In summary, the book on social studies for the first semester of the first year of junior high school moves from a promising systems approach, in which society and social life are seen as being activated by systemic factors, such as the economy, to an action approach, in which individual intentions and awareness – often objectified as values – condition the outcome of the social process. The latter way of presenting precludes a clear view of what is really going on.

Community or society?

The book for the second semester offers a rather elaborate vision of history that, in its turn, affects the principles of social construction and the image of society. Yet, for our purposes, it seems most appropriate to treat the image of history separately, and to keep our focus with social analysis per se. This is proposed in the book's fourth section, 'Man in Family and Community under Democracy'. The opening statements remind of the principles propounded in the elementary curriculum: every human being has a family and is part of a community. In being their constituent part, the individual can be compared to a small cog-wheel in a big machine. If the small parts function smoothly, the whole machinery will move efficiently. If, however, the minor parts stop doing their work, they will affect the whole, and the engine may even stop functioning. We are like these small cog-wheels: we are constituent parts of a family and society, and even if we appear unimportant, we are a part of the whole; we all have our parts to play.

This simple statement appears innocuous enough, yet it is full of hazardous implications. (1) The nuclear family is promoted as the basic element of the social edifice; (2) community and society are treated as being the same thing; (3) the social process is compared to a machine – which is a highly misleading metaphor;

(4) the view proposed is functionalistic to the bone; (5) the individual should operate in line with the requirements of the whole; if not, (6) he is a potential danger to society. This latter idea makes the vision of society rather individual- and role-centric, and thus personal, relational, and concrete.

The introductory statement still adds a few observations about democracy. They appear to be even more programmatic than the previous principles. 'All of us desire a democratic system of government, but do we understand that elections and other procedures are merely processes of the democratic system? The heart of the matter is that each and every member of society is conscious of their individual role and executes their duties accordingly, with love and commitment to the common good, from one's family to the region, from one's country to the nation' (102:88). In my biased view, I cannot possibly understand what the above has to do with democracy: the same statement can be made in the frame of any family ideology, and fits the rhetoric of whatever dictator preaching his particular brand of statism. Besides, the emphasis on role and duty makes me surmise that ideas about individual rights and freedoms, about moral autonomy and responsible citizenship, or about the rule of law and rational conflict resolution, will remain beyond the scope of the discussion. Well, let us inspect the next few pages.

The finesse of this jugglery is immediately revealed by the denial of a basic principle of sociological analysis, namely, the distinction between community and society: Whether you know each other or not, you are always a member of a community, from your household up to the world. Community is then defined as a group of people who share a place and who relate to each other, which makes sense. Subsequently, this idea is dismantled by the attempt to substantiate such relationships. They may be based on shared history; economy; government; culture; and race, such as common lineage and physical characteristics. For example, Thailand is the place of Thai people; Malaysia is the place of the Malays [sic] (92).

'Sometimes people say **society**, but nowadays it is preferred to talk about **community** because the latter stresses the idea of the importance of the **people** relating to each other and sharing a place, in the same way as a melting or gathering occurs in a single place' (93) Communities have the tendency to grow, until they become towns, empires, countries or states. While our (individual) membership in the world community, or in ASEAN may be somewhat far off, we definitely belong to our country and government, that is, we must be members of such communities, and in these we have clear roles and tasks.

The confusion reaches new heights when it is asserted that administrative boundaries define communities; even if we live in full isolation in a forest, we belong to a district, and thus to a community. This insight gives the opportunity to elaborate on the duties of community membership (subjectship), such as tasks, taxes, care for the peace, and respect for the law, customs, traditions and regulations. If everybody fulfils their duties, society [*sic*] will be in the best of order, and on this note the pupil is reminded of the simile of the engine. The stress on task and duty is reiterated on the chapter's last page and, again, we are assured that happiness will ensue from such behaviour.

From this first exercise in conceptual muddling, we advance straight into the next, when the jugglery is with nuclear family, relatedness, relatives, and household. In the process the word 'society' is smuggled back in, and is apparently not in need of further explanation. Before reaching these points, though, we are told that our home is our castle (*wima:n*, also: paradise). Ideal community living, in simple circumstances, is sheer happiness, in stark contrast with life in the adjacent street built in modern concrete where people treat each other as strangers, drink and gamble, and where the youth has lost manners and respect for elders. Even so, within the respective houses, we find families, households, extended families, relatives, and people who grow to become a kind of relatives. To be related, to share living and reputation, is called family (*khrô:pkhrua*).

The Thais have extended families because they are kind and like to help each other, whether they are strangers or intimates. The closer they are related, the more they want to stay together; they share their meals; the elderly teach the time-hallowed ethics to their grandchildren. This ideal situation is now under influence of the western family; economy and society are rapidly changing; families grow smaller; you cannot rely on your wide circle of relatives any longer; work and school are far from home. All this makes us apprehensive about the future of elderly people who will feel abandoned and lonely, who are losing their role of teachers of the young; in this way, the youth will be without experience, without a basis in life, and without ethics. Life will merely be lived in elementary, nuclear families. Already at earlier occasions we have noted that the Thai way of teaching likes to indulge in the construction of stark and unrealistic oppositions.

Anyway, before people are totally atomized, they should be redeemed by their consciousness of having obligations, tasks and duties *vis-à-vis* their fellow humans, and of their being denizens of the country. Especially in relation to the latter, people should be conscious that they can be punished for negligence and breach of rules. Such rules are defined by law, religion, tradition, regulations, and public opinion. These latter are then illustrated by elementary family law and behaviour of extraordinarily exemplary children who do not fail to say their prayers and to pay respect to the image of the king. Needless to say that this ideal, white picture is provided with a murky, black background of the evil following from gambling, wife-battering, amorous adventure, estrangement, extravagance, negligence, and lack of time to spend together. Of course, the occasion is not missed to emphasize the unequal duties of individual family members, and the observation that relative deprivation is no reason for not enjoying happiness; after all, home is paradise.

The chapter ends with four pages titled 'Our Family is Embedded in a Democratic Society'. We learn that democracy is good, because it allows us to express our opinion and concedes that everybody in society has an important part to play. Such opinions and roles are all equally important, and everybody is entitled to them as long as they stay within the bounds of majority decisions, such as the law and the regulations of the land. The latter are decided by our elected representatives. To be democratic is not a mere matter of elections, nor of the members of parliament about whom we read in the newspaper. Democracy should be in the heart, meaning that people should be willing to listen to the opinions of others, express their ideas, make sacrifices, feel responsible for the public good by respecting the laws. People should exercise their right to vote consciously, and not sell their vote for money. If democracy is in the mind, the national political process will function smoothly; yet, as long as people are not possessed by this mentality, democracy will remain a strange thing that only functions superficially.

To cultivate a democratic mentality is as delicate as the caring for a small plant. It takes many years before it grows to be a sturdy tree, and a lot of preparation and care need to be invested. The environment, so to say, must be fine-tuned to the requirements of its growth. If the family functions in a democratic manner, with opinions and options being discussed openly, it will foster the spirit of democracy. It is the same at school. The point is: can things be discussed; are people open-minded enough to listen to each other; or do they think that not to speak is wiser, in the manner of 'speech is silvern, silence is golden'? Whatever the situation in the family, in a democratic society people must be courageous enough to speak, to think, and to demonstrate their opinion. Then, if they see they are in the wrong, they should have the courage to admit it. Besides, they should respect the opinion of others. If superiors would force their opinions on us, who would still dare to think and speak? Conflicts can be put to an end by an open exchange of opinion, and by final voting on them. Although we do not vote in the family, we should also give in to majority opinion there. Anyway, in a democratic society there is no pigheadedness, no pushing of self-importance irrespective of the opinion of others. Moreover, a democratic society respects and fosters originality, and does not stick to tradition. Such originality is the fruit of free exchange of thought. If the majority agrees, such original thinking and ways of doing things may be accepted [sic].

Be this as it may, people should be tolerant, give in, sacrifice part of their interests in the name of public good and nation without asking for honour or compensation. In the final analysis, it is the fulfilment of duty that leads to reward. Such duty-conscious people live up to the standards of society, respect the law of the land, and the moral code; they have order and discipline. Outstanding examples of democratic behaviour are Mahatma Gandhi and Abraham Lincoln [why?], but everybody can be a democrat as long as they fully live up to the duties inherent in their roles.

The last chapter is about 'Our Community', and no reader will be amazed that it is packed with tasks, duties and obligations that stand out against a bevy of examples of antisocial behaviour, from polluting to vandalism, from rape to drugs. Know that your community is yours, and care for it accordingly. Yet, often people behave towards public property (khô:ng luang) as if it had no owner. To foster community development, people need respected leadership and should participate; if the task is left to officials, people will not identify themselves with it, and be unresponsive to improvements. In other words, people should be made aware of their ... [yes, you are right!], and thus behave as good subjects, in order to solve all the problems of their being a community. Your community is as your family. In caring for the physical environment, threat of sanctions can be effective. If people formerly feared supernatural and religious retribution for their transgressions, modern urbanites are more inclined to fear the police; these days, laws are more important than gods.

The final six pages are about the great community that is the nation and – predictably – the obligations of its denizens. 'We must defend the country; act according to the law; pay tax to the state; go to school; care for the environment and promote Nation-Religion-King along with the democratic system of government which has the king as its head, so that the country can persist stably and safely, and in good order, which, eventually, will benefit each and every one of us who is a member of the nation' (114). We should be wary of those who incite us to be divided, to hate the servants of the state, to disregard the law while stressing that the country is ours and that the people is its sovereign. Such persons want to destroy our good customs and traditions, such as respect for elders, and gratitude to those who assist us. In the past such propaganda has had some effect, but at present the population has achieved a higher level of education while government and people understand each other better, so that the country is quiet again.

The boring stress on duties makes one forget all ideas about rights – apart from the obligation to vote – and creates the idea that the community – be it district, country, nation, society, state – is there for its own sake, with the population as obligated subjects-servants-members. The law is there to follow, yet, how it relates to popular will remains entirely obscured. Besides, it is presented as concrete rules, in the same manner that religion offers tangible ethical rules to go by. The law, and the democratic system of government are never presented as conventional means to regulate society-in-the-abstract, that is, society where people are unknown to each other, an anonymity that results in – theoretical – equality. In the scheme of the course, such a presentation is not possible: society is family, is community, and its members lack moral autonomy; they are obligated people whose existence is defined by their being part of a group.

If the basic image were correct, the reasoning could be sound. Family may be seen as the fundamental building block of community, and membership entails concrete mutual and moral obligations. Beyond personal social life, one finds the public world of wider society. Order there depends on legality – not on personal obligation and subjectship. If that order is democratic, then the moral autonomy of citizens is required. People in and by themselves become carriers of inviolable rights, and thus of responsibilities to the common interest which, in their turn, guarantee such right. In the mix that has been presented so far, images become difficult to grasp because personal experience is not distinguished from public life at large.

Democracy and rights

The first semester of the second year is devoted to geography of Asia, and more than half of the second treats the history of Ayutthaya. The rest goes to 'Thai Government and Administration'. The summary explanation of that part runs as follows.

> Thailand changed its government from royal absolutism to the system of democracy under the king in which the king holds supreme power, that is, the sovereignty that consists of legislative, administrative, and judicial powers, and that belongs to the Thai people as a whole. He exercises that power in their stead by way of the parliament, the government, and the courts.

> ... Democratic government is government of the people, by the people, and for the people; accordingly all people have a share in the governing of the country ... In order to realize this democracy, people must respect and pay attention to the legitimate and reasonable opinions, knowledge, and capacities of others, accept (the principle of) equality, respect the rights and freedoms of others, be mindful of the interest of the majority while doing justice to the voice of the minority, and protecting its rights and liberties. It is therefore necessary that all of us understand the democratic principles, that we know the rights and freedoms alongside the obligations of ourselves and others so that we can execute the tasks of a dutiful population in order to really establish a democratic government under the king (*204*:129).

To me, this text oozes with uncertainty of purpose or direction, of the traveller who must chart new territory. Supreme power is objectified in three types, then illustrated as three establishments. It is of the people, but in the hands of the king. How this makes the exercise of it 'of, for, and by the people', sounds formulaic and woolly, at the same time that it mystifies The People; perhaps it is some deity, or suchlike. Key problems of conflicts of interest and of the common welfare are reduced, and reified, to 'majority' versus 'minority', while 'rights and freedoms' do not appear to be vested in human beings as such, but wrapped in a package [granted by the state?] that also contains the obligations, that then lead to the, by now very familiar, duties of good people. Be all that as it may, for the time being a desirable democracy has not been established. Let us see whether the substantive chapters improve upon this.

The first of these chapters is a boring repetition of the current ideology of the various monarchical dispensations the student has gotten spoon-fed during all of his school years. Later, when we discuss the image of history, we shall come back to the myths concerned and the democratic inclinations with which the later absolute kings have been credited. Anyway, since 1932, there is a democratic government of sorts that would have been more of a success if people had listened to the wisdom of the king.

The second chapter does not add much to our knowledge either. The statements cited above are reiterated; the idea of the public interest does not surface: it seems to equate with 'majority'; parliament makes laws that see to it that the country is peaceful and happy; government serves progress; and for the rest the (institution of) king – who is above politics – is eulogized. Royal projects and solicitude are mentioned at some length, from which follow the obligations of loyalty and gratefulness.

Next is the promising caption 'The Democratic Way of Problem-solving'. The text begins with the example of a village meeting about an irrigation problem. To involve the people concerned; to consult and discuss; to find compromise and a willingness on the part of some to sacrifice for the common interest, are said to demonstrate democracy at work. Reasonable, that is, non-emotional decision making, majority decisions, and consideration of individual interests belong to it. At that point the sophistry begins: If democracy is practised in the family and at village and subdistrict levels, democratic understanding will prevail up to the national level too. Here the failure to distinguish between concrete, personally known, communal levels and the abstract one of politics leads the authors into balderdash. Democratic understanding 'will enable people to behave in good conformity with being people who live under the democratic system of government which is a system of government in which the people are supreme because this system is the government of the people, that is, the people are the owner of the supreme power to rule the country'. Because there are so many people, they need – for the higher levels – to elect deserving representatives who are knowledgeable, sufficiently capable, and can be trusted. These elected individuals must be understood as the people (*pracha:chon*) who elect themselves (*pracha:chon*). Subsequently these individuals will govern the country (150). Of course, they cannot just do as they please, but have to operate within the bounds of the law in order to care for the interest of the majority while respecting the minority. This (more has been mentioned) is our action; it is the action of the people itself.

There still follow the basic principles: (1) mutual consultation; (2) reasonable exchanges; (3) mutual respect: all people are humans such as we, and as such we are equal, whether rich or poor; (4) in decision making we should bear the public interest (*prayo:t suanruam*) in mind rather than personal advantage, that is, we have to mind the interest of the majority more than (that of) the minority [!].

Whereas the last chapter is – again – about obligations, the penultimate one of the section has – surprisingly – 'Rights and Freedoms' as its subject. What we have to look at here is the manner in which these are proposed, to see how they relate to individuals – as subjects, citizens, or humans – and to wider society – as the space of the state, of the king, of 'us', or of 'the public'. This scrutiny will help us to develop a better understanding of 'dominant' ideas about democracy, society, and public world.

The first thing that strikes the reader is the legalistic language. Although the formulations are in accord with the law, it must be doubted whether they connect with the comprehension of junior-high-school students. A second point that comes to mind is the neglect of cultural context: foreign derived – objective – ideas are made to function in a setting that is person and family-oriented, and based on the principle of the moral inequality of individuals. The provincial public prosecutor, who functions in the book to explain rights and freedoms to the assembled villagers, says that 'a right ... is an abstract thing; it is a power, or the legitimate, or just, interest that belongs to us since birth; such a right is recognized and protected by the law; other people have to accept and respect our right, meaning that the fact that we have a right obligates other people not to violate or to infringe upon it' (155). Protection of the right by law and police; not to settle disputes privately or by hired killers; civil and criminal cases, are mentioned further. The important thing is that the exercise of rights should not irritate other people.

Freedom means that we are free to act in accordance with our rights as long as our actions do not cause upset to other people. If this leaves it all somewhat suspended in the air, the prosecutor specifies that people obtain their rights in accordance with the law, and that these rights belong to us as of birth, such as the right to our physical body, to our good name, to property, and so on. Some of these rights, such as the right to vote that we must exercise by ourselves, are called personal rights that perish upon our death. Other rights, such as the right to property, are passed on to our descendants.

Now, what are the rights and freedoms the Constitution specifies? The prosecutor begins by explaining that the Constitution stipulates that all the Thais have the same rights and freedoms, regardless of their position and rank: before the law, all are equal. All have (1) freedom of their body, meaning that we can do with our body as we please; if you want to be fat, nobody has the right to forbid it, but you have to keep your clothes on in public, because people are not allowed to go against our good mores or the criminal code that forbids obscenity. (2) In the same vein people are free to follow the religion of their choice as long as it does not contravene the obligations of the population, the law, and morality. (3) The freedom of abode, or domicile, means that we can do as we please in our homes, and that nobody has the right to enter there without our permission, not even the police.

(4) The right to property, within the bounds of the law. While this last formulation is a nett improvement over the 'as you please' of (1) and (3), it is full of sophistry when we come to the explanation of expropriation. This procedure is called 'to return'. This is so, because we should be aware that the king is the owner of the place, only allowing the people to use it. Although this reasoning seemingly belongs to the period of the absolute monarchy, under our democracy we still honour the king as the owner of the realm although, in reality, it now is the property of the state, with the people having the right of usufruct and property within the bounds of the law. Yet, the public interest may necessitate the situation that real property has to be returned to the state. After a listing of conditions surrounding such 'return', people still want to know what 'of the state' means. It means: 'of the country', or 'of the nation', or 'of all Thais'. I am afraid that this equation makes the state a very powerful player in relation to individual Thais. Perhaps that in the final analysis, this will appear to be the deeper meaning of 'the system of democratic government that has the king as its head'

Thai people enjoy (5) the freedom of education. Apart from the legally defined years of compulsory education, people are free to learn anything they want, and to establish schools, although they are not free to teach or learn criminal pursuits. (6) The freedom of communication, and thus its secrecy, is protected by the law. This freedom includes the freedom of the press. People are also (7) free to travel, and enjoy (8) freedom of residence. Besides, Thai citizens cannot be exiled from or denied entry to the national territory. We also have (9) the right to our family, our rank, reputation, and privacy. (10) People have the right to be economically active, to exercise a profession, and to compete freely and honestly, although some professions are the exclusive preserve of the state (police; soldier), and others (gangster) go against the grain of the law; undue exploitation of others is illegal, too.

(11) People have the right to safety and protection from crime, and they should not be deemed wrong before they are proven guilty. (12) They also enjoy freedom of expression as long as they do not damage the reputation of others, or the stability of the state; and (13) the freedom of association, all, again, within the limits of the law, for instance, the law on trade unions and worker organizations. (14) People have political rights, such as the active and the passive franchise. (15) They have the right to call meetings, as long as they are peaceful, unarmed, and do not disturb the peace of others. (16) People have the right to complain; also (17) to accuse the instruments of the state. All these rights and freedoms are stipulated by the Constitution in order to protect the people (167).

The problem with all these rights and freedoms is that people are only conscious of their own while not respecting the rights of others. It is only when this latter awareness arises that we shall achieve a stable democracy. More important than this still is the condition that the exercise of rights and freedoms should not antagonize Nation-Religion-King and the Constitution.

The latter observations, and the simple examples that accompany them – do with your body what you like – demonstrate a deficient imagination in relation to the very subject of democracy, namely, the public world. The images evoked are personal; the presentation of the rules, rights, laws, and so on, is merely formal; and finally the invocation of the Three Institutions reminds the student that he is ranked under something. The ideas of the free citizen responsible for a – shared – public world regulated by – the majesty of – the law do not surface, and how could they in the Thai cultural environment?

This is fully apparent in the Part's last chapter about 'The Obligations of the Populace'. These obligations are specified in the Constitution; they are the duties the population must perform and from which there is no exception. Everybody has the task to defend and care for Nation-Religion-King and the democratic system of government under the king, plus the obligation to go to school, to serve in the armed forces, to pay taxes, to exercise the right to vote in an honest manner, to care for natural resources and environment, to assist the government whenever desirable, and to seriously observe the law. Apart from these obligations, the populace must also behave according to good morals and customs (170).

Subtle changes in wording reveal the true spirit of the explanation. Morally good people **in** the context of the democratic government under the king become people **under** such goverment. Rights and duties go together. The mere exercise of rights equates with taking advantage of others.[3] The word 'country' as in the American saying 'Do not ask what the country can do for you, et cetera', is translated by 'state'. In the country and nation it is as in the family: we have obligations to each other. Besides, it is not just about legal rights and obligations: people should also live according to good morals and customs. An example illustrates this last clause: If a factory labourer works to the best of her ability, and the boss profits from her efficiency and efforts, she should consider to reward the worker beyond what is legally required.

All the fifteen or so constitutions stipulate the rights and duties of the population, the obligations being (1) the care for Nation-Religion-King, formulated in the worn-out mantras that pervade the social studies' curriculum. People also have the duty to care for democracy, because under this system all of us are partner-owners which enables us to foster the progress of the country. We have full rights and freedoms so that all of us live happily. Because we would like to persist in this way forever, and because we do not

---

3   The idea that rights are vested in the person per se has gone lost here. Human Rights - *sitthi manutsayachon* - are thus not mentioned at all.

know what a change in the system will bring – whether we shall be happy or not – while we know from the news that life under other systems is problematic, we must help each other in taking care of our democratic system under the king.

This nebulous reasoning is followed by (2) the duty to use the right to vote honestly. We must take part in government through our elected – capable and moral – representatives. We should elect them in an honest manner, meaning that we vote for the person whom we really want, and not for the one who pays us to do so, or to whom we are morally indebted (who have *bunkhun* to us). Of interest is (3) the duty to defend the country, or nation. This is not the privilege of any single group, not even of the instruments of state, but a task in which all of us must share. Then there is (4) general conscription (for men); (5) the duty to obey the law. The law fosters peace and comfort. Especially in big societies with many people, laws are necessary to promote progress and prosperity. (6) We must pay tax; (7) and assist the government. The government cannot do it all by itself, and because all of us are owners of the country, we must do our share. Such help is important to the government, such as exemplified by the cooperation between the state and the private sector (apparently analogous to the saying, 'What is good for General Motors, is good for America.') (8) Compulsory education; (9) the duty to care for natural resources and environment, illustrated by the ecological devastation for which 'all of us' are held to be responsible.

The non-legal duties are presented in the way familiar since elementary school. Promoting self within the bounds of morality makes us more than willing to care for our family as we care for ourselves; the family is then projected to become community and *sangkhom* (society), which ultimately becomes country and world. If everybody does their duty in caring for self, family, and community or society, they really execute their task toward the nation. We must cooperate, be diligent, patient and tolerant, economical and honest, while not taking advantage of others. We should never be the tools of foreign powers. Together we shall restore the good social values while being wary of self-seeking politicians. We must be decisive to instil democratic values, which is our most important task, resulting in a clear perception of what is personal gain and what is public interest. We should do more than just admire (*thoetthu:n*) those good individuals who exert themselves for the common good; we have tasks to the nation.

The last chapter starts with the assertion that religion teaches how to achieve a peaceful society. This is the reason why people should hold firmly to it, and practise its fundamental principles. This is not problematic, because 'Thai society has been peaceful and quiet for a long time because its population holds firmly to religion' (*104*:186). In a similar simplistic spirit, a few principles are then discussed, such as the Four Principles of Social Welfare. Differences need to be overcome; then, people can cooperate. This is achieved by giving, by being mindful of other people, such as building a factory so that poor people will find themselves gainfully employed. Non-material forms are in extending religious teaching, education, and help.

A society can only progress because of education. If the people are stupid and uneducated, they will be barbaric, cruel and ruthless. To have reason and to be reasonable depends on education in Buddhism and morality.[4] The next two principles are explained in a very individual-centred manner: to speak pleasing language, and to fulfil one's duties. The fourth rule is to understand and to be friendly with other people: even criminals have good qualities, and some people, even though they are poor, may be clever and wise. Because bad people have their good aspects too, we may consider to associate with them in order to effect in them a change of heart. Buddhists, who should consider things from all sides in order to know the truth, can easily mix and associate with all people.

---

[4]   Note the clear opposition between ignorance and knowledge, and the idea that to have reason is to have morality. In short, knowledge is dharmasastra, that is, to discern truth and right values. By itself, such knowledge refrains a person from committing wrong, that is, stupid actions.

Follow the Six Principles of Good Cooperation. Under its fifth clause we find the observation that a country with an orderly and disciplined population will experience progress and prosperity only. Even if such a country is small, yet filled with quality, it can triumph over bigger countries that lack such properties. People should also be of one opinion and avoid conflict; then society, and ultimately country and nation will be strong. Finally the Six Directions, that is, the duties inherent in different positions, or relationships, are elaborated. If everybody knows and fulfils their obligations, there will be no 'cleavages' in society, and relationships among people will be good; this demonstrates that there are principles of human relations 'that are good' (204:192). Upon these notes of deep wisdom, I shall leave the scrutiny of the Christian and Islamic insights that still follow to the discretion of the enlightened reader.

The trials of democracy:

third year

About one fourth of the third year curriculum of social studies is spent in explaining government, and in between formalities and legalities we find some observations that help construct an image of the public world. Parallel to earlier teachings about ethics, the relevant chapter begins with the objectification, or reification of the law as an agent for ordering society. 'If there is no law to protect us, who will protect our possessions? Other people may enter our house, and just pick up our things and use them as their own' (306:209). The issuing of laws, their vindication, maintenance, and consideration, constitute the power of the government that the king exercises in our name by way of the institutions of the legislature, the executive, and the judiciary. Yet, the king is above politics.

To go by democratic-constitutional principles has been a laborious task. Our fifteenth Constitution dates from December

1991. Follow summary explanations of the institutions mentioned above, the institution of kingship, the elections, and political parties. Then a chapter is devoted to the pivotal role of kingship, spelling out the legal tasks of the king, the king's role as a stabilizer at times when political infighting gets violent, and his symbolic function as the centre in which the hearts and minds of the Thais meet. By eulogizing the institution of kingship and the person of the present monarch, other instrumentalities of government are firmly relegated to the wings: without kingship, Thailand would perish in civil war. The reasons given for this faithfully follow those propounded in all history courses.

The chapter about the three branches of government is interesting because of the realism it demonstrates. After all, in Thailand we try to emulate the example of the British form of government. The three branches are called 'institutions' (*satha:ban*) 'in order for them to be extolled, to so demonstrate the great value of these establishments for society' (224). For sixty years now, parliament has been struggling along, and thoughout the fifteen constitutions its shape has been altered regularly. Currently, after the savage events of May 1992, the latest constitution is being amended in order to clear it from the excessive demands of the former National Peace-Keeping Council [a junta that came to power through a putsch]. From the narrative it is implicitly clear that the professional civil service is the mainstay of administrative continuity.

Realism informs the chapter about elections, too. While the reader is not offered any clear ideas about the inner workings of the democratic process, it points its finger to interesting weaknesses of actual electoral practice. Because representatives can only run under the banner of established parties, such parties become constituent elements of the democratic system. The stipulation that parties must field at least one hundred and twenty members, is clearly to the advantage of the larger parties, and prevents locally popular smaller ones from seeking political representation.

The multitude of parties running in elections inevitably leads to the formation of coalition governments with a reduced capacity for efficiency and stability. Following on this observation, the main problems of the democratic system are presented as: (1) Vote-buying. This practice is against democratic rules and political ethics; it leads to excessive spending and thus to profiteering from elected office which causes the corruption of politicians. (2) Most people have a very poor understanding of democracy, and vote for the wrong representatives, to wit, those people to whom they are morally obligated, or who particularly care for their home districts. This leads to being biased in favour of one's own constituency without considering the national interest. (3) People vote for persons rather than for parties. It is asserted, however, that in Bangkok public opinion rather than individuals is influencing the result of the polls.

Voting for individuals instead of for parties makes that party ideology has no meaning, and that parties are mere groups of individual people who happen to enjoy popularity in their districts. In other words, parties serve individual interests, and thus lack continuity. Every single person wants to become a cabinet member, which results in a lot of infighting and eternally shaky governments. It is these three conditions that cause governmental instability and the prejudiced behaviour of elected representatives. It is hoped that further economic development will result in better income for all and in a higher level of education. Also NGOs and the coming of age of the political parties will be beneficial for the development of our political culture. All this, however, will take a long time, yet we should not despair as long as the youth keeps acquiring a deeper understanding of democracy.

While I appreciate the critical approach towards political behaviour exemplified in this chapter, I have to observe that political ideology and platforms have remained out of the picture. Democracy is not seen as the negotiation of conflicts and social contradictions, and certain democratic premises – equality, rule of law *per se* – have remained words only without any attempt to understand them in the patronage-seeking context of Thai society.

I fear that these latter observations – and the 'ideologization' and 'politicization' of society that these entail – go against the, sometimes barely hidden, basic argument that equates the state with nation, society, country, the people, the public interest and the common good; these entities ultimately fuse in the Three Institutions that in their turn conflate in King. To guarantee the stability of all these, people should live by the law, the guidance of which strengthens government and adminstration. The last chapter, therefore, specifies a few of the laws people should know.

In the last Part, the axiom is repeated that, since a long time, the hold of the Buddhist religion on the Thais has been the cause of the country's quiet and happiness. More interesting is the observation about the use of religious teachings, namely, that they are useful to the individual, and thus to society: individuals need to work for the development of their morality first; only then they can make a meaningful contribution to society and country; if each and every individual does not develop himself morally first, how will society become civilized?

Then, under The Two World-guarding Principles, we learn that people are basically bad, egoistically striving for power, pelf and prestige, with which they exploit others and flout the law. It is only *Dhamma* – religious, or higher natural, law – that can protect the world through deep reluctance to commit evil, and fear of sin and retribution. Needless to mention, this way of teaching religious principles presents ethical law and values as causes in and by themselves. This is in no contradiction to the popular – and old-fashioned – understanding of the law of karma that is explained as being a personal attribute with concrete causes and effects. Follow still the Seven Qualities of the Moral (or wise, or good) Person, and the Ten Ways of Building Goodness. Then a few words are allowed to Confucius and to Guru Nanak, the teacher of the Sikhs.

The image of Thai history:

Sukhothai

A part of the social studies course of the second semester of the first year in high school is devoted to history, to wit, some forty pages about Sukhothai, and a summary of subsequent occurrences up to the present. As in primary school, it is difficult to disentangle history from the national, or state ideology in which it is wrapped. This is immediately apparent in the first substantive sentences about the prehistory of what is now known as Thailand: 'Our country is independent and has the king as its head. We enjoy freedom within the designated borders of our country. We do not need to wander around to seek the protection of another country, such as the people of some of our neighbouring lands' (102:3). Later on in the chapter, it becomes clear that the present unity of Thailand is not a matter of course, that the expansion of the Thais was at the expense of Khmers, Mons, Lawas, and others; that Thai groups were fighting each other; and that they took many cultural elements from those who had previously held the territory.

The kingdom of Sukhothai is considered to be the origin of present-day Thailand. Its current shape and ideals of nation-statehood make their imprint on history as presented. Often the dynastic realm is referred to as Thailand; the populace becomes nation; we and our substitute for the king's; Thai replaces Sukhothai and, later, Siam. Kings are fatherly and wise, always taking the happiness and well-being of the populace (ra:tsadon) to heart; vassal states that reassert their freedom are rebellious; conquering them is good, because it expands 'our' realm. A vast territory, and lordship over all kinds of people, is a glorious and good thing; the present borders define the commentary on the past; the monarch is the kingpin, the creator, the very centre of the realm. Religion is a good thing in itself, promoted by the king, and a tool of statecraft. Laws guarantee the orderliness of the realm, and justice for the people; the country and the nation must be stable.

The text must also be credited with giving a good deal of accurate information. To expand the realm, many wars need to be fought, yet, the alleged happiness of and the compassion for 'the people' are never questioned. It is stated that Sukhothai enjoyed prosperity and stability for two hundred years, yet half the text is about its decline. The Ramkhamhaeng inscription is taken for granted as a description of the social situation, yet we also learn that society was composed of two groups, namely, the estate of the rulers, and the ordinary people. In the same paragraph we learn about other groups, such as slaves, foreigners, and the estate of the clergy. Talking about the 'borders' of the realm is imposing another modern notion,[5] which is later corrected by more accurate information about the vassal states and their ambiguous relationship with the centre of power. The fighting of kings against kings is correctly noted, and most often implies the fighting of 'Thais' against 'Thais'. This stands at right angles with the smuggled in modern notion of the kings as nation-builders, presaging the twentieth century idea of Nation. Of interest is the importance given to culture: it is defined as the quality that demonstrates the progress of the nation; it is the nation's heritage and identity, of which the Thai language and Theravada Buddhism are inalienable parts. Yet, the observation that the writing system 'of the Thai nation' was invented as a sign of national independence sounds rather weird.

While it is repeatedly emphasized that the king ruled the people such as a father does his children – and that the populace held the king in awe, honouring, obeying and worshipping him, while being filled with gratefulness – the information is also given that the Sukhothai kings held absolute power. This observation is interesting, because further on in the texts the origins of royal

---

[5] For the older political formation, it is more accurate to speak of 'spheres of influence'. Regarding Thailand, borders in the western sense - and related definitions of the state - are a late-nineteenth-century innovation. See Thongchai Winichakul, *Siam Mapped*. Honolulu: University Press of Hawaii, 1994. Chiang Mai: Silkworm Books, 1995.

absolutism will be situated in the later Sukhothai period, that is, at a time that the realm was contracting and its power declining. As we shall see, this invalidates the very reasons given for its establishment, namely, the growing complexity caused by territorial expansion. Another interesting fact is that King Lithai, the alleged author of the *Traiphumiphraruang*,[6] was not only very active in propagating Theravada Buddhism, but tried to shore up his power by promoting the well-being of religion. It was apparently no guarantee for success, as he was losing out to the founding king of Ayutthaya.

The odd mixture of ideology and facts, resulting in the a-historical projection of the present into the past, leaves the reader somewhat bewildered, and distracts from the evolution of the Thai social formation. The part that follows, 'Summary History from Ayutthaya to the Present', does not improve upon this. Racing through history may point to some way stations, but can never reveal the track, let alone offer the map on which they are located. What the summary attempts to instil is a dogmatic periodization that, according to the text, will give the student an image of the continual progress of the country: 'At the same time we tried to care for and built our firm identity; with this the country could maintain its national independence, especially because of the sagacity of the kings and the resolve of our ancestors' (61). Leaving this quotation for what it is, the three main episodes discerned comprise (1) The Olden Times, that is, Ayutthaya up to the Bowring Treaty; (2) The New Times, up to 1932; (3) Constitutional Period. They are defined by the type of prevailing dispensations, such as, divine kingship; western administrative practice; and democracy.

The method of historical presentation is respectable because it aims to explain social and economic dynamics while hoping to demonstrate cultural continuity-in-change. Because of the Thai

---

[6]   The *Traiphumiphraruang*, or *The Three Plains of Existence According to Phra Rüang*, is the standard and, until recently, authoritative treatise on Thai-Hindu-Buddhist cosmology.

flexibility to adapt to changing times, Thailand could guard itself while its population enjoyed peace, happiness and protection. The main thing to adapt to was western power and influence, and thus western methods, manners and know-how had to be taken over in order to foster progress and development.

Ayutthaya

The second year offers the history of Ayutthaya, which is again a fascinating mixture of facts and fanciful ideology. The qualities and position of the king are presented in exactly the same terms as in the primary curriculum, and need not be repeated. Royal power is reined in by religious principles and the king's boundless compassion for his subjects; add to this the abundance of natural resources, and life under Ayutthayan reign can only have been pleasant and comfortable. Of course, if 'free', the populace had to work six months a year for king or grandee; men were soldiers for much of their time; they were severely controlled as a scarce resource; were hardly if at all protected by law; had no right to engage in significant trade; and had to produce assigned goods as a poll tax, yet, 'there was rice in the field, fish in the water' – the living was easy.

The restricted role of the common people – bonded subjects, soldiers, slaves, monks – made that much commercial and industrial activity in the capital was in Chinese hands, at the same time that the royal monopolies reserved foreign trade for king and nobility. The city-centred state grew rich and powerful, very much because of its commercial contacts, first with China and other parts of Asia, then also with Europeans, among whom the French and the Dutch played important roles. Much of the knowledge about these later times derives from European sources.

Following the official format, parts of the texts are devoted to the organization and administration of the realm; the economic and human resources of the government; the connexions with the various *müang* and tributary vassal states; the necessary, somewhat feudalistic decentralization; the *sakdina* system; commercial resources; while even some historical sources and hypotheses are critically discussed. Much of this is presented in an awfully formalistic and technical way, more as a burden to memorize than as a stimulus for the historical imagination.

All the time the presentation is palace-centred, and we get very little information about ordinary life. The constant projection of the present into the past is irritating and confusing: a permanent preoccupation with – national, *cha:tba:nmüang* – integration and stability; Siam becomes Thai; the royal realm, our country, or even nation; the balance between the three branches of government surfaces several times; on some pages the people enjoy justice (*204*:34), on others it is clear that it was out of their reach (60). Comparisons with the economic conditions of the twentieth century are frequent: capital investment and the profit motive did not operate among the people because their resources were abundant; they did not depend on external contacts; they assisted each other as a matter of course.

The focus on the king – especially interesting for the reign of King Narai toward the end of the seventeenth century, and the subsequent decline of the power of Ayutthaya – reveals the dependence on the person of the monarch, and that all the details about laws and administrative arrangements are peripheral to what is really significant: the basic institutional weakness of the realm. A powerful ruler at the centre means continuity; a feeble one, or strife about succession, presages unrest and decline. The way to keep people in place is to maintain a strict hierarchical order (*sakdina*) and to enforce 'loyalty' to the centre. Of interest is the importance of foreign trade, both as a source of wealth and stability, and as a threat; it is a pity that this basic economic factor has not been theorized, because it portends the developments of the nineteenth and twentieth centuries. What happens throughout the text is that things are repeated without end at the same time that past circumstances are idealized, almost as if such repetition and idealization would breed insight.

Although aspects of the economy are frequently mentioned, the movers of Ayutthayan history appear to be strategic considerations, the desire for expansion, and thus war. In simple terms, with near neighbours, it is perennial fighting, with further-off foreigners, it is trade. Commercial contacts have cultural and political consequences, and bring in Chinese, other Asians and Europeans, who come to occupy all sorts of new ranks and functions. Interestingly, the evaluation of these foreign influences is generally positive, although the dynamics of the economy are kept from view. Maybe this is because a more economy-focused treatment would conflict with the implicit preconception of the periodization: Ayutthaya = old = economic self-sufficiency. Political factors should explain the motion of The Olden Times, and thus the supreme importance of leadership, unity and 'stability' are explicitly paraded to elucidate the undoing and fall of Ayutthaya. This sets, of course, an important precedent for the stability considerations of the present.

Modern times

The constraints of periodization dominate the presentation of history in the third year. The Thonburi and early-Bangkok periods are old; new begins in 1855 and is over in 1932; the constitutional era lasts up to now. If Ayutthaya provided the example for the old times, western ways become the norm in the second period. In the present stage, 'we Thais imitate the ways of western countries in almost every respect' (306:1), which results in progress and development.

There is little of relevance to say about the Thonburi period, that saw the reimposition of royal power over the widely spread dynastic realm. The chapter concerned does devote attention to the obligatory details: the many wars; government, administration, and their sources of revenue; laws and justice; economy; society, religion, and culture; foreign relations (wars, imperialism, China). Since this was and is done for every period and subperiod, the information grows extremely repetitious and uninspiring. The explanation of the role of the Chinese in the early Bangkok period is of interest: They did the non-agricultural work Thais were restrained from or uninterested in doing; they even became tax farmers, and some of them joined the ranks of the aristocracy. Their power made them into a kind of mafia. Simultaneously, the role of bonded labour diminished, but since we are told that this occurred in order to make the life of the ordinary Thai more pleasant, the reader is put on the wrong foot. Again: the relationship between economy and social developments is obscured. Anyway, trading contacts with the British adumbrate the dangers, misunderstandings, and economic evolution of the second half of the nineteenth century.

It is a pity that the fascinating chapters about Thailand's modernization are divided into politics and administration; economy; and societal change. The same happens again for the democratic times beginning in 1932. Both the main periodization, alongside the discussion under preset labels tend to fracture history, and give rise to awkward reiteration. Anyway, change affects all aspects of life, and the reasons given for its necessity are most revealing, and relevant to understand the present. In order not to be overpowered by western imperialism, the Thai kings realized that they needed to bring the country up to modern standards, that is, to accept and implement western civilization. Contemporary Thai practices are described as out-of-date, primitive, and barbarian. Americans and Europeans, therefore, had good reason to insist on extraterritoriality. The latter looked down on Thai customs and the way ordinary people were treated by a powerful, rich nobility and aristocracy. Accustomed as they were to middle classes, their rights, freedoms, and citizenship, Thailand had to go a long way to reach their standards. Thus the Thai kings assumed 'the white man's burden' to civilize the country and its people, inspiring themselves with the example of the culturally advanced nations (a:raya phrathe:t), in order to demonstrate that the country could meet their level.

As a result, and against the conservatism of the ruling families, the fourth and the fifth kings began modernizing the legal system, while giving better protection to ordinary people. At the same time all sorts of outdated customs had to make place for more European-style ones. Of utmost importance were the administrative reforms of the Fifth Reign; its precursors of the democratic system, such as the establishment of advisory councils of nobility and aristocrats, were not successful. Its members lacked all originality and preferred not to endanger themselves by opening their mouths. In the end, the now centralized administration began to touch directly upon the lives of the population at large.

The sixth king discovered nationalism, its important role in a country's progress, and its economic and military mobilizing power. Up until then, Thai people had had a regional identity at best. He also experimented with democracy in order that 'the administration results in all the sorts of progress desired by the people' (90). It is noteworthy that this undifferentiated idea of democracy is still with us some seventy-five years later. This vagueness is perhaps why the reasons for monarchical actions in the sixth and seventh reign remain covered up by apologetics at best, while those given for the coup of 1932 are the same as in the books for elementary school. Yet I have to take exception with a persistent misinterpretation, probably smuggled in because of the weird periodization, namely, the idea that kings gradually lost their absolute power. The most powerful of all kings was probably the Fifth, who succeeded in reducing the grandees, centralizing the government, and unifying the realm within modern borders. This overwhelming central power not only ran counter to the interests of nobility and aristocracy, but also to those of the emerging middle classes of commoners. It is sociologically sound that the role of the latter in the transition to a modern social order is pointed out, and one of the given reasons, namely, that royal absolutism and aristocratic privileges were obstructing their development, hits the nail on the head.

It is, therefore, a pity that the analysis of modernization in the subsequent chapters shies away from highlighting the significance of contemporary middle classes. After all, it is these groups who exert pressure on the political system, who articulate problems and demands; they are the eminent product and articulators of a modernizing society; interestingly, in Thailand, they most often are of Chinese and Sino-Thai descent. This is not to say that all this is not mentioned in passing, but the description tends to put the central government in the limelight, and to enumerate economic factors without considering the roles of entrepreneurship, education, and professional differentiation.

In itself the treatment of material, economic factors – and the role of foreign pressure – is consistent: the country opens up rapidly; the export of rice becomes its mainstay. In the margin, we are also informed that the farming population remained poor; that Thai aristocrats grew rich; that government policy was an important facilitator; that foreigners and Chinese dominated the economy. In this changing economy, dependence on trade, both exports and imports, grows; all sorts of new capital and consumer goods stream in from abroad. Modern monetary means, banking, relevant laws and taxes, alongside new transportation systems, need to be developed; the role of government expands. All this stimulates – early – consumerism, exploitation of the environment, and the commercialization of relationships. It also results in class formation: capitalists versus – poor – labour, and the emergence of a middle class that articulates the desire for democracy. Full stop. Then the sensitivity to world economic happenings is illustrated, inexorably leading up to the events of 1932.

The more societally oriented chapter groups social change and foreign relations. Firstly, it is concerned with the reception of western civilization and the progress it brings. Since the western powers become increasingly aware of rights, freedom, and human equality, the institutions of bonded labour and slavery are gradually abolished. This social revolution also resulted in the creation of a free labour market; it offered chances for social mobility and personal advancement; it stands at the beginning of the formation of middle classes. Missionaries introduced western school education; it became compulsory for girls and boys during the Sixth Reign. Universal, that is, western cultural standards, say, family names and a national flag, were adopted. This summary treatment then makes way for nineteenth century foreign relations, and the need to modernize the Thai polity. This need becomes especially apparent through the various forms of prosperity prevailing among those neighbouring peoples who were governed by western powers [sic] (139). During his travels to these and European countries, the fifth king was impressed by their progress; they became the example for his reforms.

Western expansion, driven by 'the white man's burden', industrialization and free trade, demanded unequal treaties and territorial concessions, resulting in the loss of half the Thai [sic] territory. The Thais joined the Allies in World War I in order to create the basis for renegotiating the unequal treaty relationships. No, I beg your pardon; according to the book, they joined because they were indignant at Germany's very violent methods of warfare that did not consider the laws of war and humanitarianism, namely, unrestricted submarine attacks that cost the lives of many innocent people, and the use of poison gas.

The last section covers the democratic-constitutional period. It begins with a listing of its kings, then proposes to describe these years in four segments. The first is about the struggle among the proponents of the new dispensation themselves, and between them and the old vested interests of aristocrats and others. In the wrangling, ideals apparently get lost; the king abdicates, Phibun Songkhram becomes the first military dictator. He propagates nationalism, irredentism, autarchy, and the trappings of western civilization. The second segment relates about the war, Japan's aggression, and the Free Thai movement that saved the day. This brings us to the third: America did not recognize the Thai declaration of war; in 1946 there were democratic elections. Quarrelling among politicians and the armed forces is endemic; all and sundry are corrupt; nobody seems to be able to solve basic problems. It results in the return of Marshal P. and subsequent machinations.

This leads up to the fourth subperiod. Beginning with Marshal Sarit Thanarat, national economic development becomes the guiding policy. It is a time, like the preceding ones, of coups d'état, of corruption, bickering, dictatorship, new constitutions, of Cold War, and the awakening to democracy. The unruly period of open society, 1973-6, brought all sorts of new interest groups to the fore. A polarisation among political left and right occurred; infighting among the parties that composed the coalition governments was endemic. Yet, even the subsequent non-democratic government was unable to bridge, let alone transcend, the conflicts of interest and ideology. A new coup was necessary to bring effective mediators to power. Henceforth, rural development policies brought justice to the village population; the civil service reduced its exploitation of the ruralites; and rapid economic development, fuelled by foreign investment, was taking hold of the country. The clownesque and tragic fiasco of military arrogance and pedantry finally led to elections won by the Democratic Party (1992).

The same subperiodization is used to describe economic progress. Subsequently we are offered lots of facts and opinions that fail to explain how developments stick together. The early problems were foreign domination of the economy and poverty. The state tried to remedy this by establishing publicly owned companies. They proved to be a failure. Private initiative and free capitalism are more effective.

Since 1958, foreign investment drives the economy; economic growth is a good thing. Ecological and moral problems crop up, though. Foreign capital benefits from Thai labour and exploits it; it is greedy, tries to dodge taxes, exports its profits and our natural resources. The towns grow rapidly, giving rise to slums, lack of discipline, and crime. Factories pollute. In the early days the Thais lived together in good friendship and cooperation, but our shift to industrial production even affects social relations in the countryside. Nowadays people compete with each other, minding themselves only. Everybody is motivated by money, while the gap between rich and poor widens. Respect for elders and teachers, alongside belief in religion, is diminishing all the time, while tendencies to egoism are strengthening. It is most worrying to watch how senseless violence and drugs are strengthening their hold. Thus, while economic growth increases people's income, it should not focus on earning more money only; we have to take the quality of life into account and mind the environment, moral principles, education, and equality.

The last relevant chapter begins with the same lamentation; (school) knowledge is suggested to enable people to discern right and wrong, and to solve ecological problems. The whole period is characterized by the emergence of middle classes and the rapid expansion of western culture. The latter brings in discotheques, bars, cocktail lounges, karaoke bars, and other things that do not benefit our youth. They begin spending money and time there, ultimately wasting their lives and addicted to drugs. Although western ways also have positive influences, such as upon our literature and architecture, we should care for our identity and age-old heritage. This is all we are told about social and cultural change, to which the final section about foreign relations – and the Cold War – repeatedly adds that the Thai people love democracy.

Comments

The closer we get to the present, the weaker the text becomes. From heroic attempts to analyse the economy as basic to all social dynamics, the narrative slips back to moral observations and club twaddle all the time. What remains in place are a few slogans: without king, no Thailand; the king constitutes the centre of the Thais' hearts and minds; the Thais love democracy; foreign investment is good; European civilization is superior; Thailand is independent and respected; the past is untroubled, the present problematic.

Because the total presentation lacks theory and structure, the lines of social and historical evolution cannot be articulated. Arbitrary periodizations exacerbate this problem. Yet, most teachers I interviewed are not aware of these questions, and proceed to present social studies in chunks and pieces. Some of the latter are well chiselled out, making inner sense, and thus lead up to single images, but other things require so much reading between the lines that it cannot be expected to result in clear mental pictures; for instance, the real conditions of the people under absolute and feudal impositions is a forbidden question, going against the grain of the national ideology of benevolent and just kingship.

Apart from such ideological constructions, the main 'structural principle' of the story appears to be the chronology of political dispensations. Such 'structuring' allows for facts; facts to be learnt by heart, instead of a vision or theory that can be understood. Taking an anthropological point of departure by trying to reconstruct the evolution of the mental world of the people as subjects and rulers, peasants and princes, knaves, adventurers and monks, would already offer a line that connects past to present. Such a line cannot be offered by the current attempt to idealize and ideologize. If drawn, it would show the persistence of ideas surrounding power, the continuity of family ideology, and the distrust *vis-à-vis* authority, to mention a few possibilities.

'In elementary school we aim to build people. When our students go on to high school, they are abandoned, neither finding moral guidance nor discipline. The break between the two systems is very problematic' This head-master's opinion hints at the discontinuity between a moral system and a more intellectual one. Yet, we have noted that in facing problems, structural solutions are avoided, leaving social causes and effects dangling in the air, while ultimate recourse is taken to unconvincing moral and religious means that have little application in everyday life situations of students and their mentors. While I am given to lay the blame at the primary level, the problem of the non-continuity remains. Pupils in junior high are prepared for different ways of thinking. However, at least in social studies, they are not encouraged to see the bigger picture and to reason. We may thus expect that their knowledge merely roots in memorization.

The public world is represented as royal, or national, or state ideology plus boisterous politics; it is these constructs that should serve to make the evolution of society and history visible. All through the narrative the influence of external factors – trade, ideas, wars – is taken account of, yet, an understanding of the own being, of Thai culture and Thainess, is sorely missing. This means that foreign ideas – democracy for one – function in a vacuous environment, and that their adaptation to the Thai scene is left unquestioned. Undesirable traits should be kept at bay; the beautiful Thai traditions and culture should be revived; identity must be promoted. What all this substantially means is obscured – and this is as it should be – given the steadfast refusal to reflect about the own being.

Another line to draw – and possibly a more fecund one to bring order and image – is that of economic development. Now it is represented by the simplistic, and thus highly confusing and untrue, sequence from subsistence to trade to industry that is made to coincide with changing regimes. A further possibility, at least for the newer periods, is a good focus on the emergence and growth of middle classes. The line that I would like to follow is the history of ideas – which needs, of course, a good go at Thai cultures, but there is a fair amount of sources that can be interpreted. Just to say 'religion was respected' or that 'people held firmly to it', does not say anything about actual religious thought and practice; neither do statements that 'life was peaceful and abundant', whether because of resources or thanks to the Buddhist faith, inform us about the real conditions.

In other words, the Thais often seem to forget how Thai they are and remain. They seem to be unable or, at least, highly unwilling to consciously find their own models, and would be shocked to analyse, say, the current political confrontations, or corruption, as eminent examples of the Thai social process and the ideas that animate it. This deficit of critical reflection about the own being makes for many equally uncritical calls for the instatement of lost values and Buddhist wisdom, as if these represent the past. This being bound to formulaic perceptions –

including: the West is modern and prosperous, we have to follow – corresponds with the security of authoritarianism, hierarchy, formalism, rote learning, and the king-centred national ideology. The school – it is a pity to say – generally reinforces this tendency to conformity. Originality is insecurity. As a result, the recent preoccupation with national identity leads to harmless folklorization, showmanship, and the 'authenticity' of reinvented traditions. It also leaves the new middle classes with few alternatives but to follow the trends of fashionable consumerism, that is, a culture in which money is the measure of all things.

I find the abandonment of basic sociological concepts throughout the analysis very alarming. I have pointed to the fact that discarding the fundamental pair of community and society precludes explanation of the latter, let alone the means that are concocted to get a grip on society-in-the-abstract – such as laws, rights, democracy. By reducing the social process to what can be personally experienced, the theoretical imagination cannot develop, and a vision of society cannot emerge. This may explain the absence of vested interests, institutions, and their continuity, in the presentation; it also homogenizes and reifies 'the people'. To overstate it, perhaps the nation had better be analysed as a functioning market than as subjects tied to a ruler, or as a highly stabilizing bureaucratic polity rather than as a 'democracy'. Perhaps there is even something good to say about the long-prevailing statist ideology itself to explain continuity-in-change. If the nation were just left to its civilian, confrontational politicians, it might have split up a long time ago. About this 'democratic' weakness, and the importance of the king, the books are explicit, however.

Chapter 3

SENIOR HIGH SCHOOL:
IMPAIRING SOUND REASONING

The books in use for senior high school are produced by private publishing houses who religiously stick to the format prescribed by the Department of Education in order to have their texts approved. The series that I consulted is produced by the Watthana Panich Company according to the revised curriculum of 1990, originally prescribed in 1981.[1] The six books concerned have all been written by different (groups of) authors who apparently do not consult each other, which not only results in repetitious information, but also in a confusing variety of approaches. The general absence of a master scheme exacerbates this weakness, such as immediately apparent from the first book of the two that are to be used in the tenth grade.

The book's intention is to take a conceptual approach to the subject matter. Already on page two we learn that people are capable of devising and using a variety of symbols. These are things that are used to represent the meaning of other things; they may represent material objects, such as a cross to represent

---

1   Watchara Khlainathorn, Phenkhae Kittisak, Dr Tueanchai Ketusa, *Sô: 401 Sangkhomsüksa: (Social Studies 401)*. Bangkok: Watthana Panich, 1991.
     Sukhum Nualsakul, Dr Preecha Suwannathat, *Sô: 402 idem*, 1991.
     Dr Thaemsuk Numnont *et al.*, *Sô: 605 idem*, 1993.
     Dr Duean Khamdee, Nuek Thongmeephet, *Sô: 606 idem*, 1993.

crossroads, or immaterial things, such as the cross to represent Christianity. Symbols serve communication; they may be linguistic, both spoken and written; material, such as a flag; and behavioural, such as greeting. This information is given to set humans apart from animals. The subject is not pursued beyond this – it is not even related to the idea of culture. So, after some artful concretizations of the idea of society – a big community, a state? – we learn that society and culture belong together, that culture regulates social life, and that people must behave in conformity with their culture.

This basic, functionalistic view is amply illustrated by the footnotes referring to the outdated American textbooks the author(s) obviously have read at some point, and that serve to lend academic credibility to the narrative. In order to avoid any integrated view, four different objectifications ('definitions') of the idea of culture are presented – none of which even approach the Thai idea of *watthanatham* with which the students have been familiarized so far: 'Culture' is constituted by those qualities that demonstrate the progress and the orderliness of the nation (*102*:29; *204*:83). Needless to say, this procedure – let us avoid the word method – heavily taxes the students' ability to memorize things.

Accordingly, the five qualities of culture are specified as (1) culture is learned; (2) it is a response to human needs; (3) it regulates social behaviour; (4) it changes and readjusts itself all the time; (5) as social heritage, it serves socialization. Then, culture is divided into its material and immaterial variants; according to the National Culture Commission, Thai culture consists of four entities: behavioural principles; legal, regulatory principles; cooperative principles; and material manifestations. Culture can also be analysed as those basic norms that are valid for all members of a given society, versus structural, or regional, variations.

In addition, culture has the following functions: (1) it helps people to adjust to their natural environment; (2) it is a tool to create order in human society; (3) it contributes to progress; (4) it unifies the members of society; (5) it develops manners and codes that enable people to interact with each other.

This foretaste of what teachers and students have to struggle through indicates the level of the discourse: it never sees the wood for the trees. Were it only so that a single one-sided functionalist line were presented consistently, trees, or rather facts, would cohere. Then, on basis of its inner logic, an image of society and an illustration of what social science hopes to be about could possibly whet the appetite for further study. Now, however, both comprehension and curiosity are killed in one stroke. Anyway, the same suffocating and meaningless methods are followed to explain social structure, groups, institutions, and their functions. The authors do not feel any need to explain the basic unit of sociological analysis, that is, the idea of social relationships. Values and functions are only known in their positive aspects, and resound with the moralistic bias of the earlier lessons in social studies. In that way the functions of religion become (1) to integrate society; (2) to build and relay culture; (3) social control; and (4) to respond to emotional needs. Such *ad hoc* selections of qualities, and the failure to go in-depth, make the first book less interesting, and definitely less informative, than a critical editorial column in a newspaper.

Following upon the first three introductory chapters, Thai society is analysed. The 'depiction' generously mixes ideology with armchair observations, drivel, and functionalism, while steadfastly side-stepping simple Thai realities, such as hierarchy, patronage, fascination with power and prestige, conflicts and violence, and everything else a newspaper would write about. It has obviously not been written to enable the student to get a mental grasp of wider society and its public world. Perhaps it merely serves as a demonstration of the authors' erudition by generously quoting from old foreign textbooks.

Thai society

We read that the basis of Thai society – including its minorities – is the shared acceptance of Thai culture in collective life. Thai

society is influenced by its natural, cultural and social environments. While the meaning of environment, as external factors
that exert their influence, is clear from the explanation of the
natural surroundings, externalities and the own presupposed being
are confounded and confused in the discussion of the cultural and
social environments. Everything thought of as culture is first seen
as heritage; then Buddhism, India, the Mons and the Khmers, et
cetera, are mentioned. And so it goes for the social environment. It
is both the inner pattern of social relationships and, for instance,
the influence of external western ways that need to be selectively
adopted.

The special qualities of Thai society that set it apart from others
are the fact that it holds to its king as the head of the nation;
Buddhism; customs and traditions; behavioural patterns and
values, amongst which gratefulness, respect for seniors, and fun-
lovingness stand out. Certain values need changing, though,
because they function as obstacles on the way to a better quality
of life. This digression brings us to the last special quality: the
Thais live in an agricultural, countryside-based society; it is there
that people persist in the real Thai traditions.

The structure of Thai society brings its various groups and
institutions into focus. The first ones mentioned consist of the Thai
family, communities, and minorities. The family is made up of Thai
people who live in 11,3 million households. Communities are a
group of families who share a territory; they share a measure of
common ways in order to respond to the needs of their members
and to solve the problems of communal life (this is quoted from an
American text of 1968). To this the authors add an administrative
view of community; as a result, they can be analysed as rural and
urban. A recent (1973) American introduction to rural sociology is
quoted to list the seven properties of rural communities; another
text referred to specifies the seven qualities of the urban ones. In
the latter, people hardly know each other, and they are riddled by
social problems, such as crime, traffic, pollution, and the family
[?,!].

The unexplained equation of family problems with social ones, and the loose usage of the word community for both face-to-face and urban-anonymous interaction are characteristic of the conceptual confusion of the authors and the freedom they appear to enjoy from theoretical constraints. This leaves us with the last groups making up Thai society: the minorities, such as Sino-Thais, Muslims, and Christians. Although these groups have their own subcultures, their basic culture is Thai, and they join in contributing to the progress of Thai society, or so it is said.

Thai institutions consist of models of behaviour that are grounded in Thai culture in order to fulfil the needs of Thai society. The important ones are the family, education, religion, the economy, and politics cum government. Since olden times the institution of the family is the basis of Thai society because it provides the model of Thai cultural behaviour and the continuity of Thai society as a collectivity. It has forms, functions, patterns to follow, qualities and values. Needless to say, functions and values conform to what 'society' wants its members to be: children are to be educated to be **good** members of Thai society who know its desirable order and its norms; gratefulness, respect for elders, and mutual assistance belong to the latter.

This pattern of presentation is repeated for the other said institutions; it emphasizes ideals [whose?] rather than everyday life, and is thus very selective. About the economic institution we learn that it is the basis of Thai society, and that its changes affect the way of life of the members of Thai society. It is as if the economic institution is a separate actor, endowed with a will and values. This also goes for politics and government that, because they are treated as a single entity, reveal basic statist conceptions about the unity of nation and state. Its important values are: worship of the king; love of the nation; sacrifice for country and nation. Said values motivate the individual members of Thai society, and serve its continuity.

Thai society also has values. These are different from norms, and serve to evaluate the worth, usefulness, desirability, suitability and beauty of actions and objects. After a tortuous explanation and ample reference to two American textbooks, we finally hear that the eminent values of Thai society are: worship of the king; belief in Buddhism; love for Thai society; respect for seniors; and honesty. To illustrate the quality of these insights, it is still useful to quote – the often repeated – opinion, 'Belief in Buddhism. This value is an important quality of Thai society because the patterns of Thai social behaviour have their basis in its values, such as the various traditions of Thai society that are wont to be accompanied by Buddhist rites' (401:48). Apart from this interesting reasoning, the critical observer can only wonder about all the things not being said. Thai society is presented as a highly biased inventory of unconsolidated things from which all lifeblood has been drained. The students may well imagine themselves to be learning about another planet.

The fifth chapter subjects the poor pupils to a treatise on social change. After swallowing a terrible American definition from which inferences are drawn that are not implied, the student learns, thanks to another textbook still, that change comes in two kinds, to wit, social and cultural. Such change originates from internal or from external factors, but every society has its own reasons for change; seven of these are then specified. There follows a discussion of planned and unplanned change in Thai society. Beginning with Sukhothai, and by way of Ayutthaya, the early and the later Bangkok periods – inclusive of Marshal P.'s attempt to establish Thai social identity – we arrive at a detailed description of the seven five-year plans since 1961 up to the present. Two awkward definitions of 'trend' then introduce the direction of current Thai social change: the family tends to become nuclear; education is expanding. The trend in religion is that it must fulfil its functions in order that the members of Thai society will be a good human resource [sic]. Economically, we are on the way to an urban industrial society, which gives rise to many social problems. Politically and administratively the people want to participate more and more, while government must increasingly respond to the wishes of the people as a collectivity.

Social problems

The sixth chapter is about the social problems of Thai society. Quoting from an American text published in 1977, such problems are widely recognized, and people feel that they must do something about them; they can only be tackled if the members of society cooperate in solving them. The authors jump to this conclusion, and keep emphasizing – in line with their conception of ethics – that people must work together, and that the cooperation of all individuals is conditional to solving the problem.

The refusal to think sociologically, or structurally, becomes abundantly clear when the causes of social problems are listed. In the first place, it is suggested, social problems arise because of group-based differences in opinion, desires, and interests. They also stem from behaviour that deviates from social norms which results in a lack of order. Social problems originate from social change too. Societally, these three 'causes' are perfectly normal conditions, and so it seems that hidden ethical assumptions about harmony and equilibrium problematize society as process. Be that as it may, the problems of Thai society are specified as follows.

Firstly, the rapid population growth that is caused by better medical and sanitary conditions, and from planned economic and social development, results in a rising standard of living. Accordingly, the rate of population growth increased, because it was not considered in the planning [sic]; also because of the old value of having many children, combined with the absence of knowledge about population questions and family planning. The situation can be remedied: by family planning, the melioration of the quality of life resulting from education, sufficiently remunerative work, and a wholesome environment.

The second issue is the environment, which arises because of population pressure; pressure on resources by expanding industry and technology; and the absence of responsibility and cooperation among the members of society in relation to environmental questions. Solutions must be sought by instilling ecological consciousness that should also be reflected in economic development planning, and in relevant legislation. Interestingly, the political-economic factors that are the prime movers of environmental destruction remain totally beyond discussion.

A further problem is the abuse of habit-forming drugs. Again structural explanations are avoided, although a whole page is devoted to a discussion of the stuff itself. Remedies should be sought in loving parental care, in awareness to be taught at school, in counselling of children with problems, in positive newspaper reporting, in promoting the sense of self-responsibility and straight reasoning in the youth, and in the government taking effective measures against dealers while making available adequate opportunities for the treatment of addicts.

Crime is a problem, too. Causes are identified as (1) lack of emotional warmth, whether because of broken homes or interindividual distance on the work floor; (2) degeneration of moral principles; (3) faulty values, such as the desire for riches, which results in kidnapping for ransom or dealing in drugs. Sometimes people hold modern values, such as suicide [sic], in the view that this enhances their honour and demonstrates their courage, even though it was never thought to be a value in earlier days. (4) Social change, such as urbanization, makes crime easy; think of supermarkets and places of entertainment. Besides, the media are saturated with western culture, such as infectious crime on TV and the production of criminal implements. Effective measures against crime would consist of moral education; dedicated policemen; adjustment of the criminal law to keep abreast of the times.

(5) AIDS is a problem, and defensive measures against the affliction are recommended. (6) The sixth problem is poverty Since this is the last one to be treated, we might expect the analytical powers of the authors to have run out. The comparison of *per capita* income between Malaysia and Thailand demonstrates that poverty is an important social problem in Thailand. According to an American text, this relative disparity in income also pertains to interindividual differences in standards of living. Causes must be

sought in rapid population growth that results in a vast, unproductive population of children and senior citizens;[2] in a low level of education and skills; in activities that do not provide full-time employment. This can be ameliorated by economic development, such as a better communications network, land reform, and urbanization. Social development, such as fostering education and skill training, would also be helpful. The quality of life contributes to the solution too, as in promoting the work ethic by being diligent, patient, and original. All this is very cosy: we are really back in the drinking circle and its boisterous but harmless tittle-tattle. But then, there is only one Ph.D. on the team which composed this book.

These two women and one gentleman finish the text with the obligatory and often repeated wisdom about religion, namely, that it is a system of ethical teachings.

> All religions are important to the way of life of the members of a society, and have their influence on that society, expecially because religion lays down the social norms. It sets the basic standards of the moral principles, or the mores and traditions. The religious teachings set the moral standards the members must practise and follow; they help to form the ethical model of behaviour. Besides all this, religion is part of (our) emotional cravings, helping people to solve their life problems, building happiness, eradicating anxiety, diminishing fraudulence and hatred, while teaching honesty, self-sacrifice and forgiveness, which all leads to a contented society (75).

---

[2] In the case of Thailand, the number of dependents has decreased considerably for the time being. The authors ignore this in a further demonstration of their *ad hoc* reasoning. Perhaps, during their schooling, they have been saturated with the practice of multiple choice testing: It is fine as long as a blank has been filled in.

Follow twenty-six pages about Hindu, Buddhist, Christian and Islamic history, and their teachings. These are compared in the last few pages in order to demonstrate the above assumptions.

Thinking about the state

The text for the second semester is written by two authors who hold a Master's in government and sociology, and a doctorate (with the highest honours) in law, respectively. If we were right to surmise that the first book for the tenth grade attempted to introduce sociological analysis, then the second must be thought of as inspired by political science. The book begins with introducing the most difficult concept of political analysis, namely, the state, and immediately the absence of theoretical perspectives plays havoc with the subject matter. The treatment is so illustrative of a thorough mix of theoretical-pedestrian, functionalistic, teleological, and idealistic thinking that I was tempted to translate the whole chapter concerned. This being impractical, we must do with some commented excerpts.

> When people live together in great numbers, it is necessary that political cum government organization (ô:ngkon) arises, because for being together it is necessary to have rules and regulations. There must be a government or a ruler to watch over the people in order that their social life is peaceful, that they do not exploit or bully each other, because, if there is no political cum government organization and everybody can do as he pleases, those who are more powerful than others will bully the weaker ones, those who are clever will take advantage of those who are less sharply witted, and therefore the organization of government arises in order that people be together in society peacefully (402:2).

With this statement about human nature in mind – and leaving open the question of the character of the presumably more

124

powerful government or ruler – we proceed to the idea of the state. 'The being together of people originates from the smallest group, say, from a group of families, to more of them forming a tribe. When society grows further, it will increase in members and in territory, expanding from a tribe into a nation, becoming a state or a country, a kingdom, an empire' (2). Of interest is here to note the seamless transition from family to empire, in which the only variables of any importance are numbers and territory. The quality of relationships does not play a role at all, and we may surmise that the cardinal hidden assumption – that has been made explicit at previous occasions – namely, that community = society = the morally defined nation (= the state) – inspires this representation.

Then we hear that, nowadays, states and countries equate with each other, with state emphasizing the political, and country the geographical aspects. A state, then, refers to a group of people and their territory that has fixed borders, and their government that holds sovereign power, meaning that it is free in its exercise. Accordingly, a state is a society with political institutions, which sets it apart from an ordinary society. 'The meaning of "state" stresses political affairs, that is, it is organized in such a way that there is a number of people who are rulers, who hold power over all the people. The power of the rulers may derive from their might, from acquiescence, or popular acceptance. Considering the word "state", its complete meaning could be "nation state"' (2).

The state is necessary to guarantee peace and order by seeing to it that people follow its rules. 'The important purpose of having a state is the desire of the people to have a peaceful and fulfilling life, such as, having freedom; equal chances; enjoying progress; the chance to develop one's intellect, skills, and individuality; having the right and honour to be owner of the country' (2).

If anything is demonstrated at all by the above, it is that the so-called descriptive method is no method, but more like a wrong track that leads the students astray. It seems that *ad hoc* definitions do not define anything, but separate trees that never show the coherence of the wood. We remain completely in the dark about the origins of the state, and no concept has been developed to subsume the variety of its representations. It has been described as a corporate body, as society, as country, as nation state, as polity; besides, whatever has been written does not cover any Thai experience of reality. There is plenty of exploitation by the powerful, and often the instruments of state themselves are the most predatory towards the powerless; things are not well ordered according to the wishes of 'the people'. The way of life of the Thai family is vastly different from that of politically organized society, or the state; the equality of people or opportunity goes against the most obvious of experiences. Given this inconsistency, how are teacher and students ever going to learn to think?

The self-defeating character of such a self-styled, armchair functionalist analysis becomes immediately apparent when we scrutinize 'the purposes and functions of the state'. Basic among the purposes is to create orderly conditions; these result in the opportunity that people can exercise their **rights**. Order also gives rise to **freedom**, because freedom arises when the state is orderly, through principles and regulations, and when all people have the responsibility to control their own actions so as not to infringe on the rights and freedoms of other people. Besides, order gives rise to **equality**, because order creates the situation in which people will respect each others' rights. This respect for each others' rights and interests gives rise to the equal [sic] acceptance of interests or the equality of the people of the nation (4).

While this exercise in sophistry and crookedness should by now have been enough, the authors' partiality is further elaborated in the ideas that the state must aim at building ethics by teaching love and moral principles; at providing basic welfare; at building progress and stability: 'The state, similar to other valuable living things, desires political, economic, and social progress, stability, and safety, in order that the people can live peacefully and happily' (5).

The duties, or functions, of the state are predictable and do not add to our understanding: justice, equality, rights, freedoms, and the happiness of the people, are words that occur often. These happy people, as good denizens, also have their oft repeated duties. It is of interest to note that people should not create problems for the state: Work!; see to the stability of yourself and your family;[3] educate your children so as not to cause problems because the instruments of the state cannot control everything. Ideas about citizenship, public responsibility, or democracy have totally vanished from the discussion of the duties of the population. The state becomes reified as a caring father and good provider; it is never substantiated as the public realm par excellence.

Democracy

State governments are distinguished as absolutist or dictatorial, and libertarian. The first derive their power from higher sources, the second from the people; this latter ideology subsequently gave birth to democracy. If the discussion of the state was disheartening, the chapter on the democratic system gives hope again. While the way it has been written is free from historical and theoretical constraints, it does develop a sort of an ideal type of democracy. Given the conclusion, the authors appear to be aware of this. Under 'The Value of Democracy', they write:

> We could conclude that the democratic system is a system that has very lofty ideals, that it is the best possible model, and that it is a style of life that should be desired by both individuals and society ... This system values individuals by recognizing that they have freedom, and that they are equal in dignity and humanity. The fact of enjoying freedom implies that people must not be under the control of others because democracy is a system of government that holds that the sovereign power is of

---

[3] Excessive care for the own family happens to be a key obstacle to the creation of a civil culture of the public world. It justifies corrupt behaviour, and even results in the traffic jams caused by parents taking their children by car to far-away, prestigious schools.

the people and the people is its own ruler. In order that people
can rule themselves, they must have full freedom ... Democracy
recognizes the value of the individual by allowing him political
freedom and the freedom of expression (speech, writing,
criticism). Political freedom means the freedom to elect
representatives ... It also means equality: every individual
whether a millionaire or a beggar, has one vote ...

A democratic society is a society that believes strongly in the
dignity of human beings; they trust each other. The people
consists of persons who have reason and who know how to
think with discretion. They are replete with the desire to
compromise and to give and take. They share in the spirit of
sportsmanship and concede full-heartedly that things are
always changing. A society that consists of individuals who
have a democratic way of life can accordingly be called a
valuable society, a society where it is a pleasure to live
(402:21).

The great vistas democracy opens inspire the writers to train
their scope on the heavens. For our purposes it is futile to
comment on these visionary revelations; we have more to gain
from the scrutiny of the pillars the authors thought worthy of
erecting. They explain that democracy is a form of government
where the highest power belongs to the people. In practice, this
means that this power derives from the people. Everybody is born
with natural rights and freedoms, being able to think and do as
they please, but, when people congregate to form a society, they
must give up some rights and powers to those who govern; the
latter will exercise their power within democratically specified
restrictions. Good government recognizes the rights and equality of
persons; they have equal rights to participate in economic,
political, and social activities in order to advance themselves and
society as a whole. Such freedom of action, within the limits of the
law, equates with the democratic system. In order to shape their
society, people must participate and voice their ideas: after all,

their opinion is the voice of heaven [*vox populi, vox dei* !]. It is like Abraham Lincoln said, 'democracy is government of, by, and for the people' (10-1).

From these various meanings of the word democracy, scientists conclude that it has three basic meanings. (1) Politically, it signifies: (a) People have reason and moral consciousness; therefore, the quality of social life can ever be improved. (b) They are free, and enjoy rights within the limits of justice and the rules of their society (specified are the freedoms of opinion, association, religion, and the rights to one's body and property, to residence, to move, to travel, and to exercise a profession). (c) Equality of human dignity, with the right to see it respected, which boils down to equality in political participation, such as specified in the Universal Declaration of Human Rights; equality in legal protection; equality to seek progress in one's personal life; equality of social and economic opportunity (11-3).

(2) Governmentally (administratively), the basic meaning of democracy is: (a) Sovereignty belongs to the people; (b) it is exercised by the people; (c) for the benefit of the people. (d) The exercise of democratic government rests on the basis of reason; (e) on majority decisions; (f) the acquiescence, or consent of the population; (g) compromise, with due respect for the public interest; (h) equality before the law, based on the idea of equal dignity; (i) basic freedoms of the people; (j) the belief that people are capable of governing and improving themselves. The resulting forms of government are very similar, although we should distinguish between royal and presidential heads of state. Also, parliaments differ: they may be unicameral or multicameral; membership is elected or appointed; some presidents have representative functions only; in other systems, they double as chief executives (13-6).

(3) Democracy as a way of life. This means: (a) Decisions and conflict resolution are based on reasonable consideration; (b) the willingness to listen to each others' opinion and not to be prejudiced; to have (c) a democratic disposition, such as being willing to think about issues independently; (d) interest and

participation in politics; (e) preference for compromise instead of forcing issues; (f) optimism, combined with patience; (g) responsibility for the public interest (16).

All this is followed by some information about direct and indirect democratic representation, and about forms of citizen participation, from membership in interest groups and parties to elections that should be free, secret and regular, and based on honesty, equality, and general participation. It is especially important that people expose their opinion and criticism of authorities. In general, a democratic system will be promoted by a high level of education, a flourishing economy, a democratic mentality, political stability, and a sound administrative system. And so it is argued, for instance, that people who have a good education, will be reasonable; aware of being part of society; and interested in politics and news (17-20).

As we have noted before, education is expected to solve all social and individual problems, and to function as a core element in attaining a desirable future. Although there is a trace of truth in this, it should be noted that the relationship between education and the arising of democratic government is historically spurious. Awareness of being repressed, of injustice, and demands for rights and equality, have far more to do with popular pressure for democracy than levels of education, and ordinary Thais are no exception to this observation. They understand their predicament, but have little power to improve their situation *vis-à-vis* the state and the business establishment. The idealistic presentation of 'democracy', however, shies away from both historical considerations and the prevailing social situation. It must be feared that this steadfast refusal to face the own condition and the culture that informs it make the whole exercise of explaining a foreign set of ideas – and their weird Thai implementation – irrelevant.

One of the Thai qualities that shades through, though, is the penchant to see society as an undifferentiated whole, to see it as a community rather than as a place where people pursue their own interests. In the present discussion, 'The People' features all the time. Democracy is about its interest; its happiness and peacefulness must be promoted. Such an undifferentiated view plays havoc with the very idea that the practice of democracy is the most reasonable way of negotiating social conflicts and cleavages, that its arising is a response to differences of interest, and that society should not be regulated by personal whims and wishes, but by consultation and the rule of law.

The exposition of such basic weaknesses in the text – that function as obstacles to both teachers and students – may give us the opportunity to be brief about the further subject matter. The third chapter is about dictatorship, probably to offer a contrastive ideal type, and that may be why it is elevated to a doctrine or ideology. Anyway, it is a government in which the state is like God. Then we learn a lot about Hitler and Mussolini, yet one keeps wondering why the rich Thai heritage of and experience with absolute rulers and dictator-marshals is not analysed at all. The next chapter is about economy and politics. We begin by learning that all government must be accepted by the population, and that it therefore must have the welfare of the people at heart, which converts into the government's striving to realize higher living standards for the people. This demonstrates that politics and the economy are inextricably intertwined.

Following the same method as in the earlier chapters, ideal types are constructed, and evaluated, of the capitalist and the socialist order of things, that are then further characterized along the lines of democracy versus dictatorship. It promises to become more interesting when the focus of the next three chapters is on Thai realities: the evolution of Thai politics and administration, democracy, and kingship.

Polity and law

It must be boring for all those concerned that the narrative begins with the overrepeated myths about Sukhothai and the administrative organization of Ayutthaya. Moving on to the familiar reforms of the Fifth Reign – and the king's democratic inclinations [*sic*] – we hear, in contrast to earlier information, that the emancipation of the slaves was motivated by the desire to give the people freedom, that formal education was initiated to give the people the opportunity to study, that the administrative reform was a preparation for democracy, and so on, which subsequently brings us to the democratic dispensation. It is acknowledged that constitutions do not last long and that Thai democracy does not measure up to universal standards: this has to do with the contingencies of the times.

Follows the form of government according to the Constitution with – predictably – some emphasis on the obligations of the populace. The most interesting part is the rather realistic discussion of the abuse of the democratic system by powerful politicians, by coup-staging military officers, and the – hopefully – corrective role of the media and demonstrative protest. Thirteen further pages about the eternally high moral standards of the Thai monarchs and the eulogy in praise of the present king make one wonder whether the key to the Thai teaching method lies in repetition without end: the more often something is reiterated, the more it becomes true.

The second book for the tenth grade is, among other things, designed to introduce the law. Explaining that 'the law' is an abstraction, it proposes that only laws be discussed. Since the same could have been said about 'society', 'state', 'democracy', et cetera, it is a pity that this chance is missed, and that teachers and students will just have to work through fifty pages of legalities, and some familiar historical mystifications. Earlier in the book it was stated that the present Constitution is number fourteen; according to the present writer, it is number thirteen; in the previous book it was observed that we are at number fifteen. Be that as it may, since constitutions appear to function as mere symbols of modernity, it would have been an excellent opportunity to discuss Thai concepts about 'the law', about the relation of legality and society-in-the-abstract. What does get mentioned, though, are deficiencies in the Thai legal process, such as a lack of confidence in the judiciary; outdated laws; the delaying of justice. Also noted are all those who are influential enough to be above or beyond the law, which does not entail respect for legality either. In a very pedestrian manner, we are brought back to the level that states that violence and legal insecurity are bad for tourism, for the good name of the nation, and the willingness to invest in the country.

Such commonplace remarks are then further confirmed by the recommended solutions: Criminality must be tackled at its roots, namely, a degenerate mentality that should be countered by the moral education of our youth in all schools; also our police authorities, upon whom the people depend, must be more serious and efficient. Poverty, and the closing of the gap between the haves and the have-nots, must be addressed. Finally, local godfatherism should be eradicated. Many more recommendations of this kind follow to tackle the different types of crime. The last thirty pages are about the laws and the legal actions the students should know.

History and society

In the eleventh grade, social studies have geography and economics as its subjects, and these do not need to concern us here. Of more interest to our discussion is the historical-sociological approach of book 605. After a general introduction about the relation between history and society, and the foundations of Eastern civilization, Thai society is described in deep historical perspective. The last third of the book consists of a cultural, political, intellectual and economic history of the West, followed by a few pages about current international organizations.

In the opening pages it is asserted that history reflects social change, which is the most normal of social conditions. It serves as a collective memory, inspired by the natural wish to know the past. Apart from this, it is very useful in helping to understand the own being, the heritage and the present; it is a tool serving social analysis, too. Last but not least, history provides the lessons we can use to solve problems and crises in a way that is in accord with ethics and morality in order to contribute to the peaceful progress of human society.

This lofty conception of history is immediately forgotten when the bases of Asian civilization are discussed. First the reader is confronted with all sorts of bits and pieces of information about old and new China, the rise of its civilization, its expansion, and their relation to the political economy and intellectual history, before being fed the familiar nonsense of the deep-seated loyalty of the people to the Son of Heaven; both are committed to each other by the moral principles and ethics of the Confucian doctrine. Despite all this, in the twentieth century century a republic arises that apparently does away with such pretensions and starts organizing the realm along western principles. The resultant democratic system collapses when the communists take over. All this change does not need explanation. A long list of technological achievements follows, and a short exposition about the spread of Chinese civilization brings us to the end of the narrative concerned. The way India is subsequently presented does not bring us any nearer to understanding the foundations of Asian civilization either.

Then we get closer to home: Thai government-and-politics. This articulated word – presented throughout all the texts – makes it a single concept, and thus basic distinctions between politics, government, regime, administration, and state often blur. Worse yet, the king is not presented as the centre of the state, but as the heart of society. The familiar doctrinal knowledge, from Sukhothai to the present, follows once again. The king appears as eternally morally inspired, promoting and spreading Buddhism. The soundest information we get is that in Sukhothai times the stability and power of the state depended more on the personality of the king than on institutions. In Ayutthaya, the stability was served by a robust economy and flourishing trade.

History must be presented as Thai history, and none of the authors of the various texts discussed here finds it important to look at history in the terms of the participants. Sukhothai is Thailand, and so is Ayutthaya. The name Siam is hardly ever mentioned; the realm is defined by borders rather then by spheres of influence. The quasi-independent *müang* and the semi-autonomous dependencies are· referred to, but never explained at length. The same goes for the struggle for the throne and the latent threat of royal relatives, although we are told that the appointed aristocratic administrators were tightly controlled by the royal centre. Even so, the stability of the early Bangkok period derived largely from the mutually profitable equilibrium between these groups and institutions, or so we are told. The Fifth Reign's amazing success in concentrating power is indicated, and so we get a glimpse of contending, or at least opposing groups, but the whys and hows, and the dawning consciousness of the importance of modern borders, remain unexplained.

The authors use causal explanations sparingly, and often we find statements to the effect that change was necessary 'to get into harmony with the conditions' or something similar; full stop. Other explanations are ideologically inspired reinterpretations, and the view of history from the actors' point of view is usually kept hidden. History seems to serve rather than to explain the present state of affairs, and the causes and effects that moved the past remain vague. The administrative reforms at the local level (*the:sa:phiba:n*) arc said to have been initiated to give the people a voice in government. Yet, there were a few obstacles, such as shortages of money and well-trained civil servants, and obstinate vested interests that may or may not have inspired several rebellions. Anyway, slowly but steadily, the reforms became established practice.

About the Sixth Reign we find a most interesting observation that is in full contradiction with the ideology taught during the first eleven school years. The king was not a democrat; his toy-city, Dusitthani, is not mentioned; he even wrote a thesis that the monarchical dispensation fitted Thailand best, pointing to the disintegration of power in China and the disorder in Russia in the wake of their republican revolutions. He also annulled certain decentralizing measures, reconcentrating power in the Ministry of the Interior.

The seventh king was too late with the introduction of a constitution; he was overtaken by the events of 24 June 1932 that initiated the democratic period. Now, after many military take-overs, periods of dictatorship, and fifteen constitutions – a four-page list gives the details of the ten successful coups d'état – it is observed that:

> From 2475/1932 onwards, the Thai government still lacks the ideology/ideals (*udomka:n*) and the way of life that fit with democracy, because the method it uses belongs to the style of life and thinking of earlier 'days that have not changed among the majority of society. The destruction of democracy, as far as it is the model of government, therefore does not evoke a strong reaction among the people, with the exception of the happenings of 14 October 2516/1973, 6 October 2519/1976, and 17-20 May 2535/1992 (57).

These last sentences of the chapter about politics and administration raise high hopes that the authors are going to explain what they have in mind. What in the Thai way of life, what in Thai thinking, are the things that stand at right angles with democracy? How do we need to understand Thai culture and society in the first place? Perhaps that the next chapter, 'Thai Society', will fill in the blanks, and provide more insight regarding the eminently reasonable suggestions that have been made.

From an author's point of view, I thought it would be nice to keep the reader in the dark for a long time, to use this occasion to build up suspense. Alas, the observations in the fourth chapter are almost an insult to history, unburdened by any cultural considerations, and free from sociological insight. What poses as a historical-sociological analysis is at best a summary description of social groups divided into two 'estates' (*chonchan*) that, after 1932, are said to have become less well distinguished. Instead of describing structure – as the chapter promises to do – the social process is kept in the dark, its constraints and problems go unmentioned. Frequently, state and politics are equated with society and, at best, we get some ideas about political organization and social stratification. Beginning with the familiar improbabilities about Sukhothai, such as the prevailing intimacy between rulers and people, the chapter works its way through Ayutthayan times up to the present. A ray of hope glimmers when a page is devoted to relationships, opening short vistas of relating, of process. We learn that estate or class membership was not totally fixed, and that a measure of social mobility, especially in times of war, was a possibility. In Sukhothai, just and intimate relationships prevailed, and the practice of the Buddhist virtues was very much alive. The Buddhist religion and its ceremonies inspired moral principles and practices that made that people, from king down to slave, had occasion to close ranks and reduce social distance.

The patronage system prevailed in Ayutthaya. Yet the estates lacked stability because its individual members [sic] were potentially mobile: those high up could lose rank and even sink as low as to become royal slaves. Contrarily, those in the lower strata could improve their position, especially by way of serving as a soldier or joining the monkhood. This last possibility, though, was held in check by the state in order not to lose its labour force, while the absence of education was a barrier to the social mobility of commoners. In contrast, those of high rank could even improve their position because of their proximity to the king.

These, the most coherent paragraphs of the chapter, are then followed by the tumble-and-jumble presentation of the Rattana-kosin, or Bangkok, period. In its early days, the economy improves; there is a lot of war; the commoners flee from their corvée obligations; a lot of Chinese labour finds its way into the country; the position of commoners improves; religion is energetically promoted; Christian missionaries introduce the knowledge of western civilization; some of them described the prevailing social conditions. Full stop.

Within the confines of the Ayutthayan social arrangement (rulers versus ruled) that characterized the early Bangkok period, social change gets on its way during the Fourth Reign. This is apparent from contemporary laws, the early press, and the adjustment of certain customs to western ways. The ensuing discussion of the social transformation initiated in the Fifth Reign looks at the process from a statist and ideological point of view only, and thus fails to trace relationships between economy, social structure, policy, et cetera, and the reader has to make do with the by now familiar statement that 'it gave a good result in harmony with political-administrative conditions'. There are some interesting observations, such as one about the powerful taking advantage of the powerless. This eminently durable problem is one of the reasons given for the emancipation of the commoners. Another was their habit of fleeing from corvée obligations, such as military service, and thus a standing army was far more reliable. The authors mention all these things, but do not relate them, and the really important point, namely, the arising of a free labour market, is merely mentioned, never explained.

An avalanche of facts

All sorts of changes are enumerated – in education, justice, values, and customs. From 1932 onwards the momentum of change becomes most visible, with the government deciding what is, or should be, Thai and desirable. The discussion does not allow for the distinction between values and customs, and so they can be changed whenever a new government comes to power. Politically impelled choices after the Pacific War bring about an unprecedented transformation that goes on unto this day, but whereas nine pages are devoted to discuss the slow and not very far-reaching changes from Sukhothai to 1851, and while the reforms since then are still allotted a full five, the early democratic period only gets a page and a half. The far-reaching developments after the war must do with less than a page crammed with 'facts': education; universities; industry; service economy; money circulation; American style rest-and-recreation; corruption; the military-business alliance; the degeneration of morals; tourism; materialism; the appearance of middle classes; agro-business;

factory labour, and the problem of poverty. All the while we are offered gems of reasoning, such as:

> ... but war earnings are uncertain; in the long run the different types of business are likely to run out of luck with the result that problems such as many robbers, felons, and criminality ... [sic]; ... The expansion of the said middle classes is unbalanced; accordingly this will be an important problem to the progress of Thai society in general (76).

The ambition that history should help in understanding the present is obviously not part of the authors' mental make-up; what students should comprehend remains totally unexplained; instead, they are merely invited to join in with unfounded bar-room assertions.

The next chapter is about foreign relations and, again, begins in Sukhothai. Such relations may concern trade, embassies, wars, and religious and cultural exchanges. They also brought the Thais in contact with more advanced civilizations; by taking after their example, the Thais could demonstrate that they were on a par with them. This openness does indeed explain a number of things, and a theory of trade, and the wider forces that goaded it on, especially in the area of the Andaman and South China Seas, would make many interesting facts far more significant. The fact is, that the Thais were – and still are – reluctant to take to the seas, and that sea-borne trade came to them rather than that they initiated it. About such things, and the early role of the Chinese in Thai overseas contacts, we hear too little. For instance, the fact that Ayutthayan centralization, and its building of the most thoroughly organized bureaucratic polity, are connected with the benefits of (the control of) trade. Yet, like in most places in the texts discussed, the authors avoid the option of systematic treatment, and leave the reader with 'facts'. Contacts with the West are subsequently broken down into contacts with Muslims, Portuguese, Spaniards, Dutchmen, the English and the French. When nineteenth-century western expansion is to be discussed, we only hear about the immediate results as pertaining to Thailand. And so the text hurries on through the Pacific War, its aftermath, and the Cold and Vietnam Wars. The Americans pull out in 1975; Southeast Asia becomes important in its own right.

The chapter about the economy immediately demonstrates the weakness of a non-integrated approach. Dividing the discussion in chapters about government cum politics, society, foreign relations, and the economy, beginning in Sukhothai every time, before giving it the full run into the present, can only cause repetitious-ness and scatter the information. Royal trading monopolies and the bureaucratic, powerful state are, finally, related, although the trade itself remains enclosed in the previous chapter, and the organization of the realm in the chapter about society. It is clear that the population is greatly exploited and that Chinese people always seem to play a role in economically gainful activities. The discussion of the post-Bowring developments is very repetitious, and the explanation of economic factors falls far below the level of the economy text of the previous year. In spite of this, the authors try to add the aura of authority to the text through statistical figures and technical terms, like gold standard; state budget; exchange rate; and price mechanism, which they altogether fail to explain.

Anyway, the last three pages of the text quicken the pace again to rush through the period since 1932. State enterprise versus the private sector; nationalistic ideas about autarchy versus economic planning and a role for business; the increasingly intertwined interests of private enterprise, the national bureaucracy, and politics; the failure to spread development to the agricultural sector; the importance of foreign investment and its control over certain economic activities: all these are crammed in the very last page. Any mention of corruption is carefully [?] avoided. Why bother with structural explanations if only one page needs to be filled to arrive into the 1990s? Even so, we are still treated to some opinionated statements, such as 'the concentration of economic power in the business establishment is one of the obstacles to national economic growth that, as a result, advances more or less slowly'. In the very next paragraph we are informed that the rate of economic growth has steadily been higher than targeted. While most indicators of economic growth tend to go up, we are still informed that 'the rate of borrowing foreign currency is going down and the rate of population growth is also going down' (105). Whatever that may mean, the government should be concerned with a more egalitarian distribution of income.

The last Thai thing to be treated in isolation is arts and culture. The chapter starts on the promising note that art exists in order to respond to religious desire and for the sake of beauty. Accordingly, art reflects a world view, and the human condition. (It is further observed that many beliefs, arts and cultures influenced each other in the area that is Thailand today.) Well, up to the reign of King Mongkut this perspective is not used, and the student merely needs to struggle through art classifications and periodizations. When, however, the influence from China, that was strong during the early Bangkok period, gives way to western inspiration, Thailand begins to catch up with the civilized world, which is reflected in the construction of public utilities. 'Social conditions induced that the construction of temples, which was the building of spiritual public utilities, declined, and with it, the skills required to do it; architecture took after the West' (115). The big drive towards the imitation of things European is then illustrated; it also stimulated the quest for modern Thai forms. In the main, though, western forms are dominant in sculpture, music, and literature.

This brings us to the best chapter of the book, 'The Foundations of Western Civilization'. It is a quick run through cultural history, beginning with the Sumerians and ending with the Renaissance. The author concerned obviously uses a theory of civilization, and speculates intelligently about the relation between ecology, economy, and religious and political ideas. It is a pity that the theoretical assumptions remain implicit; had they been stated at the outset, comparison would have been possible, and could have invited an analysis of the origin and growth of Thai civilization, too. It would have highlighted the interrelated phenomena of urbanization, specialization, literacy, growing social complexity, the resultant hierarchicization of society, its dependence on transport and trade, and thus its economic basis, and so on. It would also have engendered the comparison of why the Renaissance gave rise to humanism, or a anthropo-centred world view, and why Thai cultural development did not (yet). This chance has unfortunately been missed, and since my interviews did not convince me that teachers hold deep insights, both they and their students are probably merely drowning in facts.

The rather powerful potential the organization of this last chapter offers is lost in the ensuing chapters about the early history of western expansion, the scientific and industrial revolutions, the Enlightenment and democratic thinking. It is facts, facts, and more facts. Treaty of Tordesillas, Magellan, Holland, Moluccas, commercial revolution, price revolution, ecological revolution, printing press, Byzantium and Moslem civilization, Copernicus, Descartes, Newton, spinning jenny, the honourability of work and trade, Karl Marx, and the influence of new technologies on the Thai army, the economy, transportation, public health, and so on. The discussion of the Age of Reason is not different, and while its connection to the French Revolution and democratic ideals is correctly identified, the chapter ends on the fall of the Romanovs, while asserting that the twentieth century is the age of the spreading of democratic ideas. A further search for the bases of the democratic 'programme' is neglected, and its basic conditions are not reflected upon. It remains facts, rather than a history of ideas and their relevance to conditions outside the countries of their birth. This deplorable way of working pervades the last chapter about postwar international organizations; they are listed, from UN to Council of Europe and ASEAN, and a discussion of the Universal Declaration of Human Rights – a direct offshoot of the Enlightenment – is not only avoided: the Declaration does not even get mentioned.

The very last semester

The discussion of social studies reaches its lowest level in the last semester of the highest grade when all integration is lost. The

142

first chapter is about the development of science and technology. Beginning at the dawn of history, it takes us rapidly to the Renaissance, and runs quickly from Gutenberg to Franklin. Since the invention of the spring by Robert Hooke in 1665, science and technology develop in tandem. Soon we arrive at the latest marvels; under the heading 'Guarding Independence and the Peace of the State', we begin with the invention of gun powder to end with the atomic bomb. Such inventions, as well as rockets and satellites, show the technology that has been developed to defend national independence and world peace [sic]. Technology does not bring good things only, but also affects the environment negatively. [The fact that it is people who cause problems, is not considered.] Technology influences society too. Machines may cause unemployment; urban-industrial life reduces personal choice, because people have to work together and within the dictates of clock time; the fact that both father and mother must work outside the home reduces the intimacy with their children. Formerly the roots of social power were in land as the primary factor of production, but in a technological society, power stems from industry, commerce and services. So, social power is rooted in landownership and in possession of other things. Technology also causes professional specializations and the division of labour.

In Thailand, technology stimulates development, also agricultural production, and the country will soon join the Newly Industrialized Countries, the so-called NICs; the quality of the population increases. Yet, that of the environment goes down, and our natural resources are depleted.

The second chapter is about 'Conflicts of Beliefs and Values'. Beliefs can cause conflicts, for example, religious convictions, beliefs in magic, philosophical doctrines that idealize war, and political ideologies. Thai society also has its beliefs that relate to nature, birth, death, illness, predictions, professions, the home, and rituals. Beliefs and values that are causes of conflict are classified as religious or doctrinal, the latter comprising nationalism, racism, and political-economic ideologies. Under 'Religion', we then find an overview of theism and atheism, with an according

143

classification of some religions and their sects, and five influences of religion on society, such as ethics, world view, arts, social reform, and conflict if adherents of different religions live in the same society. India, Lebanon, and the crusades are mentioned.

Under doctrines, we hear about those that centre on a leader, such as Gandhi, Mussolini, and Hitler; then about nationalism. This latter doctrine has the power to expand nations, also to unite people, or to divide a multi-ethnic society. Racism, Apartheid, and the White Australia Policy are given as examples of nationalism, too. Then there are politico-economic ideologies, such as liberal democracy, to which capitalism belongs; communism; imperialism, with its idea of the *mission civilisatrice*, or 'the white man's burden'. Domination of lesser groups by greater ones is still with us, although the United Nations Organization and Human Rights tend to restrain imperial ambitions.

Under 'Competition and Cooperation among Countries in the Fields of Politics and Economics', we are told that conflict and competition are normal to humankind, arising from differences between societies. They may escalate into small or big wars, but since all of us must live on the same planet, we had better compromise and share, establishing cooperation among all. The reasons for conflicts are: the arms race; different political and economic ideologies, such as democracy versus communism; the economic jealousies and resources that drive people to war, such as the ore and coal deposits of Alsace-Lorraine that caused the war between Germany and France that escalated to become the First World War. This point is also illustrated by the war about Kuwait. Cold War rhetoric about communism versus liberal democracy has it that the latter strives after morality, reason, justice, and the sharing of resources. Socio-cultural differences, grounded in nation, race, language and religion, may cause conflict too, such as in the cases of South Africa, former Yugoslavia, and the Thirty Year War.

To solve these conflicts, we have diplomacy and international law; forceful protest, such as boycotts; and war. It is better to seek forms of cooperation, such as the League of Nations, NATO, and

ASEAN. In a way, wars seem to stimulate such cooperation. Follows a lengthy exposition about World War I, from rivalry for resources, markets, colonies, and the unstable conditions in the Balkan, the heavy cost of life and goods, to the League of Nations. The latter is presented by its organization and purposes; it was ineffective, and major power rivalries continued, leading to World War II. Its causes are imperialism, nationalism, militarism, the division between major power blocks, and the weakness of the League of Nations. Again the toll is heavy, and the losses in territory and money of the Axis countries and their allies are specified in detail. Economically, the war and its aftermath were disastrous. Again, it led to cooperation, such as the Atlantic Charter, Yalta, and the United Nations. As with the League, its organization and some of its activities are elaborated on. Anyway, the latter could not prevent the Cold War. Between 1948 and 1953, tensions between the two blocks were most serious; it was the demise of the Soviet Union in 1991 that put it all behind us. Subsequently twelve pages are filled with information about the Korean War, the conflicts between Arabs and Israelis, the war between Iraq and Iran, the Vietnam, Falkland and Gulf Wars.

The next chapter goes bravely on with 'The Political and Economic Situation in the World Today' Since the textbook authors are not in the habit of knowing what others wrote in preceding or following volumes, we are treated to the same material about suspected relationships between economic and political systems that was also discussed in the previous volume 605. The way they are explained, it must be noted, is far more confused, and a blatant illustration of the dangers of working beyond the constraints of a theoretical perspective. Although the book has been written after 1991, the authors think it expedient to explain cold war ideology as a living reality: a democratic system with its free enterprise doctrine is contrasted with the dictatorial system with its socialist-communist economic doctrine.

The five-page discussion of doctrines and systems builds the sort of ideal types that we have repeatedly encountered. Besides, it is the same ideas that have been typified several times before:

statism versus libertarianism, respectively bringing together Karl Marx and Benito Mussolini versus liberal democracy (U.S.A.; Singapore) and social democracy (France; Scandinavia). These last freedom-loving doctrines may further develop towards Conservatism, and Utilitarianism in which the state does not hold any power. This mixing of concrete examples with extreme models, and the sloppy treatment of terms like state, country, government, the public system, doctrine, values – not to mention equality, legality or rule of law, and market – that are alternately used as ideas and objects, or actors, confuses the presentation.

This continues until we reach the redemptive last paragraph that states that there are no countries yet that veritably use either a capitalist or a socialist system. In the ensuing exposition about mixed economic systems, we hear that the market mechanism is at their basis, and that state intervention seeks to keep the countries concerned within the confines of government policy. Alas, a list of functions, or obligations, of the government saps the strength of these second observations; redemption becomes programmatic. Be this as it may, the relevant final paragraph clearly states that a mixed economy can go together with any political system, so underscoring that the connexion between economic and political forms is spurious indeed. One wonders what the exercise was all about.

This confusing conceptualization is followed by the more mundane news report about the world after the end of the Cold War. The Soviet Union disintegrates, and its former component states are mentioned. The countries of Eastern Europe all receive a few lines; Germany reunites; China opens up; the Thai economy booms.

This boom is said to be a sign of stability, which is a dubious statement that is not explained; it is also said to be related to peaceful and stable political conditions. The authors conveniently overlook the many coups and changes in government during the period of rapid economic development, and fail to relate Thailand's dynamic 'stability' to certain enduring institutions and their policies, such as the Central Bank and the bureaucracy. Such structural factors play a bit part at best in between the many facile – though often complicated – statements that lend their flavour to the course in social studies as a whole. Thus, while the widening of the gap between the rich and the poor is mentioned, it is not explained; and if the students want to know about corruption and the wheeling and dealing of politics, they had better consult the daily newspaper. Seven pages of international interest groups affecting Thailand, from NATO through ASEAN and GATT to OPEC, bring us to the end of the chapter; the influence of transnational companies, or TNCs, remains unmentioned.

The next is a general and Thailand-oriented chapter about 'The Development of the Quality of the Population'. Population means a group of people who live together in a certain territory and who have their own characteristic institutions and culture that are different from other such groups. The mass of people is one of the natural resources, the so-called human resource, and people are thought to be the most valuable of them, because humans are producers, users, and caretakers of the other resources in order that they usefully serve the people itself. Starting with these confusing ideas, we learn, under 'The Importance of the Population', that developed countries have high-quality populations; they live in rich countries, characterized by political stability; then, that people are needed for production; the labour force comprises those from fifteen to sixty years old; they can also be soldiers representing the power of the state. This brings us to global statistics about increasingly rapid population growth, population densities, and average incomes that show that, in 1992, the Dutch enjoyed an average income about twice as high as the French.

More enigmatic still is the statistical grouping of the so-called age brackets: up to 16 years; then the youthful of 16-44 years; then the aged. Because in the USA the 1980 percentages were 22, 48, and 30, respectively, and in Germany, in the same year, 15, 45, and 40, we are told that the age composition of the population of developed countries is almost the same. No whys, no hows, no reasons. The quality of life is then defined in three different ways; United Nations indicators are mentioned; factors making for individual well-being are briefly discussed. After an exposition on the vicious circle of poverty, there still follows a treatise on the negative impact of a polluted environment.

The last chapter narrows its scope to Thailand, and presents, once again, a quick run through the seven national development plans. This brings us to the final pages, to wit, Thai social problems. They are, (1) the unemployment of the unskilled labour force; (2) migration, that makes for the high population density of Bangkok, which further leads to traffic jams, crime, prostitution, quarrelling, slums, et cetera. To solve these problems, the cooperation of the people is necessary, as in: managing living quarters and environment in a healthy manner; taking care of the cleanliness of the own living quarters and immediate environment; sticking to traffic regulations; teaching one's offspring and their children; not littering roads or polluting water, and suchlike.

(3) There is also an assortment of societal and cultural problems. An important one is new agricultural technology. Those who cannot afford it lag behind, stay mired in poverty, and finally migrate to cities as unskilled labourers. It is the elderly back in the villages who have to take care of the young. If they take wife and children along, they will also end up in a slum, where the children have to fend for themselves because both parents must work. Drugs, criminality, and disregard for the law are the logical consequences. State and private sector must sympathize with the people, reach them by way of school and media, in order to make them realize the values of family life and child-rearing. People must realize the value of helping each other, of sympathizing with each other, not to be egoistic but to encourage one another in order that the condition of society, culture, and livelihood will be and remain Thai.

The last problem addressed is (4) politics. If the quality of life of the people is high, they are likely to choose good representatives who will act for the good of the country. The quality of the urban population is rising, and they do not tolerate military coups d'état. In the countryside, however, the quality of life is low, and the people there have a poor understanding of democracy. Government and private sector must cooperate in explaining democracy to them, by direct lecturing and by way of the mass media. Full stop. Exasperated as we are from the battering of this hail of olympian wisdom, we shall forget about the abuses of high-living politicians, civil servants, and generals: problems originate from poverty, or rather, from individual poor people.

Comments

It makes one sad to observe that the teaching materials for the fourth and the sixth grades of high school contribute little to the comprehension of things social. Of the lower grades it could at least be said that they presented – to an important extent – individual-centred moralistic and nation-centred familistic images, and so there was some – rather useless – method in the madness. The superior grades obviously aspire to offer a conceptually higher grasp of the subject matter, an attempt that fails miserably.

In itself there is not much against the so-called conceptual approach in teaching a subject as long as the concepts taught cohere, and are advanced within a single theoretical framework. In such a system of relations, a certain concept of society has to do with a connected concept of culture, to which belong specific ideas about social relationships, evolution and change, and so forth. A single theory may be one-sided; at least it allows for systematic thinking, and that skill can later be applied in pursuing different perspectives. Moreover, when you are sixteen to eighteen years old, you do not need to know everything, and even if so, where would you find teachers to accomplish such a miracle?

What happens in the course, though, is the presentation of definitions. Abstractions, such as society, culture, state, have been nailed down to earth, have been made concrete and tangible. In order to tackle their subsequent immobility, several, often contrasting, definitions are given, and all coherence is lost. The same can be observed about the perennial tendency to present the pupils with ideal types that are so far divorced from the practice of life as to have no connexion to it. Freed from the constraints of their historical roots and cultural evolution, democracy, or the concept of history itself, become meaningless clusters of words that fail to explain anything, and that cannot be applied. This way of working can never result in imagining theory and the dynamic relationships between sets of concepts. It merely collapses into the tittle-tattle facts of the popular press and the *ad hoc* reasoning of textbook writers in a hurry.

Working accordingly, 'common sense' substitutes for causality; poor people are poor because they have no education; because they lack education, they have no moral sense; they come to town, *et voilà*: crime and prostitution. They should be taught manners and morality, both by government and private sector. Such crude ethical reasoning occurs until the very last sentence of the course in social studies. In the same viewpoint, rich and educated people – politicians, for instance – must be the exemplars of righteousness and ethical living which probably explains why the abuse of power, corruption, disregard for the public interest, and hierarchy neither surface as social problems nor as inherent parts of the Thai culture of power. Basic structural arrangements are never considered, and a discussion of their actual embeddedness is conspicuously avoided, reflecting a deep-seated unwillingness to face the own condition. It is not that people do not know it; it is their refusal to think about it. Every day the newspaper is full of the facts; they are taken for granted, and the school neither fosters the attitude, nor hands down the intellectual tools, to pursue a critical analysis. Consequently, one of the stated aims of the course, namely, to firmly believe in the democratic way of life, remains unfulfilled. Where would, in this system of teaching, a democratic, socially responsible, yet morally autonomous citizen hail from?

I suppose that it is safe to conclude that the course materials have little to offer to stimulate the sociological imagination. Society, economy, state, they all remain vague, and no mental picture of the public world, of anonymous society, emerges. This vagueness is in no way clarified by the extremely boring moral prescriptions that the student has been bombarded with from his first school days onwards. These nefarious and selective recipes at best stick together in a primitive functionalistic framework in which culture is seen as the good, the true, and the beautiful. This strong bias of the presentation results in the teaching of the ethically desirable, and is based on the reification of values: values as concrete causes. By just selecting 'nice functions' (tasks), the institutions presented seem to have no negative or undesirable aspects, which makes them unrealistic and intellectually unattractive. It all results in the indifference for social studies about which almost all the teachers of this subject complain.

The image of history that emerges is not much better. The same boring run, the same boring facts familiar from the earlier years, resurface time and again. Royal dispensations are the key to periodization and are supposed to explain the development of society, economy, culture, foreign relations, and so on. It is not only so that the segmentation of time offers precariously little other than the chronology of reigns, the serious thing is that it does not explain the societal evolution and its contemporary processes. In moving towards the present, all lines seem to disappear, and the relevance of historical consciousness for the imagination of the present is totally lost.

Chapter 4

REPAIRING THE DAMAGE: ALTERNATIVE IMAGES AND REALISM

On the whole, my interviews with high-shool teachers were depressing. Most of them complained about the attitude of their students, to whom social studies were a bore. When this Dutch uncle told them to live up to this challenge, they were adamant that the students see social studies as an unimportant subject, because it does not carry much weight to pass the university entrance examination. High school, they insisted, was not an end in itself but merely a channel to higher education, the quality of schools being rated according to the proportion of their students entering university. Students were interested in passing the exams, not in the subject matter, such as history or social analysis. These latter subjects did not motivate to seek tertiary-level education either. All students would like to study subjects which lead them to well-paid employment, such as engineering, medical science, information technology, and the like; it was only the intellectually less well endowed who, for failing the grade to enter other faculties, ended up in a social field of inquiry.

From my reading of the curriculum, and from my meeting the people handling social studies – only two of them having a firm grasp of what they were teaching – I do not think it to be far-fetched to observe that school does everything to destroy the subject matter, and that teachers have few options indeed. The curriculum is overloaded; the requirements, let alone the type of questions – all of them multiple choice – for university admission are well-known and set the limits of curiosity; the classes of fifty to sixty students make interesting debate very difficult; and essential questions tend to be reduced to the level of moralistic reasoning so familiar in the Thai educational system. Thus, as long as newspapers do better in enlightening the public, what is all the fuss in school about? Moralism, nationalism, formal Buddhism, and the ideology of the state are frightfully boring. Besides, in the higher grades, what should pass for a conceptual approach merely confuses.

This educational background of their students poses a considerable challenge to university lecturers. Are they equal to the task of introducing anthropology, history, or sociology? Can they bring the social imagination to life in a manner that allows the students to develop a mental hold of societal complexity? Can they overcome a level of discussion that fits pub and club, but that leaves society beyond scrutiny and critical reflection? Because aspiring students see things social as concrete experience that they most often take for granted, a well-known professor observed that the most difficult concept he had to explain was the idea of society itself. Thai students are trained to ask moral questions, hence they find it difficult to distance themselves, to analyse conceptually and theoretically, and to realize that 'society' is a mere idea, that you can never touch or see it.

The professor concerned, and other second – and meanwhile third – generation Ph.D.s, do indeed identify the problem, namely, the difficulty of introducing a theoretical grasp of social life. It is ominous, though, that the sociology and anthropology textbooks and readers in use offer discussions at a very general level, that are mainly illustrated by examples taken from the United States of America. It is a rare occurrence indeed that the subject matter is explained by instances drawn from the own cultural and structural situation, and in this way a hurdle is created that many students have difficulty passing.

Apparently, the faculty of the Department of Humanities at Chiangmai University is aware of the background of their students. As a result, they designed an introductory fourty-two hour course on Thai culture and society for which they also compiled a reader[1] bringing together a variety of materials to illustrate and to discuss, such as serious articles, official statements, short stories, novels, and song lyrics. These are grouped according to (1) basic thinking about Thai life and culture; (2) dominant views of Thai society; (3) social change. These sections, and all the individual pieces, are preceded by short introductions. The purpose of the *Reader* is to bring together diverse explanations in order to enable the students to think about issues and subjects without being dogmatic or simply one-sided; it is meant to stimulate understanding and critical thinking. As such the editor describes it as a mere tool.

Basic thinking

It may thus be expected that the course's contents play havoc with and upset the earlier school knowledge. The student is taught to distinguish between theory and empirical material, while being confronted with challenging and iconoclastic questions.

The very first article, by the economic historian Chatthip Nartsupha, exemplifies this. In his discussion of the relationship between village and state before capitalism, he wants to explain the dearth of connectedness between the two, how they existed as separate cultural realms; this despite the fact that the state, in order to prosper, needed the tributary village, its population and productive resources. If the village enjoyed peace and quiet, it was precisely because of the non-interference of the state. Even so, three factors potentially affecting the village should be considered, namely, government, (foreign) trade, and Buddhism.

Government interest in village affairs was slight; because there was neither a land-owning (feudal) class nor a bourgeoisie, there was no reason for the state to take an active interest in agricultural production or in matters concerning the village; there was no

---

[1]   Kanika Lekbunyasin (1991)

intermediary between state and village, and the state was satisfied as long as the village contributed the levies in goods and manpower. This gave rise to the highly stable *sakdina* organization of the state which, in relation to the village, is best described as a tributary relationship rather than as a despotic system.

The political economy did not greatly affect the conditions in the village either. Although the state was heavily dependent on foreign trade, it depended for its commodities on forest produce. That is, on products that were not part of the village productive system, that was organized as a self-sufficient and autonomous economy. At best the economic systems of state and village operated alongside each other. The influence of the Buddhist religion on village life was slight. The rulers were satisfied as long as Buddhism resulted in the legitimation of their position; in practice, villagers could believe whatever they wanted. Institutional religion was a political instrument, and the state's control over religious affairs was far more decisive than that of the monkhood. In this situation, the state could really not be bothered to interest itself in the religious life of the villagers. The latter continued to honour the spirits of their ancestors, as they still do today: the inner world is symbolized by these ancestors; their ashes are kept in the bedroom, while the Buddhist representations are kept in the area where visitors and outsiders are received.

It is only in recent years that the dominant subsistence economy has been affected by world capitalism. In considering the relatively slow pace this happened at, we should consider the compromising and gradual ways of response of the various regimes to the exigencies of the times. This flexibility allowed for the gradual implementation of administrative reforms, at a time the aristocracy still held power; it permitted avoiding outright imperialism, to keep the king on the throne, and to forgive those who staged coups d'état. All this is apparent in the ways the government handles social and technological change to this day; it is socially conservative and lacks a sense of urgency.

Another factor explaining the slowness of capitalist penetration is the relative abundance of land still to be brought under the

155

plough. Compared with other developing countries, scarcity of this resource was late in arising. As a serious problem it only exists since fifteen years [the chapter was written in 1986]. The third thing to bear in mind is the arising of the Thai bourgeoisie. Originating from Chinese immigrants, they were for a long time dependent on the Thai aristocracy, and they were content to operate in the circulation economy – trade, money-lending – rather than in modern productive enterprise. Their parasitic, or rent-seeking ways of operation, still characteristic of the Thai economy, and their long-time dependency on the political powers that be, made that they did not develop ideals of their own, that they still lack a leading role in the mobilization of the ordinary people and that, in contrast with Europe, a bourgeois-democratic revolution is not in the offing.

In considering all this, we may realize why state and village have stayed apart for so long. As a heritage of the *sakdina* system, and because of the more recent factors characterizing Thai capitalist production – lack of urgency; 'abundant' resources; peculiar 'bourgeoisie' – we can now explain the inner logic of present-day Thai society, a logic that we should understand if we want to design policy for the future.

The fact of having clear ideas in mind enables *acharya* Chattheep to say very much in the space of just four mimeographed pages. His vision not only destroys in one sweep much that has been taught in school; more importantly, it opens vistas of the power of interpretative schemes in ordering historical and actual data. That such ideas should be discussed instead of just being accepted is a theme that recurs throughout the *Reader*, and professor Chatthip's provocation certainly gives room for many lively exchanges.

Although departing from an entirely different paradigm, the second chapter, written by *acharya* Nidhi Aeusriwongse is no less challenging than the first. Under the subject title 'Basic Thai Wisdom as it Appears in Rituals', the rain-conjuring procession, carrying a female cat about the village, is discussed as a symbolic representation of an economy and a way of life that are currently invalidated, resulting in the cultural crisis Thai villagers are experiencing now. The author sees rituals and ceremonies as an expression of the collective memory and ideals of a group, linking the past to the future; ceremonial also serves to face real-life problems, and what does not make immediate sense to outsiders, may in fact be a very useful response to social and economic conditions.

These historical and symbolic-anthropological considerations lead to a fine phenemenological description of the old village subsistence economy. What were the problems people were confronted with? How were their lives and work organized? How were they affected when the king forced the male population into his army? By imagining social existence, its conditions and crises, related ceremonial becomes a logical part of it.

It is clear that the old way of life is disintegrating in its confrontation with the money-oriented market economy. Of course, to be able to sell your labour is nicer than to sell off your wife and children as slaves, although indebtedness to Chinese moneylenders is different from debts to the old instruments of state. Whereas the latter were part of a cultural whole that also spelt their boundaries of action, the new outsiders were not bound by familiar arrangements. When they were finally replaced by banks, ceremonies and old ways lost their meaning completely. This is the cultural crisis villagers are experiencing: their time-honoured ways have been invalidated, and even their precapitalist work arrangements do not make sense in the new mode of market-oriented production. The penetration of the money economy has been so fast that the productive basis of culture and customs was utterly destroyed. The latter merely survive as folklore and museum pieces, taken care of by the Bureau of Fine Arts, to serve the needs of tourism. There is nothing to really replace the old culture, other than the example of the urban middle classes and their 'individualism', which is an orientation that destroys community life.

Professor Nidhi does not want to pursue his argument to its logical conclusion, namely, the proletarianization of the rural population, and the economic success of a restricted number of agricultural entrepreneurs. In its stead he refers to headman Wibun Khemchalerm who successfully experimented with a return to subsistence agriculture, evading money and the market economy.

While I fully sympathize with the restoration of the old economy and its ceremonial representations, I do not think that people will carry their puss about the village again anytime soon. What may be an elitist opt-out for a few, cannot be expected to be an option for the many; yet, it is nicer to express hopes for the restoration of dignity than to deplore the vanishing of the old ways.

The point of the matter, though, is that a fine analysis has been offered about the integration of economic and expressive ways, and about the meaning of culture in human existence. The same method could be pursued to analyse what is happening in society today, whether we are happy with our subsequent findings or not. By focusing the students' attention on this type of relationships, we move well away from the artlessness they have been exposed to in high school.

It does not serve much of a purpose to describe or excerpt the subsequent chapters. The first two examples make it abundantly clear that the people who compiled this book had sound social-analytical ideas in mind, and that they want to stimulate the imagination of their students so that they can come to grips with their society, history and culture. Whether the course and its teachers accomplish this, is not in my purview, even though some lecturers report favourably about their efforts. The point here is, that critical social-scientific thinking is available, albeit that its practitioners and audience may still be very limited.

Under the heading 'The Basis of the Thai Political Economy', we find a lengthy and exhaustive analysis of the profile, motivations, actions, and positions of moneylenders in the Thai countryside. It is a commendable piece of exploratory field research, guided by clear, practical questions. In the general introduction, attention is drawn to the fact that, in olden times, Thai society consisted of groups who held different economic, political, cultural, and even racial positions. To understand how it all stuck together, we should study productive, administrative, and cultural relations. These can be illustrated by the network of informal credit relationships. Its analysis should identify types of 'social behaviour', 'groups', and the complexities of 'the structure' of rural society. This sociological approach provides succour, shortly after the destruction of the subject in school. Society is no longer inhabited by The People as a mystical unity under a benevolent ruler, but becomes a place were different people interact, all pursuing their own interests. The authors additionally explain the economic and other motivations animating such behaviour.

Sound ideas about the Thai system of patronage serve the further demystification of Thai social bonds. These are illustrated by an excerpt of a novel set in the countryside in which ordinary people, a progressive physician, a self-confident district officer, and local influentials relate with each other. The story demonstrates that patronage belongs to a hierarchical system based on unequal exchanges. Patronage expresses differences in economic and social position in which the lesser partners show deference – call it respect – to the big people. The lower people are at the beck and call of the big shots who are expected to extend help and protection to the former in all realms of life. This alliance has nothing to do with loyalty, although it can be many times stronger than the bonds of law or morality. Patronage is a relationship between persons, not one between people and principles, or the law. The latter two have no place in the patronage system. Because the ties between superiors and inferiors root in basic social differences, the ideal of equality is absent; what is more, it is implicitly denied, being as it is a threat to the very idea of patronage.

If the first piece of fiction cast a light on individual relationships, the second, Kukrit Pramoj's *Four Reigns*, elucidates those between groups. In the introduction it is clearly stated that patronage relationships are basic to Thai society. Thai socialization drills it in to rely on dependence, and this becomes a firm attitude;

being looked after can be reassuring too. It is to be expected that this attitude does not promote bonds based on equality. On the other hand, the ensuing ties should not be elevated as a positive ideology of patronage per se; the relationships in such a system are always manipulated to serve personal ends.

The realism in facing hierarchical society can be amply illustrated by folk tales. Providing the 'hidden transcript', or a 'counterpoint' to oppressive experience and the dominant ideology, such stories reveal the tensions inherent in the relationships between unequals. There exists a vast cultural arsenal to make people acquiesce in, yea, even admire and enjoy such bonds – let us bring to mind the indoctrination in primary school. Such folk tales, literature, or ritual provide the opportunity to turn the social order around, and to vent the negative feelings that might otherwise really upset it.

There is more to this. People may even go against the flow and demonstrate success in their opposition to society. To illustrate this, the earlier mentioned headman Wibun tells his story of going it alone as a subsistence farmer who finally produces so much that he can even sell in the market. The introduction to this narrative tells us of the original mainstay of the state, agricultural production. By inducing the farmers to produce a salable surplus, it could invest in development. Be this as it may, *phu:yai* Wibun's non-conformity enabled him to lead a more placid and satisfying existence, which may give hope to quite a few other farmers.

Self-reliance is also exemplified by uncle Charly Marasaeng who created water in the arid northeastern environment, setting an example for his fellows. According to the introductory statement, the sudden and unprepared confrontation with cash crops and the money economy made formerly self-sufficient people dependent on the market and its uncertainties. By its own logic, the new productive system also led to indebtedness and dependency. The need for money fuels the migration in quest of work that results in the disintegration of families; it causes people to destroy the forest in order to plant cash crops; the consolidating force of culture and its core institutions weaken, and mutual cooperation and support give way to self-orientation. In this dark situation a few wise people saw the light of the old culture that urges people to be self-reliant. This premise implies productive self-sufficiency as a guarantee for stability in life; then, being free of debts, people can decide for themselves whether to sell produce in the market, or not. Yet, one cannot just resurrect the past, and life encompasses more than productive practice alone. It implies a world view, ideals, values, and supportive social relations. That is why uncle Charly explains that his success derives from Dhamma, from having the Buddhist principles at heart, such as honesty, calm, and altruism, and also from his effort to revive cooperation among community members, all the time with an open eye for change and productive opportunities.

The practical idealism of the last two sections is elevated to a higher level still in the next pages, which are devoted to the sweeping discourses of the well-known social critic, professor Prawase Wasi. The real Thai community and its ways are rooted in subsistence production: people used to be self-dependent. The ideological factors undergirding this self-dependency are thought patterns, beliefs, values, choices and attitudes. The changes we witness today follow from the destruction of the ideology belonging to the old way of life, and affect the philosophy of Thai communities: people have lost the capacity to stand on their own feet, and in the process most of them have become impoverished because they now depend on things they cannot determine themselves, such as market prices, rates of interest, or new technological knowledge and methods. Most observers think this is inevitable, to which the professor takes exception. He wants to emphasize that by abandoning the Buddhist principles, the capacity for self-reliance has been lost, which then caused the collapse of the family, community, economy, and culture.

The learned physician identifies four main causes for this deplorable situation, to wit, western civilization; modern formal education; development; the commercial media. Western penetration caused a market economy to come into existence; greed and unwholesomeness (*kilesa*) followed in its wake, bringing about, for most people, the loss of the capacity to care for themselves, economic ruin, and environmental destruction. Current school education does not create an understanding of what is happening with Thai society; it breeds parrots, people who cannot think, who know nothing about life and cooperation, thus causing unemployment, failure, misguided quarrelling, and stupidity. Economic development opens communities up to the world, and creates the conditions of dependency which entail poverty for the majority. The message the commercial media spread can best be labelled as anti-Buddhism; instead of contentment, people now experience excitement, and their stimulated desires, in turn, destroy the all-important economic equilibrium.

The early modern evolution of familial bonds is then illustrated by an excerpt of Dokmaisot's *The Aristocrats*. It shows the influence of changing (external) circumstances on relationships and individual ambitions. Follows another analysis of a literary work, but this time to exemplify unity and variation among the regions in the presentation of the Ramayana cycle. In spite of an apparent unity of basic themes, we find an astounding diversity in emphases, details, elaborations, and so on, that need to be explained as particular responses from specific times and places. Thus, if we consider the Valmiki version of the Ramayana as the original, we find that even the text in use in Central Thailand is nothing more than a local variation on the themes of the story.

Under 'Creating Distance from Thai Culture', a short piece of literary writing is presented to demonstrate the pernicious influence the old patronage system had on personality formation. People were supposed to be servile and accept the authority and opinions of their masters. In spite of the complexity of the system, people apparently knew their way, even in dealing with novel situations. To understand this, we need to know the abstractions (rules, norms, values; ideas, culture) they went by. It is of interest to note the author's disgruntlement about patronage relationships: he describes the death of the main character as a growing awareness of liberation from the system's fetters. This points towards the dawning of a new notion, namely, that personal freedom is important and that the bonds of patronage are an obstacle to its realization.

The last chapter about the conceptual bases of Thai life and culture treats the astrological understanding of events. This type of thinking seeks to bring time, place, direction, and occurrences together in a coordinated scheme, and also allows for the calculation of auspicious moments. The interesting point is not whether all this is true, but rather the act of coordination that makes that this ancient system can lead to the understanding of events with which we are well acquainted.

Paradigms

The second part of the *Reader* introduces dominant scientific views. It begins by·explaining its purposes. Knowledge is not built on single facts, but consists of their place in a scheme, that was already existent in the head before the facts were observed. Because such schemes may vary, different meanings may be assigned to the same data. It all depends on the interpretation of the researcher; dominant interpretations are also related to the times and circumstances of their production.

The schemes with their basic assumptions are what we call paradigms, and such models colour the study of Thai culture and society. Every researcher must always examine and put to the test the paradigms currently in use. In the following we shall critically approach the interpretative schemes prevalent in Thai studies, and question accepted wisdom. Is it true, or not, that the Thais constitute an exceptional case, especially in Southeast Asia? Is it prejudice, or not, to hold that the Thai king took the lead in maintaining national independence against western imperialist aggression? Is it a prejudice or is it true, that the Thais were the only ones not to become a colony of imperialism? Did Thai nationalism really arise sooner than it did in neighbouring countries?

This promising introduction then opens with Ben Anderson's critical review of Thai political studies in English, 'Studies of the Thai State: The State of Thai Studies',[2] which provides an excellent introduction to a variety of theoretical models then (1978) – and often still – in use. Since the approach of the author is highly critical, contradictions between and within paradigms are pointed out; the working situation of the so-called regional experts is scrutinized; their relative isolation from theoretical developments at their universities is reflected upon; the obstacles of working in a foreign cultural environment are evaluated. This should serve the students as a warning that not all that is printed in the name of science is necessarily true, and that even the most solid dissertations will fall apart under critical scrutiny, and with the passage of time. Whether this is confusing or not, it is the way we operate; we can only advance by partly or wholly rejecting established 'truth' and 'fact'. Besides, since outward influences and inner dynamics work upon the social subject under study, change is its normal condition, and what was plausible in the past may not only sound highly improbable today, but even ludicrous tomorrow.

Anderson's incisive analysis, and its ambitious implications, are followed by a series of critiques of dominant views, or paradigms. The first dead horse to receive a flogging again is the thesis, amazing without end: Thai society has a loose structure. The compilers are not in a violent mood, though, and explain that the implied lack of rigidity allows individuals to change their situations and roles easily. Yet, Thai society is not so loosely structured as these western researchers assumed, which is first of all apparent from the cultural imperatives the Thais must take seriously; people are not at all free to do as they please. Anyway, social arrangements are always on the move, responding as they do to changes in the environment. This is very clear when looking at

---

[2]   Anderson, Benedict R. O'G., 'Studies of the Thai State: The State of Thai Studies', in Eliezer B. Ayal (ed), *The Study of Thailand*. Athens, Ohio: Ohio University, Center for International Studies, 1978, pp. 193-233.

communities near cities where the influence of (rapidly) changing ways is strong. This invalidates the old order of life, and nobody really seems to know what he is in for. Because of such an observation, it was concluded that Thai society is loosely structured; had they chosen a community far removed from the onslaught of urban modernity, they would have found regularity and predictable structural arrangements. A summary of Chart Kopchitti's *The Judgement* then serves to illustrate the relatively tight structure of life within the confines of conservative conventions.

The second paradigm to be scrutinized does not originate from foreign observers, but is alleged to be a Thai trait, namely, not to look at social life in an historical manner. This means that people normally do not consider factors such as 'time' and 'place'. By disregarding the historic-cultural setting of events or ideas, all that appears to the eye becomes 'universal', changeless, and widely applicable. In that way historical events and documents are interpreted as if they happened or were composed only yesterday, or, alternatively, the present is simply projected into the past. An often heard remark may exemplify this: 'The Thais love tranquility' – which comes without questioning when and where that would be true, nor with asking under which circumstances Thais might not appreciate tranquility (*sangop*).

Such questions need to be asked, as we noted already when criticizing the loose-structure paradigm. Such a model resulted directly from the a historical manner in which the subject of inquiry was approached. History brings out the peculiarities induced by time and circumstances, but also points out the continuities. This becomes clear in the excerpt about the husband-wife relationship through time, which makes ducks and drakes of the idea of monogamy. This latter idea is a, currently influential, import from the West. Contrastively, a historical view will reveal the complexity of the man-woman relationships in depth. The fifteen pages that follow make for a delightful excursion through the worlds of European and Thai ideas indeed; as a result, even the equation *mia* = wife needs to be questioned.

Next in line is the paradigm about the uniformity of human evolution. The discussion starts with the caveat that certain models of thought become so popular as to be used unquestioned, and are even applied to situations which they were not designed to deal with at all. Such paradigms acquire the status of Truth, and exert a strong influence over how further problems are phrased. This pernicious situation can only be faced by always questioning the schemes that guide any research.

It is not only in the scientific endeavour that paradigms grow strong and need to be scrutinized. The modern state is also a zealous producer of dominant views; the propagation of its brand of nationalism to dominate the populace is a telling case in point. 'Love of nation' is seemingly a good thing that does not need questioning. The state, however, also defines the contents and the interpretation of 'love of nation', while certain individuals do hold different ideas about how to express their love of the nation. The state tries to control this by prescibing how the 'love of nation' should be felt and expressed. It propagates its view by way of the media it dominates, and through schools, speeches, expositions, et cetera.

To illustrate the point, we should consider the nationalistic songs produced between 1932 and 1982 that are full of imperatives about how to feel and be Thai. They mirror the way the state serves its own needs by defining a form of nationalism that should not be questioned and that leaves nothing to choose from. This state ideology does not consider the various situations of the population and its individuals; it is an attempt at thought control. Thus, if certain people still hold their own ideas in this matter, they will be branded as 'rebels' or people who 'sell the nation' (meaning that they are indifferent to its reputation). Having personal ideas is seen as rejecting the state ideology; this forces the producers of alternative ideas to also articulate them as a system of beliefs. These various ideas are demonstrated by the selection of songs.

Another approach to the evolutionary paradigm is offered in the next chapter; it presents a speech by professor Prawase Wasi about the 'Crisis of the Thai Villages'. The introductory discussion begins by noting that the idea of unilineary development, as it originated in the West, is spread by way of modern education and the western domination of science. The basic idea is that human society develops through particular stages, and that the European countries have achieved the highest stage. If other countries aspire to those heights, they will have to pass through the same phases as western societies, such as industrialization, the birth of the nation-state, liberal democracy, and the like.

The influence of these ideas is reflected in the way the Thai state stimulates industrialization, to which other forms of production should be subservient. It should be noted, though, that the original conditions of western industrialization do not apply here. The present policy, with its emphasis on capital investment, totally neglects cultural realities and locally available technology. While new productive methods are being forced on the country, we lose our mastery because we cannot control imported 'appropriate technology', capital flows, markets, and prices.

Policy-makers neglect the possibility of choice, even when there is plenty to choose from. Their vision is blinkered by the idea that there is only one way ahead; they reduce people to mere instruments of material development. Although other ways and ideas are easily imaginable, they seem to be kept at bay by political inertia. The monolithic view of development is at the roots of the centralization of power that, in its turn, does not consider regional and social variation. Because of this, the urban-centred authorities are also ill-equipped to solve regional or local problems. Things are centrally planned, and the concomitant mentality may prove to be a fine matrix for dictatorship to arise in. Professor Prawase's article amply illustrates the destruction of the countryside that follows from such one-sided thinking.

The compartmentalization of life and knowledge is subjected to critical scrutiny in the ensuing chapter. Departing from the premiss that local knowledge enables communities to exist in harmony with life and nature, and to face the dynamics of an ever-changing environment, the idea is put forth that such knowledge covers life in all its aspects; it is a holistic view. In Thailand, this type of local knowledge can well be illustrated by medical practice. Superficially seen, it appears to deal with old ideas about health as such, but a more penetrating analysis will reveal that these very ideas are part of a world view that relates individual health to the state of the community, the care for nature, and other things.

This type of thinking differs from modern western knowledge. The latter is based on the idea that all that can be known must be empirically present, and that phenomena are mechanically interrelated. As a matter of course this view holds that events can be explained because of concrete (empirical) causes and effects. In the search to identify causes and effects, phenomena are analysed and separated from the environment they belong to; things are broken into parts. Western medicine argues in terms of defective limbs and organs, and neglects the psyche and social circumstances as causes of illness. As a result, attention focuses on defective parts, irrespective of psychological, artistic [sic], and behavioural factors, or the social environment of the patient.

Local Thai knowledge is not only holistic, but also considers non-empirical causes, such as spirits, to be influences on natural and social events affecting human existence. As a result, respect for and correct behaviour towards spirits helps to prevent undesirable happenings and promotes the bounty of nature. In this mindset, illness arises from insults to the spirit world. Of course, nowadays modern medicine is available, although it is not always within the means of villagers. Another way of dealing with difficult-to-cure afflictions is the acceptance of them by patients and family, with the latter extending care and love to the sufferer. Such alternatives are pre-empted, however, when local knowledge is considered to be old-fashioned and out-of-date. Modern developments in Thai society tend to be patterned after and guided by western example. No thought is spent on the time-honoured wisdom and native methods of solving social problems, even though Thai people are very much in need of knowing themselves better.

A second critique of compartmentalization is advanced by a discussion of the interpretation of the old northern chronicles, *tamna:n*. In introducing the subject, the authors state that life under the influence of industrialization and scientific thinking makes for a divided and distantiated experience. This is, for instance, demonstrated by the division of knowledge into 'disciplines'. Still, we know that all knowledge is related, and that its division only serves the expedience of analysis. An integrated view should also be the basis of solving the problems of modern society. What we see, however, is that illness is treated as a purely medical question, that dams are built by engineers, and that factors that are not immediately recognized as medical or technical are simply ignored, even while it is obvious to everyone that social and ecological factors play their part in such cases. As a result, problems, misunderstandings, and faulty solutions abound. The western division of knowledge also stands in the way of understanding existence itself.

Such divisions were uncommon to the old Thais who looked at life in an integrated manner, and our understanding of the chronicles should be based on this insight. Consequently, we should not treat these writings as historical sources of data and facts. What they reveal is a world view; ethics; and connexions between all sorts of subjects, from statecraft to religion.

Social change

The third part is about social change. It begins with the present village community. Attention is drawn to the current tendency to take advantage of each other and to only take care of oneself and one's family. These developments go in tandem with dislocations in economic life that seem to drive people to gambling, indebtedness, drunkenness, and the buying of useless gadgets, leaving them without the resources necessary to acquire the things they really need. All this is illustrated by a short story by Sidaorueang, and the song *Motorcycle Girl*.

Change brought about by urbanization is the subject of the next chapter. While the mutations in the material environment in town are the most obvious, such developments bring important changes in lifestyles in their wake. It seems that the mentality of people is most seriously affected, which is reflected in their ethical and philosophical consciousness. With such changes in their world view, they will also behave differently. In the article that follows, *acharya* Sulak Sivaraksa concentrates on the question of the quality of life in contemporary Thailand. What does a good life look like? The answer to this question reveals a western (*farang*) attitude to life that starkly contrasts with the Buddhist frame of mind. This uncritical acceptance of a foreign style has many behavioural consequences, such as the addiction to consumer culture, quarrels and irritations, and upsets the individual's peace of mind. We can guess the suggested solution to all this: if the Thais become wise Buddhists, society will be whole again.

The question 'Who is in Control of Social Change in Thai Society?' is then pursued in the footsteps of John L.S. Girling, whose book *Thailand: Society and Politics*[3] is summarized in the following eleven pages. According to the introduction, hierarchical relationships are fundamental to Thai social life: they result in the patronage system. Since the fifth reign, social change has dominated life, and those higher up took the initiative. While the institution of patronage remained in place, the patrons themselves became different persons. Royals and aristocracy gave place to a professional civil service that became the foremost instrument of politics and administration. Especially after 1932, the civil service became a power in its own right, and started to control the process of social evolution: its members were the main policy-makers. Whether staffed by civilians, soldiers, or elected personnel, the system of administration grew to be the heart of politics and the Thai state; accordingly, we call such an arrangement a bureaucratic polity (*Beamtenstaat*).

---

[3]   Girling, John L.S., *Thailand: Society and Politics*. Ithaca: Cornell University Press, 1981.

From the time Marshal Sarit came to power (1957) onwards, the business establishment started to influence public policy. In the beginning, though, it was the junior partner of the state's bureaucrats who were effectively its patrons. These patronage relationships exist for the sake of expedience, and do not lead to loyalty per se. What is opportune at a certain time, may be undesirable at another, and tensions naturally belong to the patron-client arrangement. Collisions between 'patrons' and 'clients' surface from time to time, such as in 1932 and 1973. At such occasions, a whole new set of godfathers, or civilian influentials may come into ascendency and gets access to the halls of power, at the same time that patronage as a system persists.

An open letter by a group of academics addressed to all political parties serves as a conclusion about change in Thai society. In it, the cause of current change is identified in the 'strategy and tactics' of development: resources are transferred from the agricultural sector to stimulate the rapid growth of manufacturing. This injustice arises from the fact that there is no popular participation in determining the course and purposes of development; decision making is in the hands of bureaucratic economists; it is they who design the national social and economic development plans. These people form the new 'aristocrats' (*khunna:ng*). The result of unbalanced development is the impossibility of solving the problem of income distribution; quite the contrary, it is aggravated further. This is not a mere question of money, but also of equal access to the opportunities of bettering oneself. The type of development pursued also causes the collapse of social institutions, such as the family, and promotes violence as a way of solving conflicts. Development decisions should not be taken by technocrats, and a socially just strategy supported by appropriate methods ought to be initiated.

Three further choices concerning change are still presented. The first is an appeal to use the media and the educational system to foster the cause of the ordinary people instead of them serving as the handmaidens of the elite. This document, dating from the restive democratic period of 1973-6, is followed by a ten-point programme of the Communist Party of Thailand. This party was rather prominent in the 1960s and 1970s, and its policy was based on an analysis that concluded that the organization of Thai society was half-feudal and half-colonial. As a result, the outside influence of imperialism should be banned, and its tools, the native accomplices of imperialistic capitalism, should be deprived of their power in a newly reorganized society.

At the time the CPT was still active, other, less well-known people also thought about alternative solutions, although their suggestions did not gain much attention. An example is given under 'The Activities of Farmer Organizations', in which the authors identify various obstacles in the way of the emancipation of the villagers, one of them being their world view that concedes honour of place to the elite. According to the latter's rhetoric, they always act 'for the people' and 'in the public interest', although it is clear that they care for themselves only. It transpires that a new world view is needed, a vision founded on the conviction that history is driven by ordinary workers; it is they who construct society and who will decide on the ways it should change. No less idealistic is the third and last example, an article by the venerable Buddhadasa Bhikkhu with the title, 'The World Can Be Saved by the Dictatorship of Truth (Dhamma)'.

Comments

The *Reader* has been compiled to provide discussion materials that should lead to social scientific insight; its subject matter consisted of a variety of interpretations of Thai society and culture. Commented upon as paradigms, these interpretations suggested ways of thinking about social life in Thailand. Compared to the early school experiences of the students, this exercise was most refreshing, sometimes even iconoclastic. While the Thai social climate does not allow for the radicalism of naked truth, the striptease went far enough to suggest the contours of the body politic of the state and its relation to the population.

From the few remarks about history, it became clear that the state did not function as the fatherly protector of the people. On the contrary, the latter were exploited as soldiers and servants; they were a source of tribute from which the state derived a good deal of its strength. As long as such things were in order, the state could not care less about the conditions in the countryside or the beliefs of the people. As a result, the state did not propagate the practice, ethics, and wisdom of Buddhism; the latter's paraphernalia merely served the purposes and the legitimation of the state itself. This clear division between state and population resulted in social transparency, such as the presence of a state-owning class at a great remove from the agricultural masses.

The owners of the state, and its instruments, represent power; the others are expected to obey. In this arrangement, people belonged to the state, which in practice meant to identifiable 'patrons'. The patronage relationship functioned to harness the population for the purposes of the political class, and in spite of its ideological dressing, we should realize that its motivations were purely expedient. Most ordinary people could happily do without it, yet, it is at the root of a persistent vertical orientation in Thai society that stimulates dependency rather than initiative. Also, manipulation of relationships to serve the own interest should be expected; it is admired, and often longingly dreamt of.

These historical observations imply insights that can be exploited to understand present-day Thai society. They surface most clearly in the excerpt of Girling's ideas: the classes who own the state may evolve, and different types of people may become powerful, but the system of patronage, and its hierarchical relationships, continues as such. Its persistence becomes apparent in the chapters that comment on 'development'. The owners of the state exploit the realm in the fashion of the times; the environment and the rural population are subservient to their interests. They want to grow richer and richer, and they direct the economy accordingly. The so-called plight of the people is not of their concern, although it surfaces in obligatory rhetoric. As formerly, if they are patrons, they are godfathers at best; they are bosses in the service of their own well-being and self-glorification.

Because all this is abundantly clear, and not to everybody's liking, there has been, and is, a steady imagining of alternatives, from old folk tales to ideological suggestions. Sometimes religion is thought to provide redemption. What if all Thais were good Buddhists? They would cease their consumerist ways; they would stop exploiting each other; they would be wise and caring; society would be peaceful. But why would Thai people suddenly aspire to become what they have never been? Or how would they allow for popular participation and democracy? How could people possibly imagine themselves to be the owners of the state? The articles selected make it very explicit that the compilers themselves hold Thai society to be hierarchically structured, and that 'patronage' is a fine euphemism to convey the idea of the ownership of the state by a small class of highly privileged people; their enjoying special rights makes them do as they please, that is, as long as their rival fellows allow them to do so. All this is blatantly visible and known: the media provide a stage for them, and every day the ordinary people are given glimpses of the ongoing political show.

Until recently, the country had an agricultural frontier, and people were used to minding their own business; interference of the state in their lives was slight. Over the past thirty years, this situation has drastically changed. According to Chatthip, Thailand is a latecomer; then, however, it booked a flight into the future while leaving much of its cultural luggage behind. In the *Reader*, the consequences of this process for rural society receive ample emphasis, although the analysis of village culture is more theoretical and ideological than empirical.

Firstly, I think, this should have been made more explicit because, as evident from our schoolbook analysis, there exist strong tendencies in Thai culture to elevate things to a moralistic-idealistic level, and to subsequently consider this as a reflection of real life. Secondly, even if the influence of the state was slight, villages did not exist in isolation, and while it is true that in the Northeast intensive contact with 'modernity' came late, we should be careful to note all sorts of accommodations to the exigencies of time and place in the less peripheral parts of the country. What is offered in the *Reader* is an idealization of self-sufficient subsistence production that fits with an elaborate culture of ritual means, native medicine, mutual help, and self-reliance that all combined in a holistic world view that crumbled in its confrontation with a very rapid social-economic transformation. This sea change did not allow for the growth of new culture, and logically anomalousness and lack of direction prevail: self-centred individualism in the midst of communities that became societies overnight. While the model is very clear, it reeks of moralism and nostalgia.

Sulak's favourite subject does not improve our understanding either. That Thai ways of life are at variance with Buddhist wisdom – and have always been so – must be clear even to a child, yet the *acharya* finds it important to keep flogging this dead horse, possibly hoping to reanimate it with the vapour of his ire. So, the urban middle classes follow the *farang*; well, who else should they follow and pattern their lives after? They are as new as the urban jungle in which they thrive – or suffocate. There is no cultural pattern in Thai society they can have recourse to. Simply said, there was no middle-class or bourgeois culture, other than that demonstrated by successful Chinese or, higher up, by a dinosaurian aristocracy. Sulak offers the most improbable alternative imaginable: let them become wise Buddhists.

If there is a possibility for a positive cultural growth of the middle classes, they would probably have to aim for more than the superficial imitation of 'universal' urban ways. They could perhaps be inspired to follow democratic patterns, believe in equality, the rule of law, and develop themselves into morally autonomous citizens. Such utopian thinking at least aims at improving society, a thing that the ethics and wisdom of the so-called great religions have never accomplished in all the time they have been with us.

Phra Prayut Payutto

At this point it may be interesting to inspect what the Buddhist luminary cum social critic, *phra* Prayut Payutto, has to say. A recent interview with the venerable monk[4] is introduced with the observation that 'Present-day Thai society is not of itself; it has no collective conscience; it does not know where it is. What is the condition of its environment? We see a lot of aimless running about, an image of confusion'. In the absence of unity, there cannot be a sense of direction either. It results in everybody doing their own thing separately. This is aggravated by the process of globalization that fuels the competition between interests, among individuals and among national societies. Such competition blocks the road to the realization of the common welfare, and it wears people out. In contrast with this, a shared purpose would stimulate the energy of each and every one. Mutual competition thus surfaces as a core problem of our days, and we are not really equal to the challenge. We Thai people are not really go-getters, and we have no appropriate standards to measure success. People who succeed materially become vain, and lose sight of their social embeddedness and the public interest.

Whereas this interest should be articulated by politicians and the civil service, they fail to do so, blinded as they are by their own power and personal affairs. As soon as they are in doubt, they will react by defending themselves, minding their own safety, and so we suffer a dearth of great, of purposeful leaders. As a result, we waste time and fail to rise to the occasion when it presents itself. Our short-sightedness causes problems and quarrels; it keeps us wandering around aimlessly. While real wisdom and reflection would offer ways out, it is not easy to come by. Look at the monkhood itself. For twenty, thirty years we have been talking about aim and purpose, yet we do not know where to begin. And

---

4   Interview with Phrathammapidok (Pô:,ô: Payutto), The Light of Wisdom ... Prayut Payutto. *Dô:kbia ka:nmüang (The Politics Interest)* 242 (January 7-13, 2539): 4-12.

so it is with Thai society: it does not know what and where it is, let alone where it is headed. This also means that individuals feel morally abandoned, and that there is no vision of the common interest. As a result, there is little to be expected from our politicians. We suffer from ignorance, and are thus confused.

Our individual striving for the greatest profit logically results in a fascination with consumer culture that further feeds on the dynamics of capitalist production. The rat race makes us suspicious of each other and hypocritical; people stop being good; if they do something positive, it is because they expect something in return. People take advantage of each other while competing to outshine their rivals. In this atmosphere, those who are honestly motivated to help their fellows will suffer. In following the western-induced worldwide trends, we destroy our social and natural environment; all of us travel down this dead-end street.

While people in the West are conscious of these problems, they are as yet unable to reverse the trend. They are not their own masters any more. Having fallen victim to their philosophy of dominating nature, the consequences: materialism, competition and consumerism, logically follow. As long as their basic thinking – which we have accepted – does not change, it is impossible to come back to basics. In our case, we have become alienated from our roots; we do not belong to ourselves any longer. Our following of a competitive way of life is aggravated by what we do not accept from the West, namely, the rule of law, designed to regulate the pursuit of unlimited desire.

Apparently we have lost the true criteria to evaluate success: the true success of humankind is the creation of harmony; it lies in the realization of what is good, true, and beautiful. But present people are bent on material success; our politicians are businesspeople. It is most improbable that they will see the light. Do not forget that individual and society mutually condition each other. Politicians, and the people at large, are products of this material development-crazy environment. The only way out is the cultivation of wisdom, the reflection on the essence of our situation. This can only originate from individual persons, from each and every one of us.

We should not wait for a leader to arise to clean up the mess; that would be a long wait. Neither should we hope that the monkhood can give much guidance. After all, the monks are also conditioned by this society, they are not self-aware, and have the fuzziest ideas about their role. So, because of their ignorance, even good-intentioned monks come to nought. Their understanding of Buddhism is amiss. They take religion to be a thing to cling to, a source of psychic security, which in its turn panders people, and makes them feel comfortable. We do not need Buddhism for such dependency. Moreover, the very relaxation produced by religious consolation stands in the way of the will to develop insight; problems remain thus unsolved. It is like the ostrich who buries its head in the sand when danger approaches.

We, the Thai people, are more or less weak; we side-step problems, do not face up to difficulties. We are experts at avoiding. That makes us gamblers, relying on luck, instead of energetically tackling the problems of life. Every success we experience is reason enough to relax. We do things by halves, therefore not solving any problem. To put it differently, we lack direction and do not live up to challenges; the destruction of the environment illustrates these points. In brief – and that is what makes us such poor Buddhists too – we are people who go by our emotions. Some of them, such as sympathy and kindness, are very commendable; we like to trust in religion, to feel protected and comfortable; but what the Thais absolutely miss are the faculties of contemplation, reflection, and the will to wisdom. And yet, it is only because of these that people can advance to become self-reliant, self-dependent. We, however, prefer to depend on the power of 'sacred things', while leaving problems unsolved. The rising standard of living of many contributes to this wishy-washy attitude. The new generation indulges in all sorts of comforts, and has no tolerance for effort; they are easily disappointed without seeing ways out. We remain mired in superficialities and are apparently unable to solve our problems. Apart from the unlikely cultivation of wisdom, the monk concluded, I do not see any practical solutions.

Comments

In between the positions of *acharya* Sulak and *phra* Prayut Payutto, there appears to be a vast field to be explored in order to gain understanding of the current cultural dynamics of the middle classes. As I see it, both luminaries invoke more questions than they answer; the whole problematics of the human aspects of urban growth needs to be charted. It is not a monolithic field, and among the products of the educated and consumerist middle classes, we also find all the articles and criticisms that compose the *Reader*. No easy answers are possible, or should be aspired to. But as it appears, the problem of culture loss – and the subsequent generation of new culture – is not just a problem of villagers. It is a general problem of Thai society, perhaps even more apparent among all those who have suddenly donned neckties in the air-conditioned comfort of their offices than among those who are in the midst of the struggle for survival. It is not for this reason alone that I would advocate that more attention be spent on the emergence of the urban middle classes. However important the village may still be, the future of Thai society is with new people who live in a new urban environment, whether we like it or not, and these need to be understood in greater depth. Thus, if the *Reader* will ever be expanded or revised, it must be hoped that it will bring these developments, and the related growth of business and industrialization, into focus.

A related problem – and pedagogically very fertile to face is to include material analyzing Thai culture as such. What are the dominant paradigms of the contemporary world view of which the students are the unwitting mental prisoners? They have been educated to view society through a moral focus that took the idealized family as its basic model, with hierarchy, moral inequality, and obligation as its backbone. They may see study as a way of climbing the social ladder – by way of rote learning and competitive grades – rather than as the pursuit of intellectual interests and curiosity. Most of them operate within contemporary youth and consumer culture; as young voters, they tend to be critical of national political practice; they are worried about the rape of the environment but accept the pervasive materialism. Even so, they are not aware that what others or they themselves complain about is intrinsic to the fabric of Thai culture. By challenging their cultural blinders, the analysis of culture and society may become more pointed; it must be a good educational tool because it begins with what is nearest, namely, personal experience, while aiming at creating self- and social awareness. For the rest I have no qualms about the *Reader*, it gives lecturers and students an excellent opportunity to begin with the serious analysis of Thai culture and society.

An image?

The discussion of dominant paradigms notwithstanding, the *Reader* has shied away from the generalizations about Thai society that were so popular among the first generation of indigenous social scientists. In their time, Thai society was loosely structured, the people were individualistic, Buddhism spurred them on to work out their own karma and liberation, they were pleasure-seeking, fun-loving, self-confident, and unburdened by colonially induced feelings of inferiority, proud of being Thai, royalists to the bone, and carried the burden of public responsibility lightly. In spite of *kre:ngcai*, hierarchical arrangements, a fascination with rank and power, and a bureaucratic polity, a touch of anarchy pervaded social arrangements.

Within the scope of a fourty-two-hour course, not all images need to be questioned or promoted, although a discussion of the demerits of essentialism, as described hereabove, would not have been unbecoming. After all, the earlier school teachings did not shy away from creating such images, and certain books in popular use at certain universities still propagate the image sketched above. A better point for avoiding essentialism can perhaps be made: the course does not aim at constructing an image of culture and society. It wants to stimulate the imagination, at the same time that it hopes to discipline it by critical thinking. It has the potential to accomplish this.

In spite of the course's brave intentions, images do arise. The ultimate could possibly be one of cultural confusion: for ordinary people things were in place; they were sturdy, self-reliant, culture and practice were consolidated: they knew who they were. Come modern times, and it all crumbles; a few – headman Wibun, uncle Charly, doctor Prawase – develop recipes to resurrect the past ways of livelihood, but most people will need to resign themselves to a less wholesome accommodation with the exigencies of rapid change. In the process, they lack guidelines; life becomes confusing.

The picture of the past – idealized in school – is also taken apart. Patronage relationships were not wholesome; people were exploited; and patrons did not care about the welfare of their 'clients' as a matter of course. The idea of loyalty crumbled; the nationalistic interpretations of the past got tainted. Yet, patronage arrangements remain the mainstay of Thai society; they carry on into the present where business affiliated politicians have taken over from aristocrats. Fuelled by self-centred economic priorities, they are apparently behind the havoc unbridled capitalism has been playing with Thai society and its natural environment, stimulating a steady output of ideological alternatives among critical intellectuals.

Whether of confusion or unwholesomeness, these images are of things in flux, of a dynamic process that can be imagined, but that is hard to reduce to a surveyable picture. It is easier to think about than to visualize concretely. A list of 'problems', their moral causes, and facile solutions, has been avoided, and that is how it should be. If the course achieves the contemplation of the images it offers, it holds the promise that the serious pursuit of social science has begun; it is a prerequisite for democratic reconstruction. After all, it is not mere coincidence that the arising of modern democratic and social-scientific ideas took place simultaneously. From the Enlightenment, or the Age of Reason, derive such basic premises as the ideas of interindividual moral equality, and thus of natural right; and of the constructability of society: it could be mastered, be made a better place. If people are equal, and society constructable, emancipation of any underdog becomes morally and politically imperative. Sociology – that is, the critical analysis of how society proceeds – the development of reasoned political ideology, and the implementation of democracy with its inherent idea of the rule of law, will then become possible. In other words, distantiated social thinking is a necessary condition for democracy to develop, and if the course succeeds in instilling the first in the students, there is good hope for the latter to evolve.

Chapter 5

MAKING PUBLIC OPINION

Of the media, it is the press that comes closest to mirroring the public world. This proposition needs qualification. The media help construct the public world, as much as they reflect it. And what has been constructed, is. Thus, what appears in the newspapers is a particular image that people regard as the flux and flow of the outside world, yet, it is not the only depiction of it. This is immediately apparent when watching the news and imagery on television. On early evening TV, it is impossible to escape from the projection of national symbols, ceremonies, and the acts of royalty. Part of what appears on the screen is clearly the presentation of the theatre state, that is, an older image of the public world, for all to watch, but not to participate in. It figures the mutes in uniform, with some of them allowed to sing their mantras or to say their prescribed phrases. Then, later on in the programming, generals, politicians, and other big-mouthed big shots may comment on their acts and the criticisms of the day, apparently free to defend themselves. Until recently, and later into the night still, some talk shows called their bluff, and thus recreated a parallel image of the unruly public world the newspapers promote.

The press is free indeed, rivalling Filipino journalism, and in stark contrast with the confined space the governments in Malaysia, Singapore and Indonesia allow the media. It is lively, scandalous, licentious, overenthusiastic, and often shallow. There is a tendency, though, towards more investigative reporting which forces politicians to wash their dirty linen in public. Many others, who were almost unassailable until recently, now have to endure the scoff of the pen and the jeer of the popular gossip circuit. Perhaps this signals the beginning of the emergence of serious public opinion, of one carrying weight in political and social decision making. For the time being, opinion is popular rather than public, rumour rather than open discussion, but its weight is increasing, and the press is its pioneer.

Exploring an image

From November 1994 to February 1995, I scrutinized the newspapers; in the beginning of this period, I also explored them to conclude about the impression they made. How did they represent the public world they supposedly mirrored? The ensuing image is mainly based on the English language press and the popular dailies *Thai Rat* and *Kha:wsot*. The reports and commentary that stood out between 14 November and 2 December concerned tense Australian-Thai relationships in connexion with the taking hostage by the Khmer Rouge of some young tourists. These relationships based on misunderstandings flourish into the present. The Aussies seem to be experts at hurting Thai sensitivities – or perhaps serve as the favourite scapegoat to express latent frustration with those 'rice-water-eyed' representatives of what the Thais call the civilized countries (*a:rayaprathe:t*).

Other evergreens parading through the pages were: *phra* Yantra; constitutional amendments; the rising star of present (1997) prime minister, General Chavalit; the Saudi gems; military cold war rhetoric and suspicion of pro-democracy activism; EGAT and the destruction of nature; Thaksin Shinawatra; the loopholes in the law which is supposed to protect the environment; Pa:k Mu:n Dam protestors; the deplorable human rights situation of Burmese students and other asylum seekers in Thailand; Major-General

Chamlong's high-handedness and obstinacy; the continual rambling and squabbling of the elected representatives in parliament; police contempt of the public; the Bangkok traffic. Said evergreens are, naturally, not quite as perennial as the steady items serving to lend flavour and amusement to the reader, such as banter columns; the very extensive sports reporting; amulets and charismatic monks, to which *Kha:wsot* devotes at least three pages every single day.

Monks

Phra Yantra, long in the limelight in the past, and still surfacing with an occasional mention up to this day, is an archetypical example of what can go wrong with religious practice. Because institutional Buddhism is a highly sensitive issue, emotions can easily flare up. This also gives rise to the attitude of hushing the scandals that regularly surface. Their exposure is 'destroying the institution of Religion', one of the pillars of Thai nationhood. Anyway, the sequence of events surrounding the monk was so remarkable as to be irrepressible.

As a charismatic preacher, *phra* Yantra had collected himself a considerable following, especially in Thailand, but also in Europe and Australia. Like so many successful religious entrepreneurs, he apparently had easy access to his female followers. Given his Australian escapades, the initiative leading to such contacts was not always entirely with the women giddy with his good looks.

When evidence of siring a daughter and of making love to certain women became more and more compelling, his followers beat up the accusers. All the time, the monkhood's upper echelons had been very slow and overly careful in reacting, giving *phra* Yantra the benefit of the doubt. This procrastination kept the affair in the news for a year and a half, thus really undermining religion's moral authority, at the same time incensing the hard core of the monk's flock. Others grew angry too, particularly at *Thai Rat* that refused to budge and kept the priest in the news. And thus, in the

185

last few months leading up to his expulsion, a bazooka shell was fired into the newspaper's premises.

Sexual delinquency, and the claim of possessing supernatural powers, are reason enough to defrock any monk, even though the steady attribution of miraculous powers by laymen seems to have made Buddhism a booming business these days. Yet, whereas such vices may be seen as inner *Sangha* affairs, *phra* Yantra was also accused of insolence towards the Supreme Patriarch, or Sangharaja, which is a criminal offence. Be this as it may, a few months after being forced to quit, now layman Winai La-ongsuwan escaped from the reach of Thai law, and made it to America where he has re-established himself as a guru cum empire builder. In this way he added insult to injury by impersonating a Buddhist monk, a criminal offence in Thailand that, in the name of freedom of religion, cannot be prosecuted in the USA.

The basic story, and even its sequel, have all the elements that make for a most entertaining movie, yet, such publicity is detrimental to institutional religion. Together with political scandal and gory accidents, however, the irreverent adventures of individual members of the brotherhood of monks firmly belong to newspaper reporting – and sexual licence is normally not the point of interest. What is brought into focus are juicy incidents such as an abbot fired at, yet remaining unhurt. This had nothing to do with his sacred potency, but more with the bullet-proof vest he was wearing under his robes at the time. Prepared for a gangland killing, he was a rogue among rogues indeed. Yantra-like publicity befell a monk who was involved in the forging of documents to obtain royal decorations. Of late we had a monk posing for racy gay pictures; another killing a lady tourist; others abusing liquor and drugs; and someone who sat on a virtual arsenal of high-powered arms. Of course, criminals seeking a refuge in the monkhood are an age-old problem, and when exposed they will be defrocked immediately. It was *phra* Yantra's tenacity – and his large following – that made his case exceptional.

Other, very respectable priests who have been difficult to make to disrobe, were a few abbots fighting environmental depredation. As a result, such activists are readily confronted with the influential interests of those who organize the rape of nature, and an effective way is to start a smear campaign accusing the monks concerned. This even resulted in the publication of fabricated photographs in a newspaper showing the targeted man in his saffron habit in *flagrante delicto* with a woman. In many cases so much pressure is applied to such defenders of the common people or the environment that they have to leave the positions of respect they command, to vanish among the laymen.

The main category of monks attracting the attention of the vernacular press are those religious virtuosos who become famous for their meditational practices, teachings, and high age. They are seen as a kind of national treasure, and their deaths and cremations result in royal sponsorship and huge gatherings of worshippers eager to make merit. A few of such very holy monks were reported to draw crowds estimated at two to three-hundred thousand people when they embarked on their 'ascent to the heavens'. These priests, to whom, as a matter of course, sacred potency is attributed, normally consecrate amulets, either produced under their auspices or in their name. They shade over into a category of charismatic monks, also known as *luang phô*, that is, venerable fathers, whose involvement in the trade in protective potency, or *saksit* power, is more obvious. They are the great producers of talismans, powerful Buddha images, and other sources of blessing that are eagerly sought by national politicians and ordinary farmers alike. The currently most famous of these monks is *luang phô* Khun who, when he turned seventy-two in early 1995, donated seventy-two million *baht*[1] to royal charities when the King came to pay his respects on that occasion. The reputation of the monk, and of his amulets, was enhanced when he came out unharmed after his speeding Mercedes overturned. The holy man was more than just venerable, he was invulnerable too.

---

[1]   Some three million US dollars.

Such incidents, whether cremations, visits by the king, politicians seeking blessings, or accidents, are eagerly expatiated on in the dailies, but also trigger off discussions about the desirability of such publicity. It seems that those who are against the open peddling in magic, protection and blessing, and the great sums of money involved – some call it Buddha business – are losing out to those with less lofty religious aspirations. The consecration of Buddha images, the production of amulets, and spectacular merit making seem to be on the increase, in stride with the economic modernization of the country. Specialized monthlies, some six of them, report about, and serve to newly establish, charismatic monks with their miraculous powers and talismans, at least, as long as they want to stay in business. Likewise, as observed in passing, *Kha:wsot* devotes a steady three pages a day to this subject.

Constitutions

Since 1932, and even earlier, constitutions have engendered considerable publicity. This long discussion concerning the basic law of the land may seem strange to those people who opine that fundamentals are fundamentals. In the setting of Thai government, this appears to be different: to have a constitution as the foundation of the edifice of state is an ideal worth striving for, but far from accomplished. Whereas some people firmly believe in the necessity of constitutionalism and legality – and even brought down the Tyrannical Trio in 1973 because of it – others are not so sure, and prefer to find their firm foundation in the Three Institutions, and the established centres of bureauratic, military, and economic power.

The constitution debated about during the research was the ugly mongrel bestowed by the National Peace-Keeping Council (NPKC) which tried to force a strong military influence on future governments. During the drafting stage in 1991 already, the text was highly controversial and vehemently attacked in the press. Yet, military contempt for civil society had its way, culminating in the legitimation of a superbly arrogant general, and later in the Black May events of 1992. In the aftermath, the Constitution was not torn up, and up to this day amendments are being discussed that touch on the influence of the military, and matters of basic democratization, that is, decentralization. It must regretfully be conceded that many former NPKC members still exercise considerable influence in politics, and that not every democratically elected general is a democrat at heart. Be this as it may, since the advent of the Chavalit Yongchaiyudh government it has been decided that the text of the sixteenth constitution should be submitted to Parliament in August 1997.

Playing politics

At the time of exploring the press, the general-turned-politician Chavalit Yongchaiyudh held the powerful post of Minister of the Interior. In the discussions about the Constitution and democratization, he firmly opposed decentralization and the direct election of local officials. He held many other strong opinions, and because of his habit to wear his heart upon his sleeve, his ambition to become the next prime minister was hardly concealed. In this way, every single day big-mouthed 'Big Ciw' ('Big Midget') – such as he is popularly known – featured prominently on the pages. Needless to say, his ambitions and self-glorification made him an unruly coalition partner in the last Chuan Leekpai cabinet; they also made him a ready bait for a ruse by the opposition.

The general-turned-tycoon, and former leader of the 'buffet' cabinet that preceded the constitution-writing junta, namely, Chatichai Choonhavan, was still in the political boondocks. As an important figure in the parliamentary opposition, he mobilized the latter by apparently uniting it in its disgust for the ruling coalition. In a widely publicized pact, the opposition parties concerned solemnly declared that they would, under no circumstance, join the coalition in power. 'Big Ciw' took the bait, and began to press his ambitions more openly still by withdrawing his party from the government. This resulted in a rapid break of political seasons: General Chavalit found himself in the cold; Chatichai and his boys suddenly basked in the radiance of rulership.

The aftermath of this mini putsch was delightful. First of all, it moved the pens of many academic columnists who openly deplored the absence of integrity in politicians, and the opportunism tainting the political game. The important thing seemed to be holding power, and using it for the own benefit, forgetting about promises and the public interest. While there is nothing strange about these observations, I was amused, not so much by the lamentations, as by the moralistic remedies and the appeals to conscience suggested. Reminiscent of the schoolbooks, democratic ideals were contrasted with money-hungry politicians who should have been held in check by their sense of ethics and devotion to common welfare.

> Ethics and social responsibility must be taken into account if we are going to attain a truly durable change. Lasting prosperity cannot be gained if people are influenced by immoralities (*SP* 8.1.95).

> Some monks are indecent, making it all the more difficult to teach others to be proper. Similarly, the highly-honoured job of teaching turns more and more commercial ... Some teachers even ask for remuneration from their students in exchange for high or pass grades ... Today we usually hear people are getting worse. They shamelessly do what was unthinkable in the past. They no longer hold faith in heaven and hell. Such a change stems from the natural development of societies with increasing numbers but weak rules ... Men have to respect the norms of their societies. Those who violate them are taking advantage of others ... Similarly, in terms of politics, people should try to push the good to rule the bad. We have to elect the good who keep ethics and morality close to their hearts to be our representatives (*SP* 25.12.94).

The change in government also occasioned the uneasy union between Prime Minister Chuan Leekpai and Chat Pattana leader Chatichai. The wrangling within the cabinet even got worse concerning what would become the government's undoing: In Phuket rich people were given land destined for redistribution to landless farmers, and even the most fair-minded personalities seemed to be involved. The ensuing shouting matches foreshadowed a steadily more focused and investigative style of journalism, exposing virtually everyone in politics, so forcing 'traditional politicians' to dance to the beat of public accusations.

Gems

The Saudi gems were in the news too. This tragi-comedy, that even attracted the attention of the foreign media, has now lasted for several years. It is a fascinating story Agatha Christie might have relished writing, beginning with the theft of some ninety million dollars worth of jewelry from an Arabian princess. The Thai who had succeeded in taking this loot home was soon exposed, and high-ranking police talked him into surrendering his ill-gotten treasure – to them! Somehow, many in the top ranks of these 'protectors of the people' shared in the windfall and, rumour has it, duly identified themselves through the expensive ornaments their wives proudly displayed at public occasions. The society pages concerned did not fail to attract the attention of the Saudis who became especially piqued when part of the jewelry returned to them was identified as being clever fakes. To save the face of those who had been a bit sneaky, devious ways were devised to return the shiny stones anonymously. Predictably, many of the valuables disappeared again. The Saudis made it a political affair to the point of extraditing Thai labourers working there. With more and more people involved, some forging, others playing tricks, and a few knowing far too much, abductions and killings began to become part of the show, leading to the accusation, conviction, and even jailing of a police lieutenant-general.

Men in uniform

While the Saudi gems had not lost their news value yet, there was other, more short-lived news to amuse the public. What was an old locomotive, property of the State Railways of Thailand, doing on the extensive estate of a certain general and ex-NPKC strongman? Who had appropriated it, then given it away? And why? Such stories bring the arrogance of the influential to the public eye, and the top brass of army and police seem to be routinely involved in actions deemed criminal if perpetrated by others. The servants of the law appear to be well above it in spite of the oaths they swear.

Of late, the men in uniform have begun to draw a steady stream of negative publicity. Things everybody knew, or suspected all along, have now been exposed; names are mentioned; reasons given. The cans of worms that are opened are even worse than many readers ever dared think. For instance, the police robbing and killing illegal immigrants, complete with all the gory detail of how they disposed of the bodies. Or, a girl forced into prostitution seeking refuge at the station who did not survive the kind attention of her protectors; her body was unceremoniously dumped from a second story window of the precinct. Police personnel routinely prey on illegal labour, now estimated – and tolerated – at half a million. They are squeezed, and often robbed blind, all their hard work coming to nought when they are on their way back home. To counter this image problem, some initiatives are taken to create 'your friendly neighbourhood police officer', about which *The Sunday Post* observed:

> Residents there have difficulty imagining their arrogant police
> as polite and friendly people battling crime rather than serving
> vested interests – and working against the public (8.1.95).

The military does not enjoy a fine reputation either. There is a long history, of coups d'état and arrogance of power, to this. Naturally, when marshals and generals dominated, it was not that easy to voice criticism in the print media, while the army also controlled a large number of broadcasting stations – as it still does today. Yet, since the rise of business as the most influential force in politics, and after the excesses of Black May, the boys in green need to tread with more care, and that does not come easily to them.

Accustomed to being big-mouthed, many among the brass are possessed by the urge to voice their ill-considered opinions. If, for that purpose, they extend their careers into politics, they may acquire clownesque traits. Somehow they relish power and do not quite understand what democracy and civil liberties are all about. Often it seems that their minds still dwell in the cold war period, venting their suspicion of students, activists, NGOs, and the exploited and displaced farmers who bear the brunt of Bangkok-centred development programmes. When such people protest against dispossession, unfair compensation, eucalyptus plantations, dam-building, environmental destruction, military arrogance, police brutality, land reform benefiting the rich, low agrobusiness wages, unkept promises, et cetera, ranking officers are quick to reprimand them.

> Military leaders yesterday told Pa:k Mu:n protesters to settle their differences with the Government ... General Wimol Wongwanich said that in a democratic society one should know what is the proper exercise of rights and duties. What is right should take precedence over 'mob rule' where the country's laws are disregarded ... The army commander warned student activists to be more realistic in trying to achieve their purposes. He said they should not aim to create more confusion ... Gen Wimol said it was likely that the protest would end in the same violent way as the protests over the tantalum factory in Phuket some years ago, where demonstrators torched the facility. The issue will not be easy to resolve because 'there are still some who don't want the issue to be settled', he said (BP?).

Such reasoning is endemic, and not much different from the standard fare Indonesian officers regale their audiences with. Most often, the initiative is not with the government, but comes straight from the military gut, such as moving against the Hmong refugees at Wat Tham Krabok, the temple of abbot Chamroon, formerly a distinguished police officer who won the Magsaysay Award for his treatment of drug addicts. According to the same General Wimol, the monk should not put humanitarian work ahead of Thai-Laotian relations.

> I believe the monk will understand. All Thais – lay people or monks – owe their allegiance to the nation. Because without the nation even religions will not survive. *Phra* Chamroon should have cooperated (*TN* 2.11.93).

Yet,

> Saraburi provincial authorities, including the local police chief, have defended *phra* Chamroon against allegations that his temple has been used to launch operations against the Laotian government (*ibid.*).

Such as demonstrated by the last 'successful' putsch in 1991, the military still seems to operate in a mental vacuum, divorced from society, and implacably self-satisfied. Being their own measure, the high officers not only protect each other, but also grow fat on commissions and the use of their influence. Some become local godfathers who do not even need to pay for their private armies.

> Lt-Gen Prasarn is very influential in the province, and the Premier must have slept soundly at the farm, because over one hundred armed Border Patrol Police were posted there during his stay (*BP* 26.1.95).

That police and army personel run protection rackets on highly profitable illegal operations of all sorts, is common knowledge, even to the extent that it surfaces in the news as a matter of course.

> The reason (illegal) black-plate taxis cannot be eliminated is simple. 'It's because most of them are run by off-duty Air Force personnel or are relatives of Air Force or Police personnel. They have contacts at Don Muang which is run by the Air Force' ... The official requested anonymity ... 'Even police officers pretend not to see them. These drivers are protected by people in uniform and have arranged interests with local police' (*BP* 23.1.95).

Reputation

Yet, it remains military honour, and the righteous defence of it, that is part of the regular rhetoric. This honour takes precedence over the very existence of others, even if it results in a very dubious reputation regarding respect for human rights. Black May is remembered, also internationally. Yet, no military personnel, let alone those responsible, were ever challenged in court. To be in uniform is to be untouchable for the law, at least in most cases. In the same vein, villagers' rights may be trampled; the freedom of Burmese students and other refugees severely restricted; the absence of safety measures in factories, or the exploitation of (child) labour tolerated; the cosy relations of some commanders with the Khmer Rouge known; the involvement of Thai companies in the rape of nature in Laos and Burma accepted. Since such things are apparently ill-understood, the negative human rights image resulting from these practices neither seems to touch the military nor the national conscience. This is not so because people are indifferent about the country's reputation. They are worried indeed, but their 'face' itches because of other publicity. People are apprehensive of what foreigners may think of the Land of Smiles' fame for prostitution; HIV infection and AIDS; child labour; heroin smuggling and production; the murder of tourists; pedophily; and even of spectacular spirit cults.

Thailand's ongoing image war with the international media continues with the latest description of Bangkok as a flesh trade centre in the Microsoft CD Rom encyclopedia. This description has prompted another round of official protests aimed at saving Thailand's honour ... It can be said that the routine protests which are acted out with fervour by the Government are not really aimed at the foreign companies, but are intended more to pacify the voting public at home. By turning the issue of prostitution in Thailand into that of national honour and dignity, the authorities have cleverly used nationalistic sentiments to their own advantage ... How many more times will the Government have to issue protests to defend the country's honour? And for how long will the public tolerate the continued farce perpetrated by members of the Government in falling back on national dignity as a means of avoiding the real issue of the flesh trade? ...

Incidentally, the row over the Japanese sex tour guide book came at approximately the same time as the public uproar against the anti-AIDS handbook produced by the Prime Minister's Office ... Much has been said about the sexist values at home that tacitly endorse prostitution. But the vulgar messages in that handbook that treat women as mere sex objects and make light of sexual harassment – coming directly from the Prime Minister's Office – is probably most revealing in demonstrating just why the flesh trade remains such a thorny problem that refuses to go away ... Distribution of these offensive handbooks was finally halted, but without any apologies or seeming regret for the mistreatment of women implied by their production. The authorities still find the notion that sexism is socially damaging to be incomprehensible. They can only relate to the concepts of power and status. In the suspension announcement, the PM's Office apologised to the medical and teaching professions for portraying them in a disrespectful way, but not to women for portraying them as sex objects (*BP* 1.2.95).

The importance of image, and its manipulation, features regularly in the exchanges between readers by way of their letters to the editor. Occasionally, Thai citizens voice their irritation at what they feel to be outright or alleged criticism – and depending on their skill in presenting their points, they will draw flak or praise. *Khun* Suthep's letter 'Americans have a lot to learn' resulted in many reactions to the editor.

> It is good to know that my eyes are completely fooled by the Thai culture's complete acceptance of, and domination by a 'nouveau riche' culture developed worldwide by secondhand car salesmen. It is important for all of us to know that while the leaders of Thailand can subtly kill the innocent in front of the world, courtesy of CNN and the BBC, and not be prosecuted, this is a sophisticated and non-aggressive society.

> But a fundamental truth is underlined in their criticism, in that Thailand, unlike what so many Thais like to believe, is not perfect, just as any other country is not perfect. Interestingly enough, when various aspects of America were being described in his letter, I thought the writer was describing Thailand. For instance, the statement, 'Americans tend to be obsessed with money, salaries and important positions' (*BP* 22.12.94).

Of course, many opinionated and ignorant comments are made in newspapers anywhere, and especially if these come from foreigners, defences may be raised. Even so, the very exploration of the press over a short period of time raises images that are often far worse than what is observed in letters, and these are regularly commented on by the editors of both the vernacular and English-language media. Environmental degradation, the rightlessness of villagers, the loopholes built into the law, the arrogance of the privileged, the exploitation of labour – it is all there, and obviously related to rapid economic development. Commented upon in a factual manner, said things belong to social life as a matter of course, such as the Bangkok traffic gridlock also does. An occasional visionary publishes his criticisms, but the way he points to is normally one of wisdom and morality, unlikely things in any world. Even people who entered politics on a moralistic ticket, such as Brig-Gen Chamlong Srimuang, soon lose their credibility, and will eventually be exposed by their obstinacy and high-handedness. In the period under scrutiny, the issue was the way he got party member billionaire Thaksin Shinawatra into position as Minister of Foreign Affairs. And so, in stride with the police's contempt for the public, the army's disdain for human rights, politicians can negate legality, or even the prevailing opinion in their own parties. After all, having power, being a big shot, entitles one to such attitudes; they are expected and, ultimately, respected. They do not result in a negative image, such as the exposure of *Na:ng* Kae:w did.

Na:ng Kae:w is a powerful spirit residing in a big tree on the forest trail at the mountain border between Chiangmai and Chiangrai provinces. There, she has since long attracted the worship and vows of locals and travellers. As a female seat of power, she demands a replica of a penis in exchange for her favours, and these offerings may gather into remarkable piles at the shrines of such spirits. All this was exposed to the public when the new road between the provincial capitals concerned was inaugurated. In order to detract attention from this animistic place of worship, a chapel devoted to the Buddha was established a little higher up, at the very crest of the pass where it had to compete with the local guardian spirit. Anyway, this did not drive *Na:ng* Kae:w out of business, and the mandatory offerings in exchange for her benevolent attention kept accumulating. A local ceramics factory in Chiangmai even took up the production of a charming little replica for this very purpose, the traditional one being nothing more than a suggestive branch or a kitchen pestle with the top painted red.

The district officer of the area concerned was not amused. With the place now exposed to the full gaze of the many foreign tourists travelling that road, what were they going to think about Thai customs? The remedy he thought up was straightforward. He planted a sign with the admonition, 'Please offer flowers only'. The very message demonstrated that the D.O. was modern, that is, out of touch with popular practice, and nobody was going to be so stupid as to offer unwanted things that might even evoke the wrath of the powerful *caw mae:*. And so the shrine remained an irritant to local officials and modern minded Buddhists bent on taming that spirit. Finally they seem to have succeeded by incorporating her into official religion. The place of worship has since been converted into a 'Dhamma garden', with a forest monk in full residence. More than that, amulets are now made in honour of *Na:ng* Kae:w that are consecrated, that is, filled with protective potency, through Buddhist ritual. The monk sells – sorry, lets – them at 199 baht.

Presentation, appearance, reputation, or 'face' are all very important and worth investing in. This corresponds with a heightened sensitivity to insult and criticism of things held dear, such as the own person, one's family, ancestors, and founding fathers. It was, therefore, no laughing matter when the *Manager Weekly* denounced the extreme commercialization of the visual arts by publicizing the picture of the statue of the founder of Sinlapa-korn University, professor Silpa Bhirasri, with the streamer 'Sale – 50 per cent off'. It did not trigger the discussion the magazine had hoped for, and students and staff demanded the editor's 'blood'; at the very least, he should publicly retract his gaffe, and offer an apology at the statue of *acharya* Silpa on the campus of the university. Because he didn't, the incident remained in the papers for quite a while.

> Our beloved founder is being unfairly attacked. We have come together to fight against this wrong, and to regain prestige for

our University ... We feel a deep sense of sorrow for our society, especially for those who cannot resist the immorality and sensationalism of *Manager Weekly*. The writer tries to sell newpapers by defaming the image of a great man ... In the family, we must respect our parents. And in our society, the Royal family is revered above all else. So if the author cannot understand and appreciate the holiness of venerable persons, he should keep quiet instead of sharing his contemptful feelings (*BP* 25.1.95).

The image

Going back to the exploratory notes that are based on my review of the newspapers of 15 and 17 November, and 2 December 1994 – although sometimes illustrated here by imprecisely dated clippings – I then concluded that the presentation of the public world resulted in an image sketched along the following lines. According to the press, the public world is about power and politics where grandees are given to arrogance and double-dealing. These honourable ladies and gentlemen are in the habit of exposing themselves as being pigheaded, opinionated, greedy, self-serving and, sometimes, very gullible. They do not only seek the public blessing of reputed monks, but also predictions, auspicious dates, while many of them, and their spouses, are willing victims of charlatans, imposters, and genuine monks who promise them treasure. In the days concerned, the reporting was about some reputable people being hoodwinked into believing that the amulets they invested in would turn into gold.

The reporting about corruption is matter-of-fact: it is not scandalous, but fully within the range of expectations, and so are the quarrels among people charged with governing the land. Some are godfathers, others conspire with Cambodian interests; they try to amass land and plunder forests; criminals appear to have influence within the highest echelons of the military and police. In stark contrast to these privileged people stand the inhabitants of the countryside; the gap between them and the city appears to be wide; apparently the country is there to be exploited for the betterment of those in the metropolis. These things are regularly highlighted by the progressive protests of editorial columns, but apparently public opinion does not carry much weight.

Nobody really seems to worry about the way modern Thai society is portrayed to the Thai public. The ugly side of life seems to be accepted, people know about it, and probably think that it does not concern them: it is not their affair. As long as the king, national and religious ceremonies, and beautiful traditions keep existing, there is enough to identify with. Anxiety about the own image occurs when taboos are breached, when the own beautiful institutions are questioned, such as in the affair around the image of professor Silpa Bhirasri, or when certain Thai customs are exposed to the foreign gaze, such as in the case of *caw mae: Na:ng* Kae:w. Prostitution, or sexism, or the exploitation of women, and the like, do not matter, but the reputation of the country as a bachelors' and child molesters' paradise does. It is not the systematic human rights abuses perpetrated against villagers, refugees, and 'illegal' labour that are important, but Amnesty International's reporting about May 1992, the treatment of Burmese students, or the cosy relations with the Khmer Rouge. And sometimes image anxiety is merely motivated by the most practical of considerations: dirty beaches, or the occasional murder of a foreign national, keep the tourists away which is bad for the balance of payments.

People are still subjects, irrelevant nationals under the sway of personalities and parochial interests that either manipulate or simply ignore them. During election campaigns, promises are made, but the goods are rarely delivered, since the members of the ruling class have fairly precise ideas about their own interests, and only the foggiest ones about the common welfare. Authoritarianism comes naturally to them, while their sense of sympathy with the underdog approximates zero. Self-centredness is nothing new, and may even be traced to the moral particularism the school teaches.

There, individual behaviour and family membership are emphasized all the time, while no means are devised to get a mental grip on the public world in which society at large operates. This highly personalistic image of the wider social environment is clearly reflected by the representation of political affairs in the press. What is brought into focus are individual politicos and their actions – not their programmes, ideologies, and plans – at the same time that critical voices fail to articulate alternative scenarios. Thus, nobody feels puzzled by the political apathy of the general public, the popular rumour mill, the near-absence of active citizenship, and the contingencies of the rule of law.

A royal advice

Before moving on to an ordered presentation of newspaper clippings dating from a government and a year later, it is still appropriate to briefly draw attention to the king's speech on the occasion of his birthday in 1994.

> Once a year on December 4, His Majesty the King delivers a lengthy talk to his subjects on significant events which took place during the year in this country and abroad. The speech, which touches on a wide range of topics from the environment to technology, politics, social affairs and the traffic problem often contains, in a subtle and implicit manner, some thought-provoking or conscience-awakening message.
>
> His Majesty talked at length about Bangkok's problems and suggested how traffic congestion could be alleviated if travelling distances of private cars and trucks were shortened. He also offered advice on how degraded forests could be rehabilitated and restored naturally. The subject of unity was only mentioned in passing because His Majesty, in his own words, said he felt it was tiresome to talk about the subject ...

The topic of unity ... has been repeated year after year, but has failed to find receptive ears among our politicians ...

It is also open to question whether His Majesty's message on natural reforestation will find receptive ears among those business-oriented officials who appear to be obsessed with commercial reforestation and who truly believe that trees are only meant to be exploited for various industries and not for humankind as a whole. Millions of rai of degraded forests are to be designated for monoculture reforestation to provide raw materials for pulp and wood chip factories. In the opinion of our King, forests should serve the needs of humankind, and, at the same time, help preserve the ecological balance – a function that a commercial forest or eucalyptus farm cannot perform.

It is only once a year that our revered monarch has an opportunity to speak his mind out loud in the hope that conscience and wisdom can be restored in the minds of those who have the responsibility of guiding this country in the right direction, but whose vision might have become blurred or blinded by self-interest, greed, stubbornness or selfishness (*BP* 6.12.94).

Reading and clipping from 20 November 95 to 15 March 96

Politics

Nobody will need much time to conclude that the dominant reporting about the public world focuses on politics, and that politics somehow seems to equate with the actions of individual politicians. Together these make for spectacular cloak-and-dagger theatre, a wrestling match with no holds barred, while all seem to be possessed by the ambition to steal the show. The stage is set in the national capital where, since shortly, provincial politicians have entered the scene. The first to become prime minister is Suphanburi's godfather Banharn Silpa-archa. Half a year before replacing the Chuan Leekpai dispensation, he was interviewed by *The Nation's* Suthichai Yoon.

> 'I don't understand why some people still perceive me as being unclean – that I am a crook – that I am a walking ATM ready to pay money to buy everything I want ... What's wrong with me?' ... I (SY) told him: 'Some people even told me they will give up Thai citizenship if you become prime minister. They think you are capable of buying up everything you want to turn Thailand into another Suphanburi where you wield absolute power and where you can pursue whatever objectives you want despite national interest. Some people are just scared of you.'

> He nodded attentively – and seemed to take it all in his stride. Banharn is not, after all, a man haunted by self-pity. His self-confidence is matched by his unmistakable political ambition ... 'The fact that I have managed to escape the concerted efforts to end my political life must have something to do with my conviction that I have always done the right things. Don't you think Lord Buddha was on my side? ... Why is everybody after my blood?' ... Is Banharn getting himself ready to become the country's prime minister then? His answer: 'No. If I say I want to become prime minister, everybody else will make sure I am blocked.' ... What, then, stops him from becoming prime minister? 'My image', Banharn said – without a blink (January 95).

It was therefore to be expected that, when Banharn had risen to the highest elected post of the land, the public would be critical, were it only as a compensation for its powerlessness in the face of party machines, money politics, and dark influences. In *The Nation's* comment, 'Why Banharn 1 Deserves No Honeymoon', it is noted that:

Soon after the names of five key economic ministers were officially released, a consensus among commentators emerged confirming the weeks-long spectre of a potentially corrupt government, albeit one elected by the majority of Thais ... A widely respected critic was quick to warn the jubilant Banharn that more than half of his 49-member Cabinet had dubious backgrounds 'unacceptable' to the public ... Is a buffet-style Cabinet – similar to the Chatichai government which was toppled in 1991 by the military because of rampant corruption – again in the making? At the least, Banharn's Cabinet line-up has invited sceptics to be wary of the return of 'money politics', whose obvious form has been unfamiliar during the past two years and eight months of the Chuan administration (19.7.95).

After this a steady stream of criticism and disgruntlement in the media begins. As we shall see later, this irritates the political players concerned, so much so even, that they try to muzzle the hounds of the free press. The only one who consistently used their publicity to his own advantage was Deputy Prime Minister Thaksin Shinawatra, the new leader of the Phalang Dharma party. In *The Nation* of 22 July 95, he is pictured sitting in a helicopter to observe the traffic situation in Bangkok. Apparently his gimmick 'to solve the capital's traffic problem in six months' payed off immediately. The same issue also commented upon the superstitions of some of the cabinet members.

B. was scheduled to present policy guidelines to officials at the ministry about 10 AM, but according to his aide, the Chat Thai minister decided to stay home and cancelled another appointment because he believed yesterday was an unlucky day and he had to wait for a more auspicious time to go to his office ... At the Interior Ministry, meanwhile, officials were bewildered by the arrival of a Chinese astrologer ... The astrologer, a specialist in *feng shui*, the art of selecting good locations, approved the office. However, he said S. should not work alone in the room, and his aides working with him

205

should be 'fierce looking' because those with 'meek looks' would be subdued by the power of the shrine opposite the office ... Close aides of some ministers who had used the room in the past had had bad luck, it was said (*TN* 22.7.95).

When I started my systematic reading of the press, the Banharn cabinet had been in power for four months, and journalists had an abundant supply of saucy stories to relate in their columns. Outstanding were the fun about the alleged bribery attempt of a Swedish firm eager to sell two submarines; the controversy about the authenticity of the prime minister's Master's thesis; the accusations that a deputy finance minister had bought votes; the bailing out of rich people who speculated wrongly at the stock exchange, or who misinvested in certain road-building projects; and Thaksin's posing as the white knight fighting the slow-moving traffic tapeworm that saps Bangkok's vitality and quality of life. Less amusing was the inexorable stream of news about land-grabbing, log-poaching, title-deed manipulation, and other moves to cheat the country and ordinary villagers of their resources. Good fun, though, was the discussion of the price of a seat in the Senate. Would thirty million baht do?

A few of these occurrences will be referred to in the following. Yet, the ins and outs of politics are not really the most interesting things to look for in this analysis. Whereas it must be conceded that political news dominates the newspapers, we should also be attentive to the stirrings of civil society. Ideas are being circulated that seem to aim at reconstructing the public sphere of government and business, and making it a public world inhabited by mature citizens. In the following I, therefore, do not want to trace the devious paths most Thai politicians reportedly tread, but rather would stick with the acrimonious comment it draws. Important about this commentary is the remarkable increase in investigative journalism, especially about land problems, but also about the backgrounds of the scandals entangling many of the cabinet members. It is not only so that names are mentioned, but whole histories of intertwined economic interests, manipulations, collusions with the state and its instruments, sums of money involved, and so on, are exposed. At the same time, the jauntiness, conceit, and hypocrisy of the influentials involved are regularly the butt of ridicule. Altogether, the political show inspires little to take pride in.

> Corruption in public life has established itself so firmly that candidates of ill repute are winning office with the votes of the educated but disaffected. The perverse notion that the unusually wealthy – or should we say the successfully corrupt – are to be admired for their brazen greed has also begun to take root ... Time after time, the corrupt and the sometimes plain stupid are returned to Parliament with a private mandate to do exactly what they like for the maximum personal gain. It would not be difficult to compile a list of politicians who are simply not suitable; the corrupt, the criminal and a certain number with blood on their hands for their behaviour during dictatorships.

> Look beyond Parliament to the problems confronting this country: we hardly need reminding about AIDS, flooding, traffic, the stock market, inflation and the mess that we call our foreign relations with some of our neighbours. A picture that is not good is made bleaker when our gaze returns to Parliament in the search for honest people with the ability and dedication to pull us back from the brink ... So dirty has our system become that the honest leaders our country needs recoil at the prospect of standing in an election in which the disgraceful episodes of a Buri Ram nature (massive vote-buying) are considered normal (BP 5.12.95).

To consider this practice to be the norm was underscored when the deputy minister concerned observed, 'There are many vote-buying politicians elected in the last general election, but nobody has asked them to take responsibility for their actions' (TN 28.12.95). The man, however, protested his innocence in the affair that came to light when the police arrested two of his associates with the neat sum of 11.4 million baht in cash, bundled in portions of one hundred and twenty each, to which a voting instruction was attached.

Unless proven guilty, said politician must be deemed innocent. At the Ministry of Finance, he, and his immediate boss, known as Dr S., had their eyes set on certain manipulations – call it political interference in institutional affairs – that surfaced in the news a few days after the ministers took office. On 22 July 95, 'the secretary-general of the Securities and Exchange Commission tendered his resignation reportedly over concerns for the independence of the stock market watchdog ... The SEC chief's threat followed the unwelcome appointment of Dr S., which caused the Stock Exchange of Thailand (SET) to plunge 5.9 per cent ... The Finance Minister, realising his job is on the line, went all out to stop the secretary-general from resigning. The Premier's personal aide knew the departure of the SEC chief would not bode well for the volatile SET as well as the days-old Government, which has yet to declare its policy in Parliament' (BP 24.7.95).

So, on Monday 24 July, the new bosses at the Ministry of Finance 'affirmed their policy not to interfere with the stock market ... By law, the Finance Ministry has no authority to interfere with the SET's affairs', to which the deputy minister added:

> I assure you again in all sincerity, as I said before, that I have performed my duty as a representative to protect the interests of the majority. I will never interfere with the SET and I have never been involved, even once in my life, in trading on the stock market' (BP 24.7.95).

Whether the government's fantastic plan to shore up the stock market 'by deciding to have the Bank of Thailand make twenty to thirty billion baht available to pay the margin calls of investors' (BP 2.12.95) – the SET had shed one third of its value – has much to do with the sequel of the story, I do not know, but by the end of the year the chief of the SEC was forced to resign. He also lost the post of deputy governor of the Bank of Thailand. The charges against him were vague and possibly spurious. Obviously he was the victim of a fight among personalities. As a result, on 13 March 96 the *BP* could announce that the former deputy governor had filed a lawsuit against the Bank's governor and the director of the National Intelligence Agency for abuse of authority and defamation.

Apart from the politicization of the SEC, and even the Bank of Thailand, other institutions are apparently subverted by political interference too, and everything that has to do with the obvious, that is, money and resources, remains in the limelight. Consequently, Dr S. kept featuring in the news. Under the telling title 'Time for him to show his gratitude?', *TN*s editorial of 26.1.96 asked:

> Did S. abuse his power as Finance Minister? Was he pandering to the interests of senior politicians? Did he disregard the country's judicial process? ... One strong possibility could be that the finance minister is playing the game of political nepotism. S.'s appointment to the Cabinet is a case in point. He was made finance minister because of his close association with Prime Minister Banharn Silpa-archa, leader of the Chat Thai Party. So now, the time has come for the finance minister to show his gratitude to the Chat Thai Party. So what better way than Wednesday's announcement.

The announcement concerned was the order to revoke the cases to claim arrears taxes from a number of 'unusually rich' politicians, an interference clearly subverting the dedication and morale of the officials concerned.

> Revenue officials charged with the messy task of clawing taxes back from politicians dubbed 'unusually rich' feel they are in a no-win situation ... Revenue Department staff are frustrated that whatever actions they take in the back tax cases will be criticised by someone ... The Supreme Court later ordered the

return of their [the politicians'] assets, ruling the NPCK order to set up the Assets Examination Committee was unconstitutional. But the Revenue Department decided to claim back taxes from the ten politicians – pending payment of their back taxes their assets were withheld ... It was revoked on the grounds the assessment was carried out without the approval of the director-general of the Revenue Department (BP 27.1.96).

On the same day the paper bannered on its front page 'Thaksin says govt MPs have fingers in logging pie', which was followed by an extensive documentation of the allegation. But would anybody be surprised? All along the newspapers publish about politicization, abuse of privilege, land-grabbing, forest destruction, illegal logging and plantations, encroachment on this or that, the scramble for real estate in to-be-developed areas and the disregard for those ordinary people who happen to make their living there, stock-market manipulation, and the use of influence to secure bank loans to take over ailing companies. With all this in the open, a statement that 'the Banharn government appears to have no regard for proper ethical conduct' (TN 29.12.95) seems fair enough, but the people who keep criticizing it because of its absence of credibility and policy are in the wrong. What politicians and other influentials are up to is very clear, namely, to obtain a purchase on public resources.

In this quest, they are each others' temporary allies or foes, colluding with their competitors, or fighting them tooth and nail. There is nothing unpredictable about this; the only thing that changes is personalities, or patrons and their pecking order. As politicians, they are after privileges, monopolies, concessions, immunity from the law, legal loopholes, freedom from taxes, behest loans, and the like. Altogether such political behaviour may be called rent-seeking, or the conversion of public resources into private ones, and whether this is respectable behaviour or not, it makes vote-buying and other, patronage-related investments in position very credible, and the ensuing actions a predictable policy.

We could go on and on, but it is wiser to leave it at this: the image of politics is clear. Newspaper editors, columnists, academic luminaries, all of them dislike the spectacle, and propagate vague ideas of 'service to the country', 'citizen's responsibility', 'commitment to the common weal', 'legality', and such, but these appeals hold little weight among a nonchalant and self-interested public. That is the way it goes; everybody knows it; why bother?

Apparently some people, such as BP columnist Suvit Suvitsawasdi, do bother indeed. In his year-ender in the *Sunday Post* of 31.12.95, he recounts the moral consequences of Thai politics. Departing from the ploy of a rival politician playing the religion card against Phalang Dharma leader Thaksin, namely, accusing him that certain slogans used in the campaign to discipline behaviour on the road were 'a bad example to youngsters and could insult Buddhism and Islam' (BP 15.12.95), Suvit deplores the cynicism of this politically motivated move, and continues:

> This kind of mentality could affect young people who may find themselves lacking direction and be lost in a new social environment. They might turn away from their parents, teachers and religion and look instead to singers or movie stars as their heroes. Such circumstances reflect a lack of identity, ideology, spiritual guidance and fundamental beliefs ... Without those, our people would not believe sufficiently in their identity and the country might turn into a domain of singers, movie stars, nude models, prostitutes and amphetamine addicts. Society could turn to vice and people might become so used to it they feel no remorse or shame when criticised from abroad.

To many readers it may seem absurd to suppose that the example set by politicians will cause identity problems among the youth. At best, politics is an indication of the state of the public world, just as the high suicide rate is. On 22 February 96, the BP reported the suicide rate of 1994 to be 45/100.000, up sixty per cent from 1993.

However, suicide and the problems leading to severe mental stress are just indicators of a larger picture of social ills. Many promises have been made to improve the quality of schools, boost the efficiency of city officials and public health services, ease traffic congestion and stressful competition for places in universities. Pledges have also been made to tackle urban poverty, overcrowding and rural migration which are turning slum growth into a boom industry (*BP* 11.10.95).

While these problems persist, the social crisis the nation faces may also be argued in economy-oriented observations, such as during the Asia-Europe NGO Conference.

Economic growth has widened the income gap and led to a social crisis of unprecedented magnitude ... The country's top twenty per cent took most of the gains from the 'impressive progress' over the past twenty years. Their share of national wealth increased from 47 to 55 per cent while the share of the poorest twenty per cent dropped from 6.5 to 4 per cent ... Industrial workers, women and children, who work for low wages and in poor, dangerous and unhealthy conditions, had not benefited ... Now the number of working children was five million, half of them in the manufacturing, commercial and services sectors, including the entertainment and sex industries. Thirty years of growth had transformed Thai society from a 'quiet, peaceful and docile community' into one that was 'bustling, modern, industrialised and consumer-oriented' ... Through this process of change, Thailand had lost 'good traditions' and had sacrificed its heritage. Important social institutions, such as the family and religion, particularly the monkhood, had been weakened. 'The main goal today is to accumulate wealth. Money is the most important thing in life' ... Quoting the National Committee for the Promotion of Social Affairs, he said Thailand had half a million drug addicts, half a million HIV cases and two hundred thousand prostitutes. In addition, nine million people cannot help themselves.

A thesis

Sometimes the discussion of the dismal state of the public world reveals its lighter side. The then prime minister was not only a very successful tycoon, a provincial godfather, and a cunning politician with a reputation 'to get things done', he was also ambitious in demonstrating that he was on a par with the eggheads on the professional staff at the ministries. For this reason, he went back to school, and graduated in law. To commemorate this proud day, *The Sunday Post* published the main findings of Banharn Silpa-archa's thesis, *Thai political development: with emphasis on political parties' funding.*

> The Prime Minister notes that political parties in people's eyes are a tool of interest groups who provide financial support in return for favours, while politicians exploit parties as a key to social, economic and political privilege ... When in power, parties use their muscle to smooth the way for their allies' business. There are also those who contribute for future investment. Because the stakes are high, and it is hard to predict which parties are to be in power, business people usually invest in most parties. So contributions in this area are usually enormous ... In conclusion, the Prime Minister observed that political parties are formed to look after the interest of particular groups ... This makes politics immoral and creates inequality and unfairness in political contests. People lose confidence and trust ... After thorough investigation, the Premier said that under the current system, it is not yet appropriate to introduce change. Vote-buying is rampant to the point it has become part of Thai political culture (*SP* 14.1.96).

We can certainly not say that this thesis lacks transparency, and the authority of the conclusions is definitely enhanced by the fact that they derive from the highest elected politician. The press, though, did not follow up on these aspects of the thesis, probably because they merely confirm what everybody knows. In its stead, the vernacular newspapers raised another question: Has the author

> resorted to plagiarism in order to obtain his master's degree in law from Ramkhamhaeng University? ... *Siam Post* demanded a clear explanation over allegations that his thesis is similar to a research paper commissioned by the Interior Ministry ... Critics pounced on Banharn after it was revealed that the prime minister quoted a French book, *Le financement de la vie politique*, in his thesis for the master's degree ... This is a big surprise, because Banharn speaks only a little bit of English. Does Banharn have special interest in French? ... 'This matter has adversely affected the reputation of academics and Ramkhamhaeng University itself' ... But a Thammasat University professor told *Siam Post* that it's not uncommon for some top officials seeking higher university degrees to let their subordinates write a thesis for them. 'I know of one Army general who has copied the thesis of a postgraduate student', the professor reportedly said (*BP* 24.1.96).

All of this triggered off a good round of fun, with some people coming up with anecdotes about the poor foreign language skills of the prime minister. Others raised moralistic questions about the integrity of politicians, a subject that moves the pens of certain columnists *ad nauseam*. Ramkhamhaeng University students organized rallies and demonstrations to demand that the originality of the work be probed in order to clear the university's name. The rector of the institute, however, did not want to have anything investigated, and was non-committal, trying to cover up the affair with grandiloquence.

> I have to defend the university and it has nothing to do with Banharn, whether he runs the country or not. But if he is discredited over the thesis, then the university needs to be concerned because it provided him with his education ... It's not possible to make people believe in what we do. It does not

mean everyone has to believe what the critics say. But we have to stick with our principles and must not bend with society when it is consuming 'sick' information (*TN* 13.2.96).

An effective way to immunity from investigation was declaring the allegedly plagiarized research paper of the Interior Ministry a classified document that could, under no circumstance, be made available to compare it with the thesis. And, of course, the University Council concerned kept dragging its feet.

> The council ruled over two weeks ago that Banharn had not copied any of its research for his master's degree thesis, but had left one page, which should have been referenced, without a footnote. 'The council has already come to a conclusion; if we are going to reconsider it then we might be seen as indecisive' (*TN* 20.2.96)

Some prominent people tried to hush up the discussion, about which other people could in turn vent their disgust.

> He was saying, in effect, that the mass media's bloody-minded drive for the truth behind the PM's Master's Degree thesis was a disservice to the country and an embarrassment abroad. Not for a moment did he try to clarify the alleged plagiarism. He simply intended people to shut up about it because, after all, he reminded, the man is head of state, leader of the government (*BP* 2.2.96).

Students at Ramkhamhaeng grew tired of the matter too, and

> issued a statement defending the institution for accepting Prime Minister Banharn Silpa-archa's master's thesis, parts of which were allegedly plagiarized ... More than one hundred master's degree students from the Faculty of Law signed their names on the three-page statement, saying they had not covered up the truth concerning Banharn's thesis. 'We can confirm that

> Banharn, a student with whom we had a chance to mingle, studied diligently despite his seniority in politics and received his master's degree in law despite already having received an honorary law degree in 1987' ... The press should separate education from politics, the students said (*TN* 14.3.96).

If anything was uncovered by all this publicity, it was the thriving of a whole thesis-writing industry. Depending on the qualifications of the ghostwriter, the research to be invested, the number of pages to be written, original academic papers and theses can be commissioned for prices ranging from five thousand to eighty thousand baht (*BP* 7.3.96). In order to save effort and money, some students plagiarize generously, and over the years I have often had the pleasure of seeing myself extensively quoted though hardly ever referred to. Sometimes, however, those who commission a thesis that is subsequently approved of by the faculty concerned, still run into trouble during their examination when it appears that they have no inkling of what they have supposedly written. This expanded the industry: nowadays, a responsible ghostwriter also tutors his principal, saving both his sideline, and his client's face (*BP* 7.3.96).

Whatever the state of thesis writing, public emotions can easily be stirred when publicity touches on cherished beliefs. Thus, when an award-winning piece of historical research was published, it occurred that:

> About fifty thousand people yesterday rallied in front of the statue of Suranaree (Ya Mo) to protest against a Master's degree thesis which questions the existence of the heroine. The protesters submitted a nine-point letter to the governor of Nakhon Ratchasima province, in which they called for an investigation of the writer and publisher of the thesis to decide if they had been disrespectful to Ya Mo ... In the letter, the protesters demanded that the Fine Arts Department should disprove the argument to dismiss any doubts about Ya Mo's existence and called on Thammasat University to invalidate the

thesis. The protesters also asked the publisher to hand over all copies to the province so that they could be destroyed and urged people in the province to boycott all publications of the Matichon Publishing Group. They also called for a campaign against the author and branded her the province's most 'unwelcome' person. They also said a seminar should be held to counter 'ill-intentioned' people who want to destroy their beliefs. The crowd sang a song before dispersing at about 5.30 PM (*TN* 5.3.96).

Freedom of the press

From what we have discussed so far, it follows that not everybody is pleased with whatever is published, and certain people in power, emotional protesters, or bazooka-shell-firing supporters of a cashiered priest may try to dictate what is fit to print, and what not. Heavy-handed authoritarianism comes naturally to many *phu:yai*; certain subjects are beyond discussion by convention; there is a reluctance to say unpleasant things; face and reputation – which includes opinion – are untouchable; revenge is endemic. Together this makes that the value of an open press and freedom of expression are still ill-understood, and often thought to offend propriety and 'beautiful' Thai culture. There can be no doubt, therefore, that the press deserves an accolade for prising open Thai politics, a thing which was even reluctantly encouraged by previous governments. As a result, the axing of the challenging talk show Different Perspectives – dating, ironically enough, from the period of the NPKC junta – came like a bolt from the blue, or had arrogance and authoritarianism been in the offing longer?

Logically, the print media was up in arms, and rode the crest of enlightened public opinion. People cried out 'wrong decision', 'abuse of power', 'outdated action', 'undemocratic', 'let people judge', and deplored the loss of a good show (*BP* 21.2.96). In the same issue, 'progressive-minded doctors' in the Ministry of Health expressed their worries 'that the Government's action against Dr Chermsak's television and radio chat shows may lead to a political crisis similar to Black May in 1992'. According to the directly responsible Prime Minister's Office Minister, the talk show's host 'was "too arrogant" and his programme was "one-sided"'. Columnists, however, suggested the closure of Different Perspectives was 'a vendetta against Chermsak, who is seen by some government leaders as "unfriendly" towards the Goverment'. *BP*'s editorial of that day reacted bitterly:

> Is this self-professed democratic government likely to content itself with gagging the state-owned electronic media which has always been regarded as its domain and which it therefore feels should serve as its mouthpiece, despite the fact that all its radio and television stations were built with taxpayers money? Will the printed media become the next target to be muzzled? If deeds are considered an indication of intention, then the writing is already on the wall. This government is clearly not the champion of freedom of expression or a free Press as it led us to believe.

But why this muzzling or disciplining of the media? Some traced it back into the past. The TV host had pressed the wrong question shortly before the present government came to power, and now the *Post* asked 'Chermsak: A victim of Banharn's wrath?' (10.2.96). Perhaps, and the prime minister could certainly do with some positive publicity, especially in view of the forthcoming Asia-Europe Meeting where, as the host, he wanted to style himself as an important regional leader and statesman. Because of this:

> PM orders ministry to give him a high profile. 'He wants some sort of poster of himself used in the campaign; he wants his picture alongside those of the leaders of big European countries like Britain and France' (*BP* 21.2.96).

The Nation commented:

> The first coercive presentation on all TV channels focused on his visit to inspect southern seaboard projects. After the first successful force-feeding, he decided to go further. His second try was a curtain-raiser for the ASEM ... There remain so many stories which could have made the two part series fair and balanced, such as the gagging orders directed at a number of radio and TV programmes which have cast a negative light on an administration that has not gained the trust and confidence of the people (25.2.96).

It is understandable that a government leader wants to build up a positive image, certainly *vis-à-vis* foreign dignitaries. For this reason, half the town of Bangkok was closed for the duration of the Meeting, and draconian measures were taken to keep all sorts of disaffected poor people off the street, while

> Chart Pattana Party leader Gen Chatichai Choonhavan called on Democrat leader Chuan Leekpai not to censure, or bring up anything negative about the Government or its Cabinet before or during the March 1-2 Asia-Europe summit: 'Aren't you ashamed? Over one thousand important people from twenty-five countries will come here for the biggest meeting in Asia and they will see us fight and scold each other' (*Sunday Magazine* 25.2.96).

Still,

> Thai governments might be shaken by public opinion, but their longevity will always depend more on the support of their coalition partners. The Banharn Government is no exception ... Prime Minister Banharn Silpa-archa comes from the old school of politicking and personal contacts; he has never been the type of politician to pay much attention to public opinion or social pressure (*BP* 21.2.96).

Perhaps, after all, it was not the premier himself ordering the gagging of the media. He certainly tried to direct the publicity around the ASEM, but did he really care about being the permanent target of the press? Possibly other personalities were behind it, people who like to be important and to assert themselves. The Prime Minister's Office Minister Piyanat Watcharaporn could be such a man:

> Chermsak is arrogant because he thought I am too small to deal with Different Perspectives. But I am too big to become involved with such a small issue (*Sunday Magazine* 25.2.96).

This minister relishes power too, as apparent from his statement:

> Thailand is a 'patronage society'. The more connections you have, the more advantage you get. Not only politicians have escaped legal punishment, but also other influential people. This is why I want power – as interior minister maybe. It's ironically sad, though, that you need power to solve this problem (*TN* 8.2.96).

Others had been on the bandwagon since longer, such as the Defence Minister. Already on 24 November 95, the *BP* reported:

> Chavalit to ban anti-government radio programmes ... Military leaders were ordered yesterday to withdraw radio talkback programmes on stations under their control if they are used to denounce the Government.

Three months later, not only Different Perspectives had been axed, but also Chermsak's six radio programmes. On 3 March 96, the *SP* could banner 'Govt bans another TV programme: Piyanat stops contentious Vethi Chao Ban episode from airing'. No cause for wonder that the press began to try to limit the damage and perhaps to curtail its duty 'to make people in society think'. In a short time, the idea of media freedom was seriously affected.

> It's understandable the TV and radio operators are now in fear of government ban, even guest speakers invited to his Let Me Have a Say programme on Channel 9 seem to also have been intimidated not to voice their thoughts quite as directly as they used to do ... Mr Chermsak said his production team was also forced to leave its office at the Imperial Queens Park Hotel by the end of March. The owner of the hotel, according to Mr Chermsak, is also the owner of a giant distillery which depends very much on state concession ... Media Plus Co said it was told by some senior government people to terminate the programmes for fear of political repercussions (*BP* 26.2.96).

In the same issue, the editor asserted:

> By tolerating protests, we could take the opportunity to show to the world and some of our partners and aspiring members of the Association of Southeast Asian Nations in particular that we have an advanced society with respect for freedom of expression ... It might also be worth considering that foreign visitors might learn a thing or two from groups which feel their views are not to be represented in the formal talks. Bans, barricades and force of arms, as we know to our cost, cannot combat conviction.

Yet, clouds had gathered:

> The Rajabhat Suan Dusit Institute has suspended poll-taking on political issues, sparking an outcry from the opposition which said the respected pollsters might have come under political pressure to tone down their role ... The suspension came hot on the heels of the Chermsak clampdown. The institute had even conducted an opinion poll on the controversy, but the decision to suspend political polls made it likely that the results

THAI IMAGES: THE CULTURE OF THE PUBLIC WORLD

of the poll on Chermsak would not be made public. When
pressed about the issue of 'political interference', S. said, 'It's
not what you think. It's just that the current political
circumstances do not seem to be right.' He did not elaborate ...
'It seems we are entering an era of information clampdown.
This government is bringing our country into a dark age' (*TN*
21.2.96).

The press

According to a report in *The Nation* of 20.11.95, the dominant
national newspapers now claim a total circulation of almost three
million copies a day. Added to this, the business dailies claim print
runs totalling three hundred and fifty thousand, and the English-
language press a hundred and fifty thousand. This means that the
major towns and cities are well provided with newsprint. The
growth of the press has been rapid.

It cannot be denied: the press enjoys its increasing importance,
and seems to be doing well in relation to the fast expansion of the
electronic media. It is also in a self-congratulatory mood. Towards
the end of the year, *The Nation* wrote:

> The press needs more than ethics: quality is another important
> element that should be cultivated. In 1995 the press developed
> more quality news exposure, but what it really needs to do is
> internationalize itself by carrying more investigative stories ...
> 'The press is a mirror. The government must be bold enough to
> look into that mirror,' S. said ... Ch. felt this year has shown the
> press to be a leader in promoting democratic awareness. He
> said the press had created a more democratic atmosphere, and
> encouraged its audience to express their opinions and be
> aware of the society they live in. 'The press took the impressive
> role of leading society.'

The limits of the freedom of the press remain a point of contention, with the Prime Minister's Office Minister Piyanat Watcharaporn 'embodying the controversy'. According to him,

> Professional journalism in the electronic media, stalled by decades of strict state control, has begun to flourish. Investigative reports abound. Leading public figures are now asked pointed questions during interviews, regardless of how taboo these questions would have seemed just a few years ago. And anti-government critics are free to speak on TV and radio talk shows. However, media freedom is one thing and unreasonable aggressiveness is another (*TN* 21.12.95).

A few months later, when the relationship between the media and the government had cooled considerably, *The Nation* bannered 'While Banharn and Co were away, the press grew up', and opined that:

> Previously the press was seen by governments only as a public relations tool. A necessary evil that could be manipulated and put to great use by public personalities such as Chamlong Srimuang. The coverage of the bloody events of May 1992 and media openness of the Anand era gave the state media a new role, particularly as the voice of the emerging middle class. This role was passed on from the Anand to the Chuan government, which intially faced great difficulty in winning the public's confidence both in terms of credibility and expectations ... Unfortunately that relationship was not complemented by positive political developments. The July 2 general election witnessed more widespread vote buying to the frustration of the urban population and the media (?).

In March 96, the current prime minister's attempts at image building backfired. When all five government TV stations were mobilized to promote his role in the ASEM, most people found the thirty minute programme boring – and even worse, unavoidable.

'The angry calls were so frequent that the operators had to hang up the phones'; 'Abuse of power by forcing certain programmes on the viewers' (*TN* 8.3.96).

The self-image of the press does not fully agree with what its readership opines, which is apparent from a 'Letters from the People' project of the Reporters Association of Thailand. *The Nation* of 7.2.96 published the results. Many people think that:

> Thai-language newspapers are often guilty of breaching professional ethics, using improper language, conveying inappropriate messages, and having other problems in news gathering and presentation ... Many of the newspapers publish too many sexy pictures of famous models and actresses, and devote too much coverage to their sexual relationships and the backgrounds of those who have posed in the nude ... Many respondents said they could do without the extensive coverage given to gruesome tragedies, stories and pictures about crime, accidents and violence, pictures of people killed or maimed in accidents and pictures of rape victims.

> The letters accused some papers of damaging society by playing up negative stories at the expense of 'good people', and of violating people's privacy. Some of the letters also accused the print media of causing conflicts and confusion among the public, threatening the government's stability, mocking politicians and inciting them to quarrel with each other to the extent that they did not have time to perform their duties. By continuously reporting about misconduct and crimes committed by Buddhist monks, the newspapers had indirectly damaged Buddhism ... Ironically, while criticizing people for their blind faith in individual monks, the newspapers have been guilty of commercializing religion by advertising Buddha amulets.

> Some newspapers distort the news, make false accusations, lie, hide the truth, spread rumours, and make unfounded

speculations ... Some papers gang up against particular people. Worse still, some even act like the enemy of the news makers ... They ignore the plight of common people while representing influential groups, they present useless and inaccurate information, and they are concerned only about making a profit.

Public opinion

No doubt about it, public opinion is on the up, and is beginning to spread through the public world. It far from saturates it; it is still rather ephemeral, although in Bangkok, perhaps, it may grow to be as pervasive as the pollution that chokes the city. Social conscience has awakened, and labour issues, women's rights, pride in progress in public health, calls for religious reform, the hanky-panky with perks and positions on the boards of state-owned companies, the rapacity of the medical profession, the state of education and the school system, all such and many more themes regularly make it to the pages of the quality press where they are generally discussed in a socially progressive manner. Subjects that draw continual attention are those concerning the environment, and the arrogance of city-based interests versus the people of the countryside. Land-grabbing, logging, dam-building, vast infrastructure projects, and other such concessions derived from the state receive inordinate attention, not only because of the questions of social justice and the abuse of power involved, but especially because of the obvious political dimensions.

Social activism, consciousness-raising, and the role of NGOs in all this are spreading. Because of publicity, they are slowly increasing their weight. How important these factors really are, is hard to say, since much of the country outside the big cities is the sphere of influence of provincial godfathers and associated politicians who are well represented in the central halls of power. They hold that they can do as they please, at least in relation to the public, although such influentials often are the targets of each others' gangland-style killings.[2]

Sometimes planned dam projects are scrapped; sometimes the outcry against the prospect of having a garbage-and-lignite-burning power plant in the backyard is effective; sometimes organized protest against the commercial exploitation of a beautiful or precious environment succeeds; even city ordinances blocking developers may pass the relevant councils. But none of these progressive strides should be taken for granted; as soon as civil vigilance relaxes, the attacks are renewed, and more trees will be felled, more toxic waste dumped, more resorts and high-rise condominiums built. Besides, activism is dangerous, and an environmental spokesman mobilizing protest may be disposed of with the same ease as any militant labour or farmer leader. This point, and the authoritarian idea that might is right, are illustrated by the *BP* editorial of 23.1.96.

> The killing last week of TK, one of the leaders who played a pivotal role in the protest by Pluak Daeng district residents against a proposed toxic waste treatment plant in the district was a repeat of the kind of fateful destiny that all-too-often strikes that rare breed of individuals who fearlessly stand up against injustice or who dare to challenge influential and powerful figures ... Apparently, Industry Minister CS is determined to save the toxic waste treatment plant project and will press for the Cabinet's approval of the scheme. He may be overly optimistic in thinking that the murder case will not affect his decision about the project, especially the part about dumping the 'treated' toxic wastes in Pluak Daeng district.

---

2   In their chapter about 'Godfathers: Local Influence and Democracy' of *Corruption and Democracy in Thailand*, Pasuk Phongpaichit and Sungsidh Piriyarangsan detail the rise of provincial caciques, their gangland style of operation, and their achievement of second-generation respectability in the central halls of power (pp. 51-98). The book was originally published by The Political Economy Centre of the Faculty of Economics of Chulalongkorn University (1994). Chiang Mai: Silkworm Books, 1997.

The minister was quoted as saying that the General Environment Conservation Company, or Genco, which implements the project has the right to do whatever it wants on its own land in the district. It might have been just a slip of the tongue, but Mr CS's remark does raise questions. Of course, Genco has the legitimate right to make use of its land, but certainly not in a way that will infringe on the right of its neighbours or put them in any kind of jeopardy, as in the case of the Pluak Daeng district residents. Would the minister be happy with someone dumping a huge pile of garbage or 'treated' toxic waste on land next to his house simply because they have the right to do whatever they like on their land?

Civil society is fighting back, and gradually achieving an effective measure of organization. Its weakness is that it mobilizes around certain issues and causes, around symptoms of a structure of half-feudal, half-capitalist exploitation, rather than that it challenges the edifices of state and economy themselves. The democratic institutions of Thailand, dominated as they are by traditional bureaucrats, military, and business, do not offer much space for protest or even the advocacy of rights. As a result, it appears that only extraparliamentary opposition can lead to results. This situation is so obvious that the conclusion that the present political system is detrimental to the well-being of the majority springs to mind. This informs the new policy of the Thailand Development Research Institute (TDRI):

> Domestic politics was approaching an impasse where the public was blocked from having a say in the country's major problems ... The TDRI, apart from economic concerns, should devote itself to looking into political and social questions in order to reflect the public's need for political reform. As long as Thai politics remains unchanged, any effort to solve social, economic and environmental problems will all be in vain (*BP* 12.2.96).

227

Some people still propagate the moral solution to remedy the social condition, such as a lecturer at the Faculty of Economics at Chulalongkorn University who, in a letter to the editor, observes:

> Contemporary economics as taught in the universities seems to be destructive to the environment, leading us nowhere. This is evident as the quality of life is clearly deteriorating. We are faced with environmental problems of all sorts, both in the cities and in rural areas. The market system is exploited daily to serve the ends of greedy businessmen. These have amassed huge sums of money and are now able to even buy ministerial posts in the government
>
> ... Greed seems to have overwhelmed our economies in recent decades. Our materialistic society offers the poor little choice but to struggle for their survival. If we need to be in harmony with this contemporary economic system, economics cannot be isolated from spiritual values any more. Now is the time for all universities to teach ethical economics. But before that happens, teachers with a strong sense of ethics must be sought first. After that, everything will fall in place (*TN* 13.1.96).

It is true, many people – in line with school indoctrination – sincerely see society as a moral construct, and thus believe in ethical solutions to structural ills. If people are good, so will society be: 'everything will fall in place'. Others, representing modern civil society, set on legality and respect for human rights as the foundations of a desirable social order. It is not the individual as the dutiful subject of the state that matters, but the protection – against the state – of the person as a human being. It is the recognition of the unassailability of the person, formulated as intrinsic rights. So, while it is true that the practice of respecting human rights, together with the practice of democracy, leaves much to be desired, the dawning consciousness of the meaning and importance of human rights may be a discerning indicator of the maturation of the ideal of the self-responsible citizen and the gradual emancipation of civil society from the state. The development of such a civil society denotes the arising of the modern public world. Because of these considerations, it is warranted to select the human rights debate in the newspapers as the last subject to be presented here. Indirectly, it also touches upon topical issues that receive more frequent attention, such as environment, ecology, and other problems caused by the predacity of the state and the rapacity of business.

Human rights

In November 1991, the occupation forces in East Timor had a turkey-shoot on unarmed civilians at a cemetery. This Dili massacre highlighted the Indonesian government's contempt for human rights so much that it became a topic of debate in the civilized world to which also students and intellectuals in Bangkok counted themselves. They remonstrated that the Thai government should, for once, not kowtow to the big brother in the south, but protest – in the name of civilization – against its blatant abuse of power. At the time, this struck me as an interesting indication of the state of development of civil discourse. Few could then foresee that such barbarism would enjoy another field day in half a year's time, in the very streets of the capital. In November, the activists were confident enough to think that such things did not happen in Thailand any longer.

The day after Loy Krathong a year later, I found the front page of *The Nation* important enough to keep. Its centre piece figures a scene from the city: a man high on amphetamines holding an anguished hostage at knifepoint. Such unpleasant things may happen anywhere, as illustrated by the announcement 'Dutch police said on Sunday that they had broken up an international prostitution ring involving Thai women, many of them held against their will'. Three other items, though, inspired me to scornfully scribble 'Thai human rights' on that page.

The Constitutional Tribunal yesterday upheld a general amnesty granted to all those involved in the bloody May 17-21 political turmoil, ruling that Parliament's rejection of the executive decree in September will have no retroactive effects ... Military and police involved in the crackdown also could not be tried ... The Student Federation of Thailand (SFT) immediately condemned both the tribunal and the government. 'From now on, there will be no guarantee that people will not be shot dead in the streets again.'

The Interior Ministry will go ahead with a plan to resettle exiled Burmese students in a dedicated 'safe area' in Ratchaburi province ... P. warned that those who failed to report to enter the camp face being charged as illegal immigrants ... Burmese students have generally rejected the 'safe area' programme, expressing distrust in the government, which many fear will try to repatriate them to Burma.

Hun Sen said Phnom Penh is poised to counter-attack the Khmer Rouge. He also accused the KR of conducting a military build-up over the past few months to prepare for a major offensive ... He stopped short of saying he would directly ask the Thai government to stop Thai businessmen from trading with the Khmer Rouge. 'I think the Thai government is considering a curb on border trade with the KR' ... Sealing off the Thai-Cambodian border was not practicable and would seriously affect Thailand, Gen CK, secretary general of the National Security Council, warned yesterday ... 'Thailand has been suffering ever since the UN peacekeepers launched their operation in the war-torn country ... The disarmament process in Cambodia has already caused an influx of weapons from Cambodia to Thailand. An AK-47 assault rifle could be bought at the border for Bt 200-300.'

The first of these three issues is the most stirring, and on page two we read that the 'Pro-democracy front vows to fight ruling ...

The chairman of the Relatives of the May Democratic Heroes Committee was clearly disappointed ... "Oh no! Everything is finished. What kind of government is this?"' Other tidbits from the same page inform us that 'His coalition government would not endorse a bill allowing the election of provincial governors nationwide'; 'Government and a parliamentary committee are studying ways to reform the judiciary, which has been divided by a power struggle during the past two years'; and finally:

> Hundreds of bikers roamed major Bangkok streets after staging a noisy demonstration outside Parliament last Thursday to demand the scrapping of a law requiring motorcyclists and passengers to wear crash helmets in Bangkok from Dec 15 (*TN* 10.11.92).

There seems to be something fishy about the law and legal process. There also appears to be expediency in the relations with neighbours. Protesting Burmese students may mar the cosy colloquy with the dictatorship in Rangoon, while trade with the Khmer Rouge is simply too profitable to ignore.

The correct interpretation of all this may be that the development of the state, alongside the mentality driving business, is out of step with the evolution of civil society. Whereas the state recognizes the law, legality, and human rights – such as confirmed by our analysis of the schoolbooks – its practical performance in these fields is poor. One sometimes wonders whether those in power understand what it all is about. This could be glimpsed from the school texts too. There, all the time, rights have been coupled with the duties which are spelled out in the Constitution as well, and the authorities do not appear to be aware of the sophistry involved. Rights, and certainly human rights, are vested in the person. If they give rise to anything, it is responsibility, that is, the active participation of the morally autonomous citizen in the affairs affecting the rights of others and the public interest. Rights do not pair with duties as a matter of course.

The shallow official understanding of rights and what they entail is also demonstrated by the apparent vagueness of the common weal. In the view of the power-holders, they have the right to decide what is good for others, and they tend to be myopically guided by 'pragmatism' and 'expediency'. They seem incapable of a wider, let alone a democratic view. This, of course, inverts the schoolbook logic that a democratic mentality is related to the quantity of education the population enjoys. After all, most of the influentials cannot complain about their, and their advisors', qualifications, and while some of them may even grasp the gist of democracy and human rights, they are just not pleased by the prospect of their implementation. This would put the question to their authority, power, and interests. Laws, constitutions, official job descriptions, committees – and there are plenty of all of them – serve as ornaments, as emblems of civilization. Meanwhile, officials, politicians, and businesspeople do very much as they please.

> It came as little surprise when the Police Department was voted the most corrupt government agency in a recent opinion poll conducted by Chulalongkorn University's Faculty of Economics. The survey shows that most of the 2,300 respondents believe that politicians and bureaucrats, especially in the Land Department, Defence Ministry, Interior Ministry, Industry Ministry, Finance Ministry, Land, Customs and Land Transport departments, among others, are only marginally less corrupt ... A realistic approach would give the Commission to Counter Corruption enough 'teeth' to turn it into a real tiger. But without public support and a collective conviction to deal with the problem in earnest, the CCC will still be fighting a losing battle. And rampant corruption will still remain a fact of life (*BP* 7.3.96).

> Top official silences man accusing top aide (*BP* 10.1.96).

> Ex-MP Klaew pays the price for honesty (*BP* 12.3.96).

The life of OM illustrates how a hard-working doctor can be persecuted by the state for doing her duty in protecting the public's health. For many industrial workers, Dr O is a heroine. But for some factory owners and a number of her colleagues, she must be made to look insane ... Dr O has appeared before the Labour Court to defend her decisions on the cause of illness of hundreds of factory workers. The cases have lasted years. In one case, the lawyer representing the business operators tried to prove to the court she was insane ... Her senior supervisory doctor told her to change the report 'for the sake of the investment atmosphere', and then began putting pressure on her to resign when she refused (*BP* 12.3.96).

It is easy to find such clippings almost every day. The laws do not apply to those who draft them, but are a means for them to assert themselves *vis-à-vis* others who stand in their way. Those low in the pecking order bear the brunt and are virtually without defence against those who run the state. Yet, things are changing: 'Six victims of the March 1991 chemical fire at the Bangkok Port are being aided by the Law Council of Thailand in suing the Port Authority of Thailand for millions of baht ... It is the first time in Thailand that a state agency has been sued for compensation. The Port Authority has declined to comment on the case' (*DPF Newsletter*, February 96). Whether the victims' action will have any positive result, remains to be seen, but civil society is developing instruments, such as the Law Society of Thailand; human rights lawyer Thongbai Thongpao; the House Justice Committee; the Students Federation of Thailand; and the Committee on Human Rights and Justice, that are able to fight back. Interestingly, appeal is not just to Thai law, but to a basic sense of justice, and universal human rights. Recent happenings in Suphanburi, the very province represented by the former prime minister, illustrates this. This province – often dubbed Banharnburi – is renowned for the grandiose projects of its godfather, and a new government centre should add to its lustre. To the authorities concerned, the fact that land is needed to build it on seemed a matter of minor importance.

Poor villagers are being forcibly evicted amid threats of violence to make way for a new government centre in their province ... On January 10, 1994, they were notified by Suphanburi Governor AY that 384 rai of land (62 hectares) they occupied was public land, and it would accommodate the new centre ... According to documents shown to the committee, the villagers are legal occupants as they possessed *Sor Khor 1* and *Nor Sor 3 Kor* land papers. And they had also paid local land development tax since 1954 (*BP* 26.1.96).

Suphanburi authorities violated the rights of villagers evicted to make way for an administrative centre ... P. quoted the provincial police chief as saying: 'It's the premier who wanted the land. Who can do anything?' (*BP* 9.2.96).

The Government yesterday came under fierce criticism as students and a House committee demanded it stop using violence against people and stop violating their human rights and freedoms ... He said letters would also be sent to Amnesty International, the United Nations' human rights organisations and the ASEM to pressure the Government to stop violating human rights (*BP* 24.2.96).

Officials' use of coercion to induce villagers to allow them to grade their land in exchange for compensation was considered to be depriving other people of their freedom. Furthermore, no compensation was ever paid, which is a breach of contract. Moreover, seeing that villagers' property was being destroyed, responsible officers failed to arrest offenders although damaged parties had pointed them out. When damaged parties reported incidents to the police, they failed to accept the reports or accepted them but failed to proceed in due course. Failure of government officers to perform their duty is a criminal offence ... The House Justice and Human Rights Committee decided the authorities must stop any act in violation of the law, comply with the law immediately, and stop harassing people (*BP* 25.2.96).

The government, though, is not impressed, and feels uneasy about the principles of democracy, human rights, and open society. Authorities still use the Anti-Communism Act to intimidate people and to force their will and projects on others, while business considerations and political expediency – call it pragmatism – tend to carry the day.

Trying to appease Indonesia in the name of 'ASEAN solidarity' has now become the main preoccupation of Thailand. What's disturbing is that the Thai government, when in the company of authoritarian regimes, seems to be almost apologetic that it is a democracy ... But the leaders of ASEAN have uttered virtually no protest and instead have turned their backs on East Timor and its people. ASEAN's total silence on a crime against humanity has posed a disturbing query concerning the regional grouping's conscience, moral justification and collective attitude towards aggression committed by one big country against a small and defenceless neighbouring nation (*TN* 25.1.96).

A big setback for Burma's pro-democracy movement. Burma's military leaders, considered pariahs throughout most of the world, have however found themselves as welcome guests at this year's meeting of ASEAN foreign ministers in late July ... For ASEAN, rather disgustingly, nothing matters more than profits ... In this region, however, nightmares become realities when there's money to be made – regardless of whether despots respect their own people (*TN* 10.3.96).

International human rights group Amnesty International said yesterday Thailand tried to block it from releasing a blistering attack on 'appalling' rights abuses and repression in China ... Later, between 70 and 80 riot and regular police prevented Amnesty representatives from approaching the Chinese embassy with orders to bar their entrance and stop them from depositing the report in the mailbox (*TN* 14.3.96).

From these observations and remonstrations in the press, it is abundantly clear that certain positions taken by governments do not necessarily reflect the views and opinions of the more enlightened citizens. These want to be emancipated from the authoritarian impositions of the state, and their appeal is to the rule of law and respect for human rights. Yet, the past weighs heavily on the so-called democratic dispensations in Southeast Asia, and public opinion is still weak enough to be ignored. The point here is not to grumble about actual practice – no state anywhere has a clean human rights record – but to rejoice at the fact that Thailand recognizes the rights and freedoms of the citizen, and that an emerging civil society begins to assert itself in order to demand what it is entitled to. The opinion of this public is sharpened by the perceptive reflections of human rights lawyer Thongbai Thongpao in the *Bangkok Post*, and by professor Vitit Muntarbhorn in *The Nation*. According to the *acharya*, respect for human rights in Thailand is hampered by:

> First, the vestiges of paternalism, especially the cultural discrepancies enjoyed by the elite over the less-well-to-do and by the bureaucracy over the people at large ... Second, the hallmarks of authoritarianism, witnessed by the twenty-two coups and failed coups experienced by Thailand since 1932 ... Third, the manifestation of excessive nationalism, used and abused by various authorities to create a certain nationalistic State entity ... It has also resulted in many national security-related laws, such as the Anti-Communist legislation and revolutionary decrees, which confer an inordinate amount of power to State authorities ... These remnants of the past are compounded by the modern trend of globalization which is not always positive. For example, the cross-frontier sale and trafficking of humans ... and transnational operations which seek to exploit and channel those resources to global markets

and international consumerism without adequately protecting the interests of the locality (*TN* 10.12.94).

The long list of obstacles and remedies the author suggests in the second part of his column makes it clear that much remains to be desired, and that Thailand will not be a paradise of legality anytime soon. But hopefully it is on its way, and all sorts of thinking people mobilize to press for less arbitrariness and more decency in the practice of social life. Concerning the parallel NGOs' meeting in advance of the ASEM, we could read:

'The situation could certainly backfire and will not be good for the country's international image if the NGO meeting is banned. We sent a report to the Government urging a reconsideration of the order' ... The liberal-minded security officer said it was a pity to learn some senior government officials were so narrow-minded that they viewed NGO meetings as a threat instead of a constructive way of helping promote democracy (*BP* 29.2.96).

'Some cabinet members have dictatorial minds. The prime minister himself should take charge', Democrat secretary general Maj-Gen SK said. 'Demonstrations are normal in a democracy and people have the right to demonstrate peacefully as long as they do not interfere with the ongoing Asia-Europe summit' ... Arresting the demonstrators was a violation of the criminal code as well as the constitution as it pertains to human rights ... The police action has also damaged the country's image. 'This country might be seen as a brutal state which disregards the basic human rights of its citizens' (*BP* 2.3.96).

Human rights issues should be discussed in the ASEM ... According to *Siam Post*, 'Although the meeting will emphasize economic cooperation and various aspects of development for the sake of world peace, we must not forget that such development cannot be attained without serious efforts to tackle child labour, child prostitution and other human rights problems' (*BP* 29.2.96).

Overall, asserting a well-thought out Thai position would be the most effective way of demonstrating Thai leadership. Instead, Thailand's position has tended to follow the Asian herd. And, in fact, the Government is less liberal in its view of freedoms than the Thai public. Worse, in the way that it has treated visiting NGOs, the Thai government has shown itself not to be such a good host after all (*BP* 1.3.96).

Unfair treatment under Anti-Communism Act ... Provincial Governor YV stated that 'I therefore make void the letter calling to reprimand all teachers and would like to inform all government school teachers that their initiative to give advice and help to villagers in trouble is a praiseworthy one and should be strongly supported' (*BP* 21.1.96).

The political and bureaucratic elite – in contrast to the business elite – are very backward. They have a very limited vision and their lives are confined to their constituents and departments respectively. When combined, they act as a substitute to what we used to know as the power of the absolute monarchy (*TN* December 95).

It is good to hear that voices of generals, security officials, police officers, provincial governors, political leaders, and so on, can be heard in the chorus of civil society. It is not just students or NGO activists who are vocal. What all these people insist on is human rights, the original ones, and in the Thai discourse there is no sympathy for the Asian values variant propagated by China and the neighbours in the south. Professor Vitit formulates it very clearly:

The list of so-called Asian values – such as 'strong government and political stability', 'respect for authority', 'economic development rather than political participation' and 'economic rights rather than political rights' – suffers from a variety of essential weaknesses which give rise to a misconception about Asia ... It is not so much the puzzle concerning 'what are Asian values' but 'who is making the argument' which is really the key to our understanding of the subject. A number of governments (you-know-who) have, for their own political ends, capitalized upon the Asian values argument to legitimize their action against the population and as a testament to opportunism ... The Asian values argument is very much a state instrument which some less-than-democratic governments use to gloss over their excesses and lend credibility to themselves, while dampening popular participation and democratic aspirations (*TN* 8.2.96).

Thus, when Dr Mahathir shows up to deliver his diatribes against a decadent West, he draws a chuckle and a sneer when he asserts his vision: 'Mahathir rides again to defend his values',

In his opening remarks to a conference of business people in Bangkok, Dr Mahathir leapt upon his trusty hobby horse and went off at a gallop: Some Asians still feel colonised by the West, he said, some of us in Asia are still overawed by the West. The West this, the West that. Somehow it all seems very familiar. But it is an odd sort of roar to hear from the leader of a country that appears happy to belong to a group of economic tigers and aspires to the pinnacle of development by the visionary year of 2020 (*BP* 6.3.96).

The above editorial then comments on the thought control going on in Malaysia where the government is apparently afraid of a free press; the eminently Burmese (Asian?) Path to Socialism; the East-Timor and Cambodian tragedies. Such comments make it to the opinion pages every time an intergovernmental meeting is held. In the period running up to such occasions, academics and NGO activists demand that their voices also be heard. They take the

Singaporean notions of 'order, stability, consensus, discipline, the family, education, and deference to authority' to task. Do such ideas really contrast with alleged western individualism, anarchy and decadence? Or is it the state, asserting itself against its subjects under the cover of an ideology that equates the state with family, under the further pretext that individual family members need not be protected from its violence? As a result, 'Asian academics have questioned the debate on Asian values and debunked the western analysis that East Asia's economic success stems from them' (*SP* 21.1.96). This criticism was voiced at the Europe-Asia Forum where members of the Malaysian Strategic Research Centre and the Institute of Policy Study in Singapore clearly demonstrated that the opinions of heads of state are not necessarily representative of public opinion. Besides, such subaltern voices are eagerly published, because, if Asians are to be proud that their vast continent is the cradle of virtually all civilization, then they had better realize themselves that its great traditions are essentially humane. Hence the opinion of Malaysian Deputy Prime Minister Anwar Ibrahim:

It is indeed sad to note that some Asians, wearied by aggressive pontification on human rights by Westerners, and disgusted by the glaring contradictions between their sermons and their practices, sometimes overreact by denouncing the very idea of human rights as if that notion is totally alien from their own tradition. Nothing can be further from the truth. It is certainly a betrayal to ideals of Asian freedom fighters such as Rizal ... In the last Sermon the Prophet declared that the life of a man and his property is inviolable and sacred till the end of the world. Life and property are the foundations of liberty ... Thus, let us be reminded that in our xenophobic obsession to denounce alien ideas, we may end up by denouncing the fundamental values and ideals of our own traditions. Those ideas and humanitarian ideals are universal, they belong to all, and are a monopoly of no one ... In fact, the pursuit of economic prosperity cannot be separated from the quest for democracy and civil society. Only a vibrant and functioning civil society can minimise, if not totally eliminate, excesses – be they related to power or wealth – and provide the framework for a continuous battle against abuse of power, corruption and moral decay (*BP* December 95).

The idea of the primacy of 'Asia' as the fountainhead of enlightened humane thinking was also brought to the fore in the written speech – the Thai government blocked his entry – by East-Timorese activist Jose Ramos-Horta:

> Governments in the region cannot continue to pretend that there is not an Asian public opinion demanding that human rights and the environment be placed high on the agenda at every political and trade meeting ... After all the people of Asia, not the Europeans, are the victims of human rights abuses and are seeing their cities, villages and forests destroyed by a collusion of multinationals with local elites ... Human rights are not a western invention. For thousands of years, while Europeans were still living in caves, concepts of human rights and justice were already articulated in the teachings of the major Eastern philosophies and religions. That Asian elites should reject the universality of human rights, democracy and the rule of law and pretend that these are European impositions is really to give too much credit to the Europeans and, in a perverse way, to betray the rich Asian catalogue of values that have been deeply enshrined in the teachings of Islam, Buddhism, Hinduism and Confucius (*TN* 27.2.96).

Chapter 6

SOCIETY IN FICTION

This chapter is about the images Thai society reflects through contemporary fiction. We shall be concerned with the presentation of relationships, institutions, and change, more so than with the stories themselves. The books were selected because their authors deliberately want to evoke critical pictures. In order to accomplish this, they tell stories, and they do that well; their narratives read easily and are accessible to the public in search of entertainment and recognizable confrontations with life as it is thought to be lived.

The quest for images is not guided by the desire to review the books in any way. Although it will be necessary to say something about characters, settings, and plot, we shall mainly be concerned with the messages the authors want to convey. Often they are rather offhand in getting these across, and the reader is repeatedly confronted with all sorts of improbabilities: at the singular occasion that the police wants to raid the house, the habitual drunkard is as sober as a judge; the mother who was said to be illiterate, does the family firm's bookkeeping a hundred pages further on; et cetera. Another peculiarity that never fails to amaze the western reader is the absence of psychologically convincing characterization. Of course, emotions do play a prominent part, yet persons are cast more in terms of role than of motivation, 'Botan's notable, 'modern' efforts at psychologizing notwithstanding.

Her two novels presented here were recommended by herself for their social-critical content. The first, *Stunted* (*Maidat*, literally *Dwarfed Trees*) is a critique of the common educational practice that deforms and disfigures to the extent that it constricts people instead of opening them out. *Victims* (*Yüa*) is about working parents, neglected children, and the consequences of the vicious temptations to which the young are exposed. The first book must be immediately recognizable to most readers who went through Thai schools, with their emphasis on discipline in the lower grades, and cramming from kindergarten up to university. The second will be less experience-near for most, but seems to confirm the alienation between generations; youth culture and its wild escapism; and other social problems the newspaper reader is familiar with.

'Botan', Stunted *(Maidat)*.
Chomromdek Publishing House, 1990.

The book begins with a short explanation of its title, *Dwarfed Trees*. Grandfather explains his lifework, and hobby, of cultivating Thai-style bonsai trees that can be potted as plants and are made to grow the way the cultivator wants. Chom listens politely, as becomes a child *vis-à-vis* an adult, his fantasy taking him along independently. He is bored of the old man's self-contented relating about his life in the service of a prince, which made him a servant of the crown rather than an ordinary gardener.

The importance of serving government or crown, of titles and rank are immediately clear, but the hope that his son – a headmaster – would be granted a title, such as *khun*, or *phraya:*, belongs to a previous era. Instead, the father of the narrator is proud to be a civil servant and a teacher, and wants to be addressed as such, rejecting the current inflation of the sobriquet *acharya* ('professor'): 'I neither predict the lottery, nor do I teach tailoring or hair-dressing; I am not a university professor, and I do not hold a degree of monastic learning either'. Teaching and supervising others is his lifeblood, twenty-four hours a day, from the time he took responsibility for his younger siblings to his having a wife and children. Of these, the boys should study up to the highest levels: 'When you get them young enough, you can shape them any form you want'.

Chom is the middle one of five children, and although his father educates him with the rod, he is relatively neglected. He goes his own way by moulding clay into animal figures in the old house behind the family's abode where his grandfather stays and stunts his trees. He neither takes after his father, nor does he merit the attention the latter showers on his two elder sons. These, Chaya and Chan, are good learners. They train at a private school, not their father's, and know that they must prove themselves through relentless study and superior grades. But Chom does not respond well to formal education. The only time he 'enjoys the honour' of being regarded as a good pupil is when he prepares to enter elementary. In the grade-school entrance test, he finishes last, and from then on he is consistently grouped with the feeble pupils. Yet, he likes being in school more than being at home, because the teachers treat all the less gifted students with equanimity, while those classed as superior have to compete with each other.

His old man blames lack of resolve on Chom's part for his poor showing; students are either devoted and diligent, or dismissed as lazy and undisciplined. As a result, the elder two curry favour with father, bringing in prizes and top grades. Chom, however, is seen as not living up to the family's reputation, and his artistic talents go unrecognized. The remaining two children also receive much parental attention, and not merely for their scholarly competence. The fourth child is a girl, and thus the parents' darling, while the youngest boy is endlessly pampered because of being the baby of the family. It is the mother who indulges herself in caring for the latter two.

Being the odd one out, Chom keeps to himself and avoids family life, particularly his authoritarian and disciplinarian father. Mother does not spend much attention on him either; during his early days he was left in the care of a nanny, while the only new clothes he ever got were his Boy Scout's uniform. In training himself to go it alone, he avoids becoming like a disfigured tree. His main source of comfort is his modelling, and the attention of aunt Chailai and her husband, Phak, who came back from America with a Master's in child psychology. With the above as a background, the author has brought the main characters in position, and the narrative can subsequently be expanded in accordance with the message she wants to convey.

In the second chapter we find some information about the school system, a subject that also regularly surfaces in the newspapers because of the demands for educational reform, the traffic jams caused by parents taking their brood to distant, superior schools, the zoning and residence regulations for school admittance, and so on. The father-headmaster has his personal reasons for sending his children to the best schools he can afford, but the decisive one is that certain private schools simply have higher standards and place more emphasis on English, the key to advanced studies later. To go to a missionary-run institution is too expensive, though, and does not agree with the idea of being Buddhist. Anyway, the two elder sons are in the best school of the subdistrict where they train in the useful subjects of arithmetic, mathematics, science, and what have you, while Chom only excels in drawing and modelling to the detriment of his chances to ever earn his keep.

Chom devotes himself to his calling, and saves every penny to buy utensils, such as a complete set of brushes, pencils, paper, while enjoying the encouragement of his art teachers. When he makes it to the next grade by the skin of his teeth, his father is so incensed that he not only receives a severe thrashing – which only hurts his body – but also his equipment is destroyed, which hurts the child in his deepest depth. The excess of his father brings him closer to his granddad and his mother; it also sets in the near-total avoidance of father and son, even though the child still craves for daddy's recognition. 'Then and there I lost my childhood, it was taken away from me. I had to become an adult, capable of taking care of myself.'

His art teacher is supportive, and tries to clarify Chom's predicament. He subscribes to the idea that everybody is the owner of his own life, that others do not have the right to shape and mould it according to their wishes. Those are the ways of the past, when parents thought they were the owners of their children's lives. They were stunting the growth of their offspring so as to cultivate conforming and obedient people devoid of curiosity and ambition of their own. This fitted with a peaceful, yet stagnant way of life. Then, however, artists were still in demand, there was patronage for their skills, and their profession was honourable as long as temples were still decorated with intricate and elaborate murals. Nowadays people pursue science only, 'And even I, as an art teacher, feel as superfluous as the teacher of physical education'.

Then the character of the father is further worked out. He is a person who identifies himself with the grades of his children in an extreme way, and thus has his day of glory when the eldest finishes the primary grades with the highest honours. It makes Chom wonder how it is possible to cram and recall so much information: Chaya is almost like a dictionary. In receiving his distinction, he declares that his greatest pride is that his prize brings happiness to his parents.

Immediately the next son, Chan, is burdened with the success of his elder brother when the expectation is stated that his success will be equal to Chaya's when graduating next year. This terrifies him, because he is aware that he cannot cram like his brother, and will thus lag behind in both Thai and English. These subjects are taught by way of grammatical rules, devoid of logic and comprehension. Yet father, as a teacher of Thai, stresses language too, and is particularly keen on his sons' doing well in English. It is explained that in his younger days he failed to gain the king's scholarship that would have given him the chance to study abroad; he lost out to a rich man's son who had studied at a western school, and thus was better in English. This traumatic episode resulted in the inferiority complex that now makes him drive his sons. Be this as it may, a family party is organized to celebrate Chaya's success and to glorify the proud father. When Chom does not show up, people think that he is jealous of his brother. To his sister he explains he is not, he is not his brother's rival in any way. He simply does not have the new clothing required to show up at the celebration: 'The way I look will cause father loss of face'. And so does his preoccupation, art.

The burden of carrying parental hopes and ambitions is illustrated by the further career of Chaya. After grandfather's death the old house, where Chom had also moved in, is replaced by a smaller structure for the two elder boys. There school continues: its purpose is to cram. They study evenings, weekends, receive extra lessons, and tutorials for English. Especially the oldest one gets totally obsessed by grades. He was so upset when a Chinese boy bested him by one point, that he did not speak to him for a year. He is turned into a narrow-minded fanatic. All this weighs heavily on Chan who is more playful and somewhat less gifted; he fears father's judgement for perceived failure, and the resulting castigation. It thus comes as no surprise that all children have their reasons to keep things hidden from their stern and rigid dad, and that the second boy begins to feel bitter about his older brother. The author then puts the following consideration in Chom's mind: 'Yes, I am lucky escaping from the old man's attention, but it makes me like an orphan. Yet, whether it is my feeling cheap or the pressure put on my elder brothers, both of these are equally harmful for children'.

At home, father keeps urging the boys on, although he is more relaxed regarding his daughter who is not expected to be either gifted or to want to pursue higher education. This contrasts with Chaya who crams to compete for an overseas scholarship, in which he succeeds. Before being admitted to a British university, though, he needs to work on his English first; then, after a year and competitive examinations, he can be admitted to one or another of the halls of learning. Of the Thais, certain individuals make it to the prestigious universities, such as Oxford and

Cambridge; Chaya, scoring less high, is only accepted at a more ordinary school. This leaves him so desperate as to cut his wrists. His father's ambition, and the narrow confines of his own world, have driven him to suicide which, in its turn, signals the beginning of the old man's undoing.

Meanwhile, Chom has made it to an arts-and-crafts school, and gets more and more absorbed in his artistic pursuits, which also reflects in the way he dresses and takes care of himself. Often he stays at school for days on end, devoting himself to his work, while more or less neglecting himself. Then, one day, he is visited by Chan and Choet, his sister, who want to know why they see so little of him. At the school, they also meet Chom's female companion, Ladawan, who is mistaken for his girl friend, thus attracting Choet's curiosity. When she visits again, she is introduced to Pariyet, Ladawan's elder brother, who is a very talented student painter at Sinlapakorn University. Her beauty enthrals him; secretly she consents to be his model.

Ladawan and Pariyet are the legally unacknowledged children of a successful businessman who maintains three families. His abundant resources provide luxury to all his dependents. The mother of the two is kept in grand style, while being totally resigned to her passive existence which is filled by nothing more than embroidering and a retinue of servants. The interesting point is that neither parent is greatly bothered by the artistic inclinations of their two children; on the contrary, they enjoy the freedom, and the money, to open out and educate themselves, which they seem to do quite well.

There is a snag, however: often young people are carried away by emotions that interfere with considered decision making. Choet loses herself totally in being in love with Pariyet. When he wants to pursue his studies abroad, she wants to join, and thus marry him. Being underage, she needs her parents' consent, and this opens the opportunity for the father to show his prudishness about a long-haired artist, son of a whore, without a father, and other sobriquets that are protested about by Chom. According to his view, it is not the children's fault that they are born, and if receiving money by a mistress, or rather, a second wife, qualifies her as being a prostitute, then all married women, save for those who eloped, can also be rated as whores.

Pariyet is emotionally affected too. Having plenty money of his own, he disappears to Europe, and does not send word to anybody. This aggravates the pangs of love Choet suffers. She is pregnant as well, having wanted to consummate her passion before its subject was to leave. Certain that she will be forced from the parental abode if her father would find out about her condition, she connives with Chom and her mother. Moving in with Pariyet's mom seems to be the best way out.

In the course of the story, the father first loses his eldest son with whose success he had identified himself. His tyrannical and rigid ways make that the second boy, who resembles him most, opts to leave the home to settle in a students' hostel. Chom was already written off, and his art prizes, recognition, and respectable income do not impress him. The youngest boy outmanoeuvred the father by taking up a study place in the provinces. Now even Choet leaves the house, and when the father discovers this – and the connivance of his wife in the matter – he wants to chase her away from the home. It is the total break-up of the family, and the end of the dignity of the man. Liquor becomes his companion, he loses his job, and takes a former prostitute as a mistress. From then onwards, mother and Chom will live in the small 'cram shop' behind the house.

When, long after the birth of Choet's child, Pariyet is heard from again, he appears to be in Italy, and drug-addicted. With Choet watching over his rehabilitation there, they both perish in a car crash. Meanwhile the youngest, Chim, gets involved with a very rich lady student in Khonkaen. When this affair runs into obstacles, he comes home and sulks, starts drinking with his father, gives up studying, and finally becomes a male model and a rich widow's gigolo. Then mother resigns, and takes refuge in an upcountry temple. Son Chan is somewhere abroad, pursuing studies, but has dropped out of the narrative, and so the only ones to survive the rigidity of family, education, or abundant money, are

Chom and Ladawan who become the substitute parents of Choet's baby. Being self-assured and self-dependent, they represent the future Thai style of life the author hopes for.

Images

The deeper image that emerges is that of a society driven by the quest for rank and prestige, in which the old idea of titled position has given way to the preoccupation with diplomas and profession. University education, and a degree, are the marks of accomplishment, graded according to the prestige of the institutions and faculties concerned. Holding a western degree in medicine is to be at the apex, while a diploma in sociology from one of the local open universities is only moderately honourable. Yet, all Thai degrees are legitimated by the royals handing over the diplomas, and the scramble for that distinction is intense indeed. We have noted teachers complaining about the absence of real interest in the subject matter on the part of students: they cram for reaching higher rungs on the educational ladder, and parents organize their children's lives accordingly, beginning with extra lessons in kindergarten, then on through primary and secondary school with the aim of passing the university entrance examination in mind. Schools are graded in such terms: the best are those that get the greatest number of their students admitted.

Competition does not finish at the level of higher learning. It is being accepted by the prestigious faculties that counts, social sciences and humanities thus gathering 'second and third rate' students. It is the distinction that is important, not curiosity or interest in a subject. Then, with knowledge based on cramming rather than understanding, a whole thesis-writing industry could arise, supplying the desired Master's theses for a fee. Anyway, only twenty per cent of the high-school graduates is allowed to enter university; the others are apparently stigmatized for their failure to be admitted there. Disgruntled and disappointed, they flock to professional schools and teacher training colleges, and it is very obvious that their learning is taken far less seriously. This explains Chom's self-evaluation through much of the book's length. Repeatedly he ponders whether he should try to enter university. When Ladawan goes on the Sinlapakorn, he stops relating to her, obviously feeling inferior to her, being a mere trade-school student. Even when professional honour and success have already come his way, he still discusses the idea of pursuing formal higher education with his mentor, and it is only in the very last two chapters that he really is a free man.

The drive to achieve prestige through education, and the pressure parents and teachers exert on their wards, have been realistically portrayed. They are experience-near, so to say, and Chaya's suicide fully fits in with this situation. An almost unheard of occurrence some thirty years ago, Thailand now ranks near the world's top in self-killings, part of it motivated by the hopelessness that grows with age or chronic unemployment, but most suicides occur among young people pushed through school.

Recognizable, too, is the importance of money; it is treated in a very matter-of-fact manner. For Chom, his earning it is a measure of his worth: 'I now receive the same as a young government official with a bachelor's degree'. Having much money places one in a position where one can manipulate the law, an arrogance that, in a certain episode, is countered by the rank and prestige of being a senior civil servant. Does money bring happiness? Two out of three well-endowed students destroy their lives in spite or because of it. Most telling are the reactions to the deaths of Chaya and Pariyet. The suicide in London is commented upon as a wasted investment; years and years of study, equalling many hundred thousand baht and, because of the scholarship, of taxpayers' money. The father's investment was also high, not to mention the care both parents lavished on their children. Apparently, Chaya did not realize how much he was indebted to his parents, and the scholarship givers. His taking his own life becomes a short-sighted and selfish act.

When Choet and Pariyet's accident is brought to the attention of the latter's very affluent father, Chom and Ladawan immediately agree, in his presence, that the cremation had better take place in Italy, because it is much cheaper to fly the ashes home than the bodies. It is there and then, too, that Ladawan complains that she has money, but never had a father: 'He was at best a guest who joined us for dinner on Saturday'. Having money, or the scarcity of it, and how it affects relationships – spoiling, pampering, love bought, drudgery, no time for each other – is a minor variation of the main theme of the novel, namely, how family bonds and educational practice stunt and deform people. To bring this message home, the author touches on the hidden ideological foundation of Thai life: the family. The critique of it; explicit psychologistic reasoning; and the proclamation that everybody has the right to his own life, are recent themes, and will be new to most of the readership. It is very clear that the author does not believe that the strict authoritarian structure of the family is beneficial in any way. The emphasis on relative position, and the obligations it entails, make people secretive to each other, and very vulnerable. Overidentification of parents with their wards, their possessiveness, and their devotion to the latters' success, result in what is called love without intimacy. The resulting relationships are impassioned yet distant.

To argue this, the writer resorts to the extraordinary step of voicing explicit criticism against the father, and some more subdued remarks against the mother. Whereas it would seem to be Chom who has the best reasons for this – 'He stole my innocence' – it is especially Chan, Chim, and the mother who are used to 'chastise' the father. 'You killed your children'; 'You treat them as mere possessions for your own glory'; 'You think the others are your right'; and the like. Whether directly addressing the father, or in conversations among the brothers, Chom remains ambivalent about these strong opinions: 'After all, he is our father. It is sinful to talk that way'; 'He behaves like he does because he loves us'. Of course, he has to grant that the criticism is to the point, but it is also sinning against the parents. Since critique of the mother is even more of a taboo in Thai thinking, her negligence of Chom, her frequent possessiveness, her self-serving care for the children, are merely made explicit, at the same time that it is Chom again who shows most filial devotion to her. He is the exemplary man: independent, master of himself, and mindful, of his parents and others.

The author does not succeed in incorporating psychology in her characters, apart from the grossest of emotions, such as anger because of insulted egos, or the waywardness of young people trapped in love affairs. The various persons figure as roles, and the psychological explanations – a novelty anyhow – are very explicit, yet stand apart from the rest of the story. The only one who matches role with psychology is the father-headmaster as an extremely rigid authoritarian personality; what this causes in others, however, is more than openly proclaimed, and such may be necessary because psychology is new to Thailand. And so is the idea that people need to develop their own potential, that they have the right to do so in modern society.

To what extent the writer will be successful in convincing her readership must remain an open question, and the idea that education, and thus becoming 'a child the nation desires', means stunting and dwarfing is still deeply embedded in the school system. Virtually all primary schools prominently display the word Discipline on their facades, while a headmaster observed, 'In elementary, we shape people and form their character. In high school they are left to their own devices, and hardly enjoy the benefit of discipline and moral guidance'.

The author chooses to disagree with this opinion. The headmaster's view is old-fashioned, equating rules and discipline with ethics. People are not made just by discipline and cramming; they stunt and substitute rigidity for ethics. It produces the dehumanized people of our technology and money-driven society, with its tensions and depressions, loneliness, confusion, and broken homes. What is needed to keep social life worth living, is a sense of ethics rooted in the individual, and that is respectful of the personhood of others.

The author accepts social change, such as western breakfast habits, instant food, jeans and youth culture, and is even very explicit in condoning premarital sex. The problem with young lovers is that they get carried away by their emotions, not the fact of making love. Similarly, she does not get excited about minor-wifehood, or the male practice of visiting brothels. What she is against is men treating their wives as furniture, as private property to be enjoyed at their will and whim; that reduces them to unpaid prostitutes indeed. In the book, she stays clear from commenting upon family ideology, although it is evident that she opines that much needs to be changed if Thai individuals are to bud and open out in response to modern life; their selves, their imagination need to be stimulated. People should read, not the stupid funnies, or the cartoons about spirits and the supernatural, but quality books. They should not numb their brains with the soaps of jealousy and violence on Thai TV, or the insensate and ruthless entertainment of the Chinese and Japanese movies shown. She firmly believes that such senseless and exciting features have a negative influence on receptive young minds, as we shall see in her next novel.

'Botan', *Victims (Yūa)*.
Chomromdek Publishing House, 1991.

The book begins with the unambiguous positioning of the main characters and demarcation of their circumstances. Nakrop and Ruethairat are married; they have two boys, Rit and Ron, who are sixteen and fourteen when the story opens. A little over ten years ago they still lived with her parents in the Khlong Toei area. At that time Nakrop was working his way through Thammasat University. The events of 6 October 1976, when right-wing extremists attacked and slaughtered the students there, sets him up against his conservative father-in-law. As a result, they cannot stay together as an extended family, and he buys a house on the outskirts of Thonburi on hire purchase. This puts him in debt to the bank; his boss guarantees the loan. The massacre of students, and his being ensnared in financial obligations, kill his ambitions to advance by way of study. He, and his wife, will have to work without end to pay the instalments and to send their children through school.

Nakrop's firm is in the Latphraw area, and it takes him three hours to go there; an equal amount of time is needed to make it back home. Besides, he is assigned to work in the provinces three weeks a month. Ruethairat cannot enjoy much family life either. She holds a responsible job in a department store, working from ten to eight. She reaches home at night some two hours later. The daily care for the home and the boys is entrusted to Sai, a nineteen-year-old impoverished relative who, in the course of their growing up, has lost all authority over her two wards.

It is the time of the holidays, and the three adults discuss the problem that has cropped up because of the arrest of Ron. The police took him in, together with some other gang members, when they were involved in a fight among the rowdies of the lane on which they live. Sai explains that the boys spend little time at home, and that the youngest likes to associate with the rough and disorderly youths hanging around in certain places in the street. He likes a rumble and a boxing match, to watch cock and fish-fights, and to join in motor-cycle racing; he also has fun sidelining as a passenger-van boy. He is given to violence, and regularly threatens Sai to let him have his way. She shows the stitched scar on her leg, a result of his kicking.

The other boy, Rit, is quieter, and spends somewhat more time at home. He goes out to play football, but when that is not possible he spends his money on firecrackers and rockets. The neighbours are irritated by the noise. Of late, he has taken to gambling at an illegal den a few houses further up the lane where everybody earning tuppence is seen trying his luck. If he wins, he buys cigarettes; when out of cash, he intimidates Sai to give him a share of the house-keeping money. Naturally, Sai is also afraid of the consequences if the boys suspect her of informing the parents of their behaviour.

The father tries to look at all this more positively. 'That's the way young boys are. If we are very strict with them, they may even run away from home. Let us be happy that they are not using drugs; that is worse than an occasional brawl. Besides, when the new semester begins, they will be in school'. Yet he worries about Rit's gambling, and decides that he will discreetly inform the police about the den, even at the risk of Rit's arrest. He, and the mother with him, agree that forbidding and admonishing will be of no avail, and that even if the children would be under the supervision of grandparents, they would still follow their own whims and wishes.

The situation does not get better because of Bangkok's severe flooding, which keeps the school from opening and renders sports fields and facilities useless. The question boils down to: How do we keep the children out of mischief and in the home? Why don't they read, listen to music, watch TV? Perhaps a video recorder would be a way out. Of course, such an investment will be expensive, and add to the burden of paying instalments; moreover, tapes need to be rented, but if it keeps them at home and away from drugs, it is worth it. 'Such as girlhood is violated by rape, so boys will be destroyed by drugs'. And thus, a video enters the home.

After this enticing picture of life in the City of Angels, the story can begin to unfold. In developing the narrative, the author makes it a point to highlight the tremendous contempt the boys have for Sai. Even though she has cared for them over many years, they refuse to demonstrate any gratitude or consideration. She is a mere convenience, in the employ of their parents, and they will not acknowledge that she is a relative with a right to respect; they will not condescend to assist her with any task around the house. They are males, superior, brawny, and ... physically stronger. When she insists on her honour and right, she is reminded of her two brothers in jail because of drug offences.

For a while, Rit is kept at home because of serious injuries to his hands, sustained in fleeing the gambling joint when it was raided by the police. But the movies the parents hired are boring. Ron, however, is given different types of cassettes by his rowdy friends that make video more exciting; soon he is carried away by the extremes of violence and cruelty he watches. It whets his appetite for action; one day he catches a cat with the sole purpose of enjoying the thrill of killing it. He dumps the carcass in the unused well behind the house.

Rit nauseates at the insensate reels his brother relishes, but is tickled to life by the hard porn Ron is also supplied with. It stimulates his desire to try it out. On his first visit to a bawdy hotel he is cheated of his money. A few days later he needs more of it to visit the doctor, which brings him in the situation that he must reveal his condition to Sai. When considering the risk and cost of commercial sex, the boy starts eying her differently; after all, she is a budding lass. He makes holes to peep at her in her bedroom and in the bath. In order to satisfy his need for money, he is driven to search for his mother's secret chest to steal some of her jewelry.

The author takes pleasure in describing the pornographic perversions and the gory violence the boys witness on the screen. It would be better if they exhausted their energy with sports, and Ron could calm down if he joined a boxing school. Yet his mother disagrees: he could get hurt. And what is the remedy for sexual awakening at a time when boys are supposed to study? The parents do not see real solutions. Meanwhile heavy flooding aggravates the situation; even the refrigerator has to be carried to the higher floor, while water brings in mud and dirt at the lower level. It is Sai who has to clean there every day.

The chore is made worse by a leaking waterpipe in the bathroom. To repair it, a large wrench is needed, and Sai wades through the flood water to a neighbour to ask for one. Then she needs Rit's assistance to tighten the pipe. Since the rusty bolt does not easily respond, both Rit and Sai need to exert force, which results in Sai's dress tearing. Meanwhile Ron has also come, and while his eyes almost pop from their sockets, Rit is even inspired to rape her at seeing, then touching, her nakedness. In the ensuing melee, Ron pacifies Sai with the wrench. They dispose of her body as was done with the cat's.

Naturally, it is strange that the girl disappeared without her purse or clothing missing. Perhaps she made off with a man. She might also have been raped and killed; after all, there are many toughs in the neighbourhood. For the time being, though, a replacement is to be sought because somebody must do the housework and take care of the boys. That is Sawing, another impoverished relative. While she muses that Rit and Ron are perfectly able to lend a hand with the chores, their mother pampers them, and seemingly does not think it to be man's work. Sawing is also interested in other things, such as becoming an in-law of the family. She easily seduces Rit to make love. As an experienced woman she has no difficulty to turn his head, and in his desire to be near and ingratiate himself with her, he even takes on household chores, a thing that is not lost on Ron who ridicules his brother. When Ron knows how matters stand, he gets even more aggressive; in the ensuing quarrel, and in a demonstration of contempt for Sawing, he threatens that she may soon go the way of Sai. Upon this disclosure, Sawing flees, the police comes, and family life is devastated. The endless effort to pay for the house appears senseless.

The last chapter connects back to the first. Hard-working parents have no idea of the environment to which their children are exposed. They do not even know what goes on in their own home. Sai became the victim of the boys, the boys the victims of their surroundings, especially of video films. Why is it possible to buy such movies in Thailand? Why does the police tolerate the import and distribution of these products of western culture? The *farang* floods the developing world with his filth; his type of civilization is no better than wilderness. But our society follows in that wake; our mores are destroyed. We are all victims of this age.

This seems to be in line with the musings of a violent and ultimately self-destructive Ron. 'What is the meaning of the life of a cat, of a woman, and even of myself? There is neither light nor happiness in the future. Look at our parents. They slave without end, their faces are sombre and sad; they are always short of cash. They are ever tired and irritated. If I look at their way of life, I do not think that I want it'. And with this in mind, he makes off for the fleeting excitement of the cockfight.

Image

To the readership of Thailand's sensationalist press, the images 'Botan' evokes are familiar, and hardly in need of commentary. The lines are clearly drawn, and the fetters of hire purchase are certainly well-known to many contemporary Thais. In principle, it is not really much of a contrast with those in the villages who are perennially indebted to moneylenders. Her basic message seems to confront the reader with a picture of hopelessness, of lives without perspective, of feeling beyond redemption. There is no authenticity in the lives depicted, the most genuine, perhaps, being the life of Sai. In spite of her unenviable predicament, she knows where and who she is; watching television soaps brings her comfort. The boys need more sensation. They seek increasingly more powerful kicks, fleeting heights of sensation that can never be sustained, leaving one hung over and craving for the next high. Whether they are on drugs or not, they are junkies, devoid of future, of meaning, wholesomeness and sense. Such is the image of contemporary life in a side lane in Bangkok: drudgery without end, and no goal to reach.

Wô: Winitchaikun, *The Upstart (Se:thi: mai).*
Watsatree, 1990.

The story is presented as the autobiographical narrative of Phian Panyak, whose first name, meaning Perseverant, is not uncommon, but whose family name, It Is Hard to Pedal a Bike, can only be understood through the history of his grandfather who tried to earn his keep as a tricycle driver, finally dying of poverty and exhaustion on the bench of his *samlor*. As such, his descendants should be reminded of his penury, and make merit for him, for the old man did not have a penny to turn for that purpose. Anyway, the lives of us who are born in deep poverty are meaningless and wasted. We even cannot afford the luxury of sticking together. Each of us has to fight his own battle, and it is thus quite amazing that I still know this much about my family. The only ones I am familiar with are my father, mother, and elder sister.

Stark contrasts are drawn between those who take pride in their pedigree, and enjoy health and refinements, and those whose lives do not count and remain unacquainted with its comforts. Phian is born at the bottom of the pile; well, perhaps not quite so. His family is allowed to live in a hovel in a rich man's lane because the father is an honest, hard-working fellow who does the gardens, and so there is some regular income. Before he went to school, Phian joined his old man at his chores, and then he was often given errands to run for their well-off casual employers. Mother is good at cooking, peddling rice and curries; Phim, his sister elder by ten years, makes sweets that she sells in front of their hut. Of course, if the young boy is not helping his father, he assists his mother or sister, and thus he never enjoys the running around and playing of other children.

Phim marries Choke when she is twenty. Her husband is a clerk in a government office who obtained his education at a temple where he stayed on until settling down with Phim. They choose a dilapidated row house on a busy street with the idea in mind that she can set up her food stall right there. A fixed place is not only more convenient than peddling, it will bring in more money too. It is the beginning of the ever-expanding fast food concern Phimchoke. Before going from rags to riches, though, their father is crushed to death by the car of a drunken student returning home from his graduation party. The ten thousand baht offered in compensation seem a huge sum for somebody who only earned a few hundred a month. This money takes care of the matter, and without ado the young man involved can go on to further his studies abroad.

Not long after this event, mother and son leave their shack, and start living together with the other two in a stone house on the same street, all of them 'working as if they were Chinese' to make it a success. Like Choke, Phian also proves to have a keen sense of money, and how to earn it. This involves giving free meals to the local policeman, targeted sales promotion, strict bookkeeping, the experience that employing poor, pilfering relatives is bad practice, and that kickbacks and occasional presents are more realistic than trust in the law.

When Phian finishes high school, Choke urges him to go on to university, arguing that it will open the door to a career in the bureaucracy. 'You will be a master of people; it is the realization of prestige'. But Phian is not interested in these things; he is familiar with Choke's colleagues who patronize their fried-chicken restaurant. He finds them unworthy; they are unreliable, do not pay their bills, get drunk, and go to brothels. He feels better about being in business, building up personal networks, and working them to their enterprise's benefit. In that sphere, the arrogance of office does not count; on the contrary, even if it is ultimately about money, it is pleasant manners and understanding the soft points of interlocutors that lead to successful negotiations. Thus, if there is something to say for studying, then it should be related to his line of work. He continues his education with night classes in a business college.

At that time, Khim confronts Phian with the problem of his 'awful' name. She is the daughter of another upstart in the same street, *thawkae:* Leng, the Chinese immigrant who now runs an expanding drug store. Upon entering the Faculty of Pharmacy, she changed her name to the more melodious Khanang. Startled at the revelation, he realizes that she has a point. He becomes aware that this aspect of his appearance is not ideal for purposes of associating with people higher up. Yet, where do you get a new name from? Finally, a more sonorous name is selected based on his original one: Phiree Pancakhon. Phian Panyak was the emblem of poverty; Phiree Pancakhon is the symbol of success, of a man who does not need to feel inferior to anybody. It is the name on his royally bestowed diploma.

The family has been doing very well, and nothing prevents Phian from pursuing a Master's in the States. Among the Thai students at the college, he is accepted as a rich man's child, which suffices as an excuse for his being there. Meanwhile he becomes very secretive about his origins and background, because Thai people are second to none in admiring status. To establish oneself, though, it is sufficient to show that one is rich, and to spend accordingly.

At a students' party, Phian sits at the same table with young, spoiled, fragile, and conspicuously beautiful Kôi, and her elder brother, Kông, who practises as a physician in New York. The doctor is very pleased with his life in America, and critical about the situation in Thailand. During their further conversation, Phian is struck by the fact that brother and sister address each other with the formal *khun*, and that they attach great importance to family names, parental status and background. He has landed in the company of members of the old aristocracy, and almost blows his cover when he fetches them cookies of his own making. 'How come you can make such delicious sweets?' Already his harmless avowing that he took after his mother makes it clear that high-born women are not trained for the kitchen. Phian feels increasingly uneasy; it is as if they try to pry into his past, with him defending himself by keeping it all deliberately vague. Somehow, he still has to learn to identify himself with Phiree Pancakhon.

In the following, we get all sorts of information about Kôi and her milieu, about honourable versus ordinary employment, about the tendency of aristocrats to keep to themselves, not to open up to others, their pomposity and reserve. To be in their company is to be uncomfortable: one has to mind one's presentation all the time, and can never relax. Even so, Kôi's weak learning and lack of interest offer Phian opportunity to help her with her studies, while she explains that private sector employment is not a firm basis in life. The ideal of her circles is to enter government service. All this does not stand in Phian's way to start courting her. His mind is set: She is the girl for him to marry.

He comes back to Thailand with a Master's, and among the people meeting him at the airport is Khim, now teaching at university. Her father is also there. Then the focus shifts to the confrontation between the upstarts and Kôi's family, personified by her mother, and between the formers' seemingly unlimited resources and the taste and requirements of the latter. Everything needs to be done in first-class fashion with the cost involved never a question, and while Kôi appears to be interested in the paraphernalia – and not really in her husband-to-be – Phiree pays and provides. At the wedding reception, only a few of the people invited by Kôi's mother turn up, and the atmosphere is ominous and uncomfortable. When the couple is to retire to their newly built home, the bride has to be persuaded by her mother to follow her husband. The mother promises to be there the next morning. She does indeed show up, and begins running the home and the servants. Phiree is at best a guest in the alienating comfort of his air-conditioned English-country-style house, with mother and daughter living high on his resources.

The latter two trick him into paying their going on a European holiday, and this gives him the opportunity to leave his eerie marital abode, and to relax as Phian in the house above the restaurant where it all began. Again he meets Khim who, as *acharya* Khanang Atsawaphanitsawat, lives out of town in a university staff apartment. On a day off, he goes there; her company is a comfort to him. On his way back, he gets into a bad accident. It is only grudgingly that his wife visits him at the hospital, and not even very often at that. As a result, his wits are restored, and he sees his situation clearly. After the divorce and its 'honourable settlement', he is back home, unburdened. Phiree becomes Phian again, Khanang Khim; both began poor, and struck it rich, their child is the offspring of upstarts. Will that make a difference to their son?

Image

Written as persiflage and satire, the story makes a butt of the high-living of the urban nouveaux riches and the general obsession with money that even old families are willing to sacrifice their reputation for. By giving up their authenticity and background, life gets as uncanny as the countryside-style villa

Phian built. At least, he survived his adventure, and came back to a style of life in which he could feel at home again. Yet it may be expected that in Bangkok's rat race with its overwhelming supply of prestige enhancing gadgets and gimmicks, many will simply be sucked into the future, having lost all attachment to their past.

The future is a real problem in a new urban environment filled with equally new individuals who are only dimly aware of where they hail from and what they are heading for. In the previous story by 'Botan', she pointed to the hopelessness of the white collar workers of the lower middle class, and the moral vagueness in which its progeny finds itself. But even if there is enough money, that is in itself no guarantee for a meaningful existence. It may spur people on into senseless status seeking while they are really destroying themselves. Life in the big city seems to be deficient in genuineness, and only few keep or come back to their senses. Because of its superficiality, it is a dehumanizing experience.

Next to this overall image, the novel opens many glimpses into set practices. The pretence of civil servants is unmasked; the law is not accorded much respect; in the modern urban setting, it is agility and expedience that carry the day, and the practice of offering tea-money is firmly entrenched. The part that money plays gets blown up to seemingly realistic proportions: it is the very fuel that propels urban society into its polluted future.

Wimon Sainimnuan, *The Medium* (*Khon song caw*).
Tonôô Co. Ltd., 1988.

Wimon is considered as belonging to the new generation of writers. He is an author with a message that he explains in the introductions to his novels. These are set in the subdistrict Khokphranang, a rural environment fully exposed to the modern economy. This Central Thai setting, and the characters that bring it to life, are said to exemplify the country as a whole. Thailand is a place that is out of alignment, a disequilibrium that is caused by people taking advantage of each other through cheating, corruption, and playing tricks, whether by the manipulation of the law or the exercise of naked force. This affects the minds of people; they lose hope, or they turn ambitious and aggressive; others resign themselves to their fate. Is there anything we can do about this other than to fight for ourselves and be patient while going our way? Probably not. We live in unjust surroundings where we often feel oppressed, sad, sombre, restless, and hassled, feelings that Wimon releases by writing, and by thus communicating with his partners in distress, his readership (Preface to *Kho:kphrana:ng*, 1990).

In the prefatory notes to *The Medium*, he declares to be interested in what it means to be human, or in the permanent drama of life of people fettered in ever changing social conditions. According to his vision, the constants of the human condition remain the same, such as scarcity, discrimination, exploitation, and the negative impact of these on the human mind; they can readily be observed, whether in communal, national, or international life. If solutions are found, they prove to be temporary only, a new problem substituting for the initial one. Real melioration or progress simply do not seem to be possible, which the author then illustrates by the contradictions inherent in so-called development activities that always evoke new problems. While these bring money to some, the environment is destroyed, relatively peaceful conditions make way for stress, egoism, urban living, unemployment, crime. All attempts at betterment merely lead to our society, or humankind in general, going to the dogs.

One of the current trends is the dissolution of the possibilities for solidarity. This fragmentation, and the accompanying hopelessness of many, have little to do with differences in intellectual capacity because of unequal chances for education. These days, education does not fertilize the mind, but aims at reproducing people who lack originality and conform to the wishes of those who control society. It is non-conformists – either because they never finished school, or because they dropped out – who are at risk. The power-holders manipulate and confuse us with their half-truths and lies, and nobody seems to see clearly any longer. Their propaganda and the empty entertainment of the mass media are like drugs, alienating us from real communication while leading to individual loneliness. As long as people fail to face the question what it means to be human, they will remain shackled in the self-perpetrating circle of suffering, mistaking imitation for authenticity.

In his novel *The Medium*, the author sets out to illustrate these thoughts by concrete examples that demonstrate, among other things, the power the of delusions that ultimately consume us. They are represented by the authority and prestige of position, belief in things sacred and supernatural, gullibility, falling in love, anxiety and, of course, greed. Their interplay is set into motion by the yearly problem of flooding.

Kham is sombre and tense; his wife, Kalong, is worried too. They need to take their animals to high ground, but the new abbot, Nian, has forbidden the farmers to take their pigs and buffaloes to the temple. The priest seems particularly concerned about the impression this would make on the many visitors who come to make merit there. This is related to another man-made mound where a huge banyan tree has grown, which subsequently became the place of worship of *caw phô:* Sai. Its reputation attracts worshippers from afar. This does not impress Kham; living close to the riverbank, he simply needs a dry spot. Kham's resolve worries his wife, and other villagers. It is brought to their attention by Mek who argues that Kham's action equates with insulting the *caw phô:* who is held in awe by all the people of the subdistrict. Kham's behaviour, therefore, is a blatant show of contempt for his fellow denizens, notwithstanding the fact that the place of worship is on Kham's own land.

Mek is also moody. Since some time he does not sleep well and is curt to Phayia, his wife of five years. He is affected by his falling in love with the greatest attraction of headman Thôngma's sundry cum coffee shop, the lovely Nongphanga. It was there that he went in his Sunday best, stopping on the way to pray for the assistance of *phra* Sai. It was there and then he noted Kham and

266

his animals. This causes the headman to call on Kham, and we witness the typical scene of a confrontation between the arrogance of a superior and the hardheadedness of a small man who has no way out. The headman is adept at handling men, and keeps his cool. He changes his line to the sacredness of the place. Kham argues that such holiness is just in the minds of people, that it was his ancestors who built the mound, that he does not believe in the *caw phô:*, and that he has no other solution to the problem. Deep down, the headman agrees, but he gets on his high horse because he also has his own interests in mind.

'By not believing, you are destructive'.

'To believe is a personal matter'.

'You wait and see what will happen. You'll experience something terrible'.

'Again, that is up to me'.

'You have the nerve to dare me?'

Losing his own nerve, the headman draws his gun. Still, Kham remains defiant. 'I shall show you how sacred that place is'. At that moment his child falls into the river, and drowns. At the coffeeshop, the incident enhances the prestige of the *caw phô:* and the reputation of the headman who is said to really care for the villagers.

The parallel scenes that are developed take place between Nongphanga and Mek, and, alternatively, between him and his wife. At the shop where the headman holds a virtual monopoly on all kinds of goods – the garlands and incense needed to worship the *caw phô:* being an important line – Mek confesses his love, then tries to get a hold on the headman's daughter by offering her a golden necklace with a heart-shaped pendant. At home he is not so sweet: he badly batters his wife, and orders her to stay in the house and not to meddle with his business.

Meanwhile Kham suffers from the opinions of the villagers who hold him responsible for the death of his son by invoking the wrath of the *caw phô:*. He does not sleep, does not eat, feels miserable and weak. He is also very angry at that darned tree that even prevents him from using his own land as he sees fit. People only began attributing sacredness to the spot when a travelling monk was forced to defrock when committing adultery there, and then honoured the tree with his saffron robe. He broods on revenge: he will cut the tree! Arriving there, he feels feeble, almost to the point of fainting. An old worshipper there sees his ax, and advises him to rather seek the forgiveness of the powerful spirit. All that does not stop him from going at the tree. As soon as his ax touches it, he loses consciousness as if overwhelmed by a spell. When he comes to his senses, he remembers this as a most terrifying experience that was pervaded by the stench of incense. It is explained that he was possessed by the *caw phô:*.

As a result, people grow very interested, concocting all sorts of fantastic stories about the spirit and his power. For instance, the headman is credited with lots of merit (*bun*) because the spirit addressed him directly, and it is believed that it is a boon to all that *phra* Sai, a former deity, had the goodness of coming to reside among them. To be near to such a source of sacredness could certainly help in finding winning lottery numbers. And so, awe readily mixes with greed.

Meanwhile, feverish and enfeebled, Kham makes it back home where he falls in a delirious sleep in which he meets *phra* Sai. 'You lost'. 'I did not lose; I had no choice'. 'That is the same thing. Now you will be my servant. That is your choice'. Kham remains defiant, 'No way'.

When he comes to himself, the water is rising, and he wants to take his animals to the enchanted place again against the protests of Kalong who advises him to ask for pardon. Only a few steps on his way, he faints. Then he falls in a deep sleep. The next day, the flood waters force him to bring his animals up the mound, although he begins to feel uneasy about it. Upon his return, his wife suffers severely; she is in labour. Because her condition only seems to worsen, he decides to see aunt Mian, the old midwife who told him to seek the spirit's mercy a few days ago. Now she punishes his swaggering and disrespect in face of the sacred by refusing to come to see Kalong. It is her husband who persuades her to accompany Kham back home. There the mother-to-be gradually reaches her wits' end, a thing that aunt Mian blames on Kham's brazen behaviour. Finally he vows to become the spirit's servant if his wife will be saved.

From then on, he is the medium of *phra* Sai, and the villagers start behaving nicely and respectfully to him. Before Kham can function properly, they have assembled in his house where the conversation is dominated by the headman, who seems to smell business, and aunt Mian, who happens to be a ritual specialist too. While the people present would like to seek answers to their problems and wishes immediately, they are advised that Kham needs to go through a Buddhist ritual first to confirm his status. The ways to approach the *caw phô:* still need to be clarified, such as what to offer to attract his kind attention, and especially, how much money that involves. When they are gone, he still expresses his doubts and rebelliousness to his wife. She reminds him that his vow has saved their baby's life; having no choice, he resigns himself to be the spirit's servant.

During the first session, the medium performs convincingly. Dressed as a 'brahmin', he is soon possessed. The *caw phô:* has a particular voice, and appears to be a heavy smoker. The first subject he brings up is the money to be offered for consultation – which also indicates a lucky number. For the other offerings needed, from cigarettes to incense, he strongly recommends that they be bought from the headman's store. Before leaving, he comes with the typical lottery predictor's ploy: 'I cannot give straight numbers. It would ruin the organizers who also trust and worship me. Interpret my signs. Those who win, have understood. Those who do not see them, do not understand'. Then Kham re-emerges. His face expresses sadness and suffering, as if to demonstrate that he has become a slave for the rest of his days.

Soon, however, Kham looks cheerful. His new calling frees him and his wife from peasant's drudgery. They are thriving. Kalong takes pride in him, and showers her honoured husband with attention. She is a true believer, and grateful to the *caw phô:*, the very source of their newly won affluence. Still, they are not rich, and Kalong fears that the headman will stick to his threat to evict them from their land that has been mortgaged to him. Kham puts her mind at ease by arguing his influence as *phra* Sai's spokesman. Besides, the headman does good business because of his mediumship. The very way he puts it shows the growing awareness of his power; he is in business; and with Kalong and their child treating him with increasing reverence and awe, his power over them grows too.

At this point the parellel story is woven into the narrative. The more Mek is frustrated in his love for Nongphanga, the more he drinks, and the more he tyrannizes his wife; upon coming home late, he seems to take special pleasure in battering away at her, and subsequently raping her savagely. In spite of his threats not to leave the house, her torment drives her to seek the advice of the *caw phô:*; she wants to charm her man back to tenderness. As it happens to be, Phayia and Kham are lovers of yore, but for whatever parental objection, they never got married. As *phra* Sai, the medium inserts that special medicine that will make her irresistible to her husband. Soon they fall into the habit of doing this on an almost daily basis, to which Kalong, as a true believer, does not object at all. It does start some rumours though, and the wronged Mek begins brooding on revenge. He publicly vows to have Kham killed, and conspires with the weak-minded shop assistant, Lamsan, to dispose of him.

This threat does not quite agree with the interests of headman Thôngma. He is depicted as a successful big shot: he lives in a beautiful house surrounded by a vast garden with lots of flowers tended by his wife; he sits in a rocking chair, smokes a pipe, and drinks foreign liquor. He is a cunning man too: he knows his villagers, and how to speak in a manner that commands their respect – and let him have his way. He'll never speak his mind, though. So, in a confrontation with Mek who complains about his being the buffoon in town, he advises him to have trust in the *caw phô:* isn't his wife growing more radiant by the day? He also knows that Mek is a dangerous man, often guided by impetuous moods, and so he proceeds to warn Kham. When the latter foolhardily maintains his double identity – 'What can the *caw phô:*

be afraid of?' – the headman has keener ideas. Not having the *caw phô:* around would be bad for business; thus, people should firmly believe in this sacred personage, at the same time that Mek's allegations and the villagers' gossip could damage the reputation of, and so the respect for *phra* Sai. On top of this, the headman is more than annoyed by Mek's overtures to his daughter, even worrying that such an unworthy type could abduct her. He takes his touching her hand as a personal insult, as a threat to his position and honour. In brief, Mek is a nuisance.

This conclusion is reinforced by Lamsan who comes to tell the headman that Mek is raising the hue and cry, causing upset among the villagers. He is publicly vowing to kill both Kham and Phayia; he ridicules the *caw phô:*, and mocks the people's beliefs. Besides, his rude and drunken behaviour at the shop inspires fear in Nongphanga while Lamsan has become the defenceless target of his insults and violent abuse. The young man's anger and fear are further aggravated by the headman: 'Mek is going to kill you, not only because you revealed his plan to kill Kham, but more certainly so now that he knows that I'll give Nongphanga in marriage to you'. The headman lends him a pistol.

When Mek's body is found under the banyan tree, villagers suspect Kham first, 'If you want to have the wife, you have to shoot the husband'. But then, when could he have done it? 'Let us consult the *caw phô:* to find out'. The headman is not so enthusiastic about this idea, and he hurries to Kham to let him know. In this and a few other episodes, the manipulation of the *caw phô:*, and the identification of Kham with the spirit, or the spirit with its human medium, becomes abundantly clear, the medium influencing certain women and the headman, and vice versa. Anyway, the only thing the *caw phô:* reveals is that the killer will expose himself soon; seemingly, he understands the headman's needs.

Lamsan panics when police comes to investigate. When he is taken away, Nongphanga pleads mercy, 'He's not all there'. When he wants to explain himself, he is intimidated to admit his anger with Mek only, and not to implicate Nongphanga: 'It will make her

271

suffer', and that is the very last thing he wants to cause her. Why? In the second part of the book, and especially in the chapters following this virtual end of the story, the author wants to expose the manipulation of people by those who are clever and sly, to demonstrate how holding power leads to its abuse, and how life is a play of delusions. Lamsan is deeply attached to Nongphanga, not just because of the headman's promise. The feeble-minded man is the product of an adulterous affair of his mother with the young Thôngma, long before he became headman. The mother entrusted her three-year-old tot 'for a day or two' with Thôngma; she was never heard of again. His unwilling father took care of him as if he were an orphan, a fixture of the house; when Nongphanga was born, twelve years his junior, he became her playmate and nanny; in short, she became the emotional anchor of his life. At this time, though, he is sacrificed for the headman's ambitions. When he is freed from jail, nobody is there to meet him.

Many pages are devoted to cunning and egoistic motives. The story of how Kham as *caw phô:* talks Phayia into being his lover is absolutely delightful. Later she, and a budding young girl of thirteen, are ordered by the *caw phô:* to be his retinue – on pain of his displeasure. His stature has grown greatly because of Mek's murder: the headman fears his revelation, and thus tries to bribe '*the caw phô:*' with a big sum of money and Kham with his title deed. 'They' accept these, but both the *caw phô:* and Kham warn him of the threat of Mek's relatives who, according to 'them', suspect the headman to be the mastermind; they have vowed to kill him. Exploiting his anxiety, the *caw phô:* advises a safe way out: go westwards, and stay away for a good while. Kham promises to provide a safe place for Nongphanga and her mother. This makes the medium the most influential man in the village. Now he can have it his way. He relishes his power. 'I am the *caw phô:*!!!!'

Wimon Sainimnuan, *The Subdistrict* (*Kho:kpbrana:ng*).
Tonôô Co. Ltd., 1990.

The story takes place in the same setting as the above, and several of the characters we met before surface again. When it begins to unfold, we are again confronted with the problem of the yearly floods, and the damage they cause to the crops. As a result, Bualôi's situation has steadily deteriorated, almost since the day he married Fuangfa. Praying for a better result this year, he feels optimistic. The signs augur well. Besides, his buffalo is in calf; better still, his wife is pregnant too, and is expected to give birth next month. Hopefully it will be a boy. He feels confident, because he has done all he can to make sure that things go well: he went to *caw phô:* Kham to ask for medicine; obtained – after a long wait – *luang phô:* Nian's holy water; he also demonstrated his respect to both *phra* Sai and the priests at the temple. Everything portends fine.

The circumstances do not seem to be guided by the omens. The flood waters rise rapidly; Fuangfa is in labour prematurely; neither holy water nor medicine nor sacred formulas relieve her severe suffering. It results in a caesarian section, and she is placed under special care. At the hospital, the dirt poor peasant worries about the consequences; he feels insignificant as compared to the nurses there. At home the water has risen dangerously; he has to mind everything: the animals, his girl child, the kitchen. Yet, the main cause of his confusion is the question where to find money for the medical bills. The *thawkae:* of the rice mill will certainly refuse because he is heavily in debt there; neither has he been able to repay a cent of his substantial loan from *caw phô:* Kham. Selling his animals would deprive him of his last source of income, because he is not going to harvest his crop this year: the flood is destroying his rice already.

The subdistrict boasts a well-known temple where, especially since a good road was built, business is booming, attracting people from far and wide. Its monks are well taken care of and in splendid condition. *Phra* Can is its moneylender. 'We only see people here when they are in trouble. When everything goes well, they forget about religion. Yet, who are we not to help them?' With all the respect due to a man of the robes, and in praise of his kindness, Bualôi is made to sign a promissory note of 3,900 baht, receiving three thousand, the rest being the interest of the three-month term of the loan. He is advised not to think of this as usury, but rather as a form of merit making to help the temple. On taking his leave, the monk still adds, 'Do not cheat a priest. If you do so, you'll suffer eternally in hell'.

The depth of Bualôi's poverty is not only illustrated by his and his wife's worries about the medical bill, but also by his decision to walk the two kilometers from the market to the hospital in the heat of the day. This tires his little daughter, who dawdles and lags behind her father. At such a moment, a reckless driver skids from the road, fully hitting the girl of whom nothing but bones and blood remain. In the ensuing confusion, he somehow loses the money he borrowed from the temple. He needs to go there again. His new debt is 7,800.-

'The driver fled the scene', but the owner of the car is willing to offer compensation, and Bualôi hopes that the cost of the cremation will be covered. Being overwhelmed by problems and disaster, he is not fully with it, but feels uneasy about 'earning money over the dead body of his child'. It is not in his hands. In a very congenial manner, the police officer who negotiated the case can promise that Bualôi can look forward to receiving thirty thousand baht! When he comes to receive the money, he has to wait a while with a young police captain who draws his attention to a big merit-making festival his superior is sponsoring. This officer on duty persuades him to contribute a thousand or two to that occasion as a sign of his gratitude. When he tells the ranking policeman that he wants to join him in making merit, he is dissuaded from doing so, 'Your position is difficult enough, and I am merely doing my duty'. On his way out, he tells the young captain what transpired. 'Yes, so he is; our superior is a very good man. But I can help you, and see to it that you make a contribution to the *kathin* festival'. Bualôi entrusts the captain with a thousand, and thanks him profusely.

Upon reaching his house, he sees *caw phô:* Kham's assistant chatting with his wife. 'How much did you get?'; then the conversation dwells on his debt, and the hopeless situation of small farmers experiencing bad harvests and always short of money to invest in next year's one. Even the boon that befell him is elusive: when the assistant makes off with ten thousand, he has only paid the interest accrued to his loan. To do better with his debt to the temple, he returns *phra* Can his loan two months ahead of the term. The monk, however, refuses to accept the money offered; he wants the full 7,800 baht, because ... The priest's sophistry, and Bualôi's signature on the promissary notes, not only intimidate the latter to pay the full sum, the man of religion succeeds even in making him feel grateful. Comes the cremation of the little girl. Also those who surround such a ceremony have their tricks and fees: the monks should be given a little extra; flowers go separately; there are bills for use of the morgue, for electricity, water, temple wardens, and suchlike. When all is added up, the mourning parents have paid ten thousand instead of the four or five they budgeted.

Apart from all that, the abbot had Fuangfa called when at the temple shortly before the cremation. He explained to her that she could make extra merit by contributing to the repair of a leaky roof. It netted him a thousand. Then Bualôi is invited to show his face at *thawkae:* Bunchai of the rice mill, to be investigated about his debt with him. The owner is depicted as a successful man, his office air-conditioned, and smoking a pipe. Explaining that the money due is accumulating, the rich man asks for repayment. When Bualôi tells him that he has no cash, he is reminded that a considerable sum was paid to him as a result of his pick-up crashing into his daughter. Bualôi clarifies how the thirty thousand was spent, and that he is as poor as before. Then it dawns on the *thawkae:* what way the sixty thousand baht he agreed with the police chief – 'a lot of money for a little girl' – went.

Next in line to drop by is headman Thôngma to ask for a donation because he needs to defend the honour of the subdistrict by entertaining the district and provincial officials who are to visit soon. He came just in time to receive some of the last cash. To top it all, Bualôi is asked to contribute to Kham's ceremony in honour of the *caw phô:*, and so his obligation to mind the goodness of one of his creditors is activated. Kham's assistant claims one of the two sows for the purpose, and it takes Bualôi a good deal of pleading to rather contribute their litter, 'What income would I have if I cannot breed?', which results in his being squeezed of his piglets; at that, he has to be grateful still.

Comments

Many more serious contemporary novels take issue with society, and are a relief from the soaps shown on television. The latter are mainly concerned with generation conflict, jealousy, slapstick, and a good deal of face-slapping. Usually, the action is set among the young people of the newly rich, and from what we have discussed so far it is clear that *Wô:* Winitchaikun's work qualifies for such representation. Its value is more in entertainment than in drawing clear pictures, although her criticism of current parvenu lifestyles is clear. Yet, it goes too far to read this book as an objection to a society where money appears to be the measure of all things.

The Upstart can probably best be understood as a depiction of the dangers of extremely rapid social mobility that alienates people from their roots, even forcing them to seek new names and new identities with which they do not feel at ease. If from hovel to row house is a realistic possibility still, from the same shack to the air-conditioned comfort of an English-style country house on a lane off Sukhumvit Road is too much of a leap. It places the self at such a remove from origins and authenticity that one is without comfort or direction. Beyond the reach of rooted meaning, life suddenly needs to be filled with foreign gadgets and styles that money can buy. It is the readily observable condominium and Spanish-villa wrapping of the lives of those who are upwardly mobile, who wear neckties and follow western fashions, who endure the traffic in flashy cars equipped with urinal, and sometimes even give birth there. It is the complaint of those who say that 'the Thais' lack originality, always imitating the westerner, in awe of the wonders of technology, while forgetting their culture. It is commercial society, more like a market than a community of people, that advertises its ways in the proliferating lifestyle magazines that tell the newly rich how to spend their money and how to fill their lives. The way out the author proposes is to move back to the row house, to become Khim again, to enjoy being Phian. For many in actual urban society that road seems to be closed, however.

'Botan's critique of education, at home and school, will be recognizable to many readers. Thai practice hopes to force people into role models rather than trying to stimulate their creativity and self-motivation. Of course, and in full agreement with Bourdieu and Passeron, all pedagogic action aiming at the reproduction of culture may be seen as symbolic violence – and at that, what parents and schools exercise is a legitimate form of such violence too, a form that in its turn is part of the culture itself.[1] But in moving from stimulation to conformity and drill, we may imagine that forcefulness increases, with 'Botan' criticizing the extreme practice of disciplining and cramming. For many parents these days, children seem to equate with their results at school, and the pressure the system places on the young is such that Thailand scores among the world top ten as far as the suicide rate goes.

It is clear that the author touches on a familiar point. Of the five children, four are thoroughly disfigured, and three more or less perish because of it. The second son finds his way in conformity, in being a standard type of university lecturer. His case is unproblematic; in him culture has been reproduced successfully according to the canons of 'legitimate symbolic violence'. The

---

[1]   See Introduction, page 17, note 6.

casting of the middle son, the artist, is in itself not problematic either. Although in relation to the family, his is a lonely position, it is precisely his relative independence that offers him the chance to mature as a personality, to see clearly, to be responsible, and to be able to make his own decisions. The problem the author confronts the reader with, is her declaring this character to be the hope of Thai society if it is to evolve in the right manner. The direction she points out is revolutionary rather than evolutionary, at least, as measured against the social studies curriculum we reviewed in the earlier chapters. Exemplary of the dominant ideology, it does not appear to want to stimulate the unbounded imagination and the self-motivation of students. It rather aims to keep people in place as desirable subjects, at the same time that elite families send their offspring to very special or international schools, and to higher training abroad.

By declaring Chom to embody the hope for the future, the reader almost loses sight of the other artist, Pariyet, and the two younger siblings. What happens to them seems to be an increasingly common occurrence. Their education has not prepared them to deal with existence as it is. These three cannot stand on their own feet; they all escape, and are obviously incapable of self-conviction. I think this to be very common among the present school youth. The regimen of discipline, cramming, and competition; of endless moral lessons, slogans, and state ideology – it is real enough. School is neither a place to be yourself, to relax, nor to take liberties. Its yard is clean; the students wear a uniform, as if to highlight that it is not their place. In private, they will discard the standard dress as soon as they can, to be close to themselves again. On the other side of the school fence they find another world, where pupils freely throw their garbage around. Life is different on the two sides of the school walls, and school education does not bridge the gap.

For the second son, Chan, this does not pose a problem. The inside world of his education agrees with a presentational, wooden world of officialdom outside. He apparently fits in with this remnant of an older Thai society that is under attack by modernity and development. But the three characters of Pariyet, Choet, and Chim do not fit in anywhere, neither with themselves, nor with old or new social life. One loses himself in drugs; the other in her tormented self; the last becomes the gigolo of an older woman. They have not been prepared to take their own decisions in life. Their education does not provide the moral guidance they need. In wider society they appear to be abandoned; they easily get lost. The old ways, in which Chaya and Chan have been trained, have become invalidated, as symbolized by the father-headmaster going to seed. Yet, what is to replace them is still unclear, Chom's individual success hardly being a model others could pattern their lives on. There is something greatly amiss with Thai education, but how to remedy it, how to restructure it so that it agrees with the times, is far from clear. Caught between the certainties of the past, and an elusive present that few can clearly imagine, it seems that Thai society is wandering aimlessly into a future dominated by the forces of the market, over which individuals hold perilously little influence.

What such a society looks like, was the subject of 'Botan's other novel, *Victims*. She took a narrow focus on the lives of two teenagers whose moral guidance seems to originate from hardcore video films and their personal moods. What they chase after is immediate satisfaction, regardless of the consequences. She depicts a society depleted of moral considerations, hard, without scruples, in which not even honest parental effort leads to reward. The only way to go is down.

This extreme pessimism, in which everybody is a victim, of the environment, of the workplace, of the bank, of lust and contempt, of the own moods, and so on, leaves the lighter side of life beyond view, other than in such remarks as, 'Let us be happy we live here. Here the problem is rowdyism only, whereas Khlong Toei, where we came from, is saturated with drugs'. Not a single individual is a carrier of hope, and those who are dutiful, perish. In *Stunted*, Chom made it to the full, and so provided a contrast. In *The Upstart*, many people arrive at the good life. Bangkok is not just hell, there is also humour, mobility, and success for a few.

It is thus of interest to consider the ambitious attempts of Wimon Sainimnuan who openly declares that he writes about modern Thai society as a whole. As we have seen, he is not filled with optimism, but his representations may be interpreted to stand for traits, experiences, practices and positions that commonly occur; they are part and parcel, perhaps even the very nature of the contemporary Thai 'human condition'. Wimon is not the only one who says so. According to the literary commentator Sakun Bunyathat:

> Every letter of Wimon Sainimnuan's writings is part of a shower of shot that, with a sudden shock, pierces and destroys the deceptive mask Thai society presents these days while fully exposing its despicable figure.

To this Mala Khamchan adds,

> The work of Wimon Sainimnuan always urges us to be critically aware of the deeper qualities of Thai society.

The 'Land of Smiles'?

The picture that emerges after reading the five novels concerned is very much along the lines set out by Wimon. Life in wider society, yea, even among people who are closely related, is a life of people preying on each other, of people insensitive to the feelings of others, of people needing others to boost their fortune, ego or sense of self-importance. The honestly motivated ones are at the mercy of the rest, and usually do not fare well. All experience appears to be delusive.

This unpleasant condition, in which especially the less influential are exploited by those with more power, seems to relate to the strong sense of inequality that these writings emphasize. It is the palpable importance of life's hierarchical dimensions that explains competition, the scramble for diplomas, the goal to achieve power, and the ambition to have face, status, honour, and reputation. Often it seems that money – obtained by whatever means – is all that is needed to achieve such success in life. Then, being on top justifies contempt for others, ruthlessness, disregard for the law, and yields recognition and admiration, the more so if one is a clever manipulator of presentation, or mask.

The most sincere individuals appear to be those without social paraphernalia or credentials. As soon as they are touched by whatever form of progress, they seem to rapidly lose their innocence and with it, their humaneness. On the whole, individuals do not appear to be their own masters. They live at the hands of others whom they need for status validation. The exception was 'Botan's Chom who, standing on his own feet, survived the onslaught of social demands, obligations, and deformation. To develop such an independent personality appears to be exceptional, though, since all the other characters we met are very much subject to their circumstances. They are amoral exploiters of opportunities, and thus, of the people they meet on their way. Doctors, abbots, monks, policemen, headmen, nurses, fellow villagers – all take advantage of others, and are busily making money. Even in the family, relationships are not really comforting. Parents are distant towards their children, forcing their ambitions on them. The only bond described as intimate was the one between the mother and Choet, in spite of the daughter successfully hiding her love life until she was well on the family way. After that, their contact seems to languish. With the exception of the couples Bualôi–Fuangfa, and Phim–Choke, the husbands and wives we met do not seem to share intimacy or sincerity.

While depending on each other for recognition, self-validation, and exploitation, people remain secretive to each other, everybody going their own way, pursuing their personal purposes, irrespective of the consequences to others. In this way they are hardly ever self-contained personalities, or self-respecting individuals, but rather narrow-minded egoists, manipulators of chances, rather than respectful of the 'generalized other' or the public interest. They operate in a society that appears as a competitive market place. In such a setting money and advantage gain paramountcy, and it is very few people indeed who keep their cool, stay clear, and are not dominated by pecuniary and expedient considerations. It appears that present-day Thai society is not a place to relax, to smile, or to breathe freely. While it offers opportunities to some, many just drudge. For all it seems that the pressure is on.

Chapter 7

WITH COMPLIMENTS OF THE NATIONAL IDENTITY OFFICE

Thailand in the 90s is a book produced under the auspices of the National Identity Office of the Prime Minister, Royal Thai Government. It was composed by an honourable Editorial Board among whose members we find at least five holders of Ph.D. degrees. Since the book is written in English, we may expect an official and authoritative introduction to the country addressed to an international audience that may, for whatever reason, have an interest in it. We therefore presume that all possible care will have been taken in its presentation, not only because of the target public, but also because the Thais themselves are very aware of the importance of appearance. Besides, in these days of open communication, it could reasonably be hoped that certain things that Thais may take for granted will have been made understandable for those English-reading foreigners who see the world in terms of their own background and experiences.

In view of the above observations and the expectations it promotes, the volume becomes a curious document full of surprises. It is at once delightfully Thai because of its mix of unquestioned ideological statements alternated with unflagging realism, and because of the way things Thai are presented as matters of course. Somehow, few concessions have been made to foreign understanding; besides, much of the publication has been produced with a remarkable lightheartedness that is punctuated by an amazing mass of spelling errors and faulty English. All this notwithstanding, two fifths of the volume have been devoted to present the country's unfolding economic miracle, apparently to anticipate the interests of potential foreign investors. Be this as it may, let us first review the book, consider the image it evokes, and then comment on a few of its points.

Its very first page presents us with a picture of their majesties and their four children at a time they were considerably younger than in 1991, the year of the book's publication. This is followed by the title page and the table of contents. A glance at the latter shows us the way the information has been structured. A historical overview is followed by introductions of the monarchy, the land and its people, and religion, thus presenting the reader with the three pillars of Thai nationhood. Two chapters are devoted to education and the arts respectively. Then the structure of the economy is discussed, followed by government and politics, international relations, and further chapters about distinct economic sectors, including tourism.

History

Where the Thais came from, or whether they were around all along, remains a moot point, but it is clear that they were well-established and organized by the middle of the thirteenth century when Sukhothai began to dominate much of the area known as Thailand today. The Thai high culture of those days was an amalgam of Theravada Buddhism, animism, Hinduism, Mahayana Buddhism, and Khmer ideas about statecraft, while we should not underestimate the power of the own atavistic contributions to this cultural mix. Sukhothai can be regarded as the cultural precursor of the present. As a 'golden age' in Thai history, its rulers were liberal in respect to the population; it was a time trade and the ceramics industry flourished; the Thai script evolved into its definitive form; the kings were devout Buddhist rulers who made merit on a large scale; the evolution of Buddhist sculpture reached a zenith of elegance and stylized beauty.

It is pleasant to discover that all this history, together with an ample supply of alternative hypotheses about the origins of the Thai race and the Ramkhamhaeng inscription can be given in less than five pages. Were such only the case at school! As it happens, the information is even richer than the standard fare because of the alternative views mentioned, and because of the recognition that to start Thai history with Sukhothai is arbitrary indeed. Of course, we do not escape from the established chronology, and thus move on to Ayutthaya. That city was not created out of nothing, but founded in an inhabited location were people were thriving on maritime trade. When kings imposed their rule, the city-state embarked on a highly successful career of military and political expansion; the social organization of the realm became highly complex and strictly hierarchical. The kings ruled according to the Buddhist Dhamma and, at the same time, were god-kings whose sacred power was associated with the Hindu gods Indra and Vishnu. The king was 'honoured and worshipped by his subjects more than a god'.

No attempt is made to resolve the contradiction between Buddhist and Hindu ideas of rule but, at least, we are being spared the ideological nonsense school children are regaled with. The point is important, though, if we want to understand the position of the king in hegemonic Thai culture, and a few more words of explanation here, that is, in Ayutthaya, could have helped to explain the monarchy which, according to the text, is 'often difficult for outsiders to fully comprehend'. Anyway, much like in Sukhothai, the king and his realm could flourish because they operated at the hub of a far-flung commercial network. The China trade was profitable enough to recognize Chinese suzerainty, to send tribute, and ... to receive luxury goods. Muslims from India were also prominent among the Asian merchants. They were joined by Persians and Japanese. All these foreigners were free to worship as they pleased, and some of them became important court officials.

Commerce got a boost when Europeans established direct contact with the East; especially the Dutch East India Company played a vital role in Thai exports. Its monopolies on certain products are mentioned, but not commented upon. The aggressiveness emanating from the westerners has, instead, been illustrated by the French: to be too much outward-looking and cosmopolitan could court danger. On the whole, however, as long as trade was thriving, the kingdom would too, and relations were usually peaceful, in contrast to those with the near neighbours with whom war tended to prevail; among these, the Thais had most trouble with the Burmese.

The sacking of Ayutthaya was redeemed by the half-Chinese general *phraya* Taksin who rallied the Thai nation during that time of crisis. For his supplies and to bolster the economy, he needed trade, in which the Chinese dominated. He was also deeply religious and studied meditation to an advanced level. Following an internal political conflict in 1782, general *Chao Phraya* Chakri was chosen king. As the first ruler of the present dynasty, it became his task to reconstruct the Thai state. He was a devout Buddhist, and intent on the firm re-establishment of the Buddhist monkhood, allying church to state and purifying the doctrine. Experts re-edited the Buddhist scriptures and codified the laws. The king's stress on accuracy and rationality stands at the beginning of a reorientation of the intellectual outlook of the Thai elite. The social organization of the realm did not change, though: manpower control and patronage remained at its basis. The new capital reminded of Ayutthaya, not only because of its palaces and temples, but also because of its ethnically highly diversified population. The cosmopolitan awareness of other cultures extended into arts and literature. And while the Burmese remained a threat, they could be held at bay at a time that the monarch succeeded in re-establishing the kingdom's prestige in the region: Chiangmai was incorporated, and Siam's suzerainty was recognized by the northernmost Malay states.

Under his successor, arts, especially literature and woodcraft, flourished. Then, when the third reign set in, we find a fine example of Thai power crisis management: Prince Mongkut did not contend his experienced brother's assumption of the throne, and remained a monk for the whole of his reign. In that position, the priest-prince travelled extensively, seeing for himself how ordinary Thais lived. He also founded the Thammayut sect of the Thai monkhood. At the time of the third king, western imperialism began to assert itself, and Siam's freedom of choice became more and more restricted. Although the monarch still managed to keep his monopolies while refusing to grant more trade to the European nations, he had to allow for the entrance of foreign missionaries. These proved to be a boon to Prince Mongkut who, being the scholar that he was, studied Latin and English, astronomy, science and culture with them. This was a fine preparation for his dealing with 'the challenge of the West' when he succeeded to the throne.

As Rama IV, King Mongkut embarked seriously on a technological and organizational reform based on western models. To this purpose he employed western experts and advisors. One of them, the English governess Anne H. Leonowens, wrote about her experiences. Her books, however, have resulted in several misunderstandings concerning the king's character and reign that were popularized by the musical 'The King and I'. This Hollywood production portrayed the monarch as a 'noble savage' rather than as the scholarly, conscientious and humane man he was.

The far-reaching reforms instituted by his son King Chulalongkorn gave direction and shape to what modern Thailand was to become. He was eager to learn from the West, and kept its colonial encroachment at a distance, even seeking support from Germany and Russia when he visited there. He also travelled in his own country in order to ascertain its social conditions for himself. He abandoned the custom of prostration in the royal presence and, under the influence of Buddhist morality and western examples, he gradually abolished both the corvée system and the institution of slavery, which resulted in a momentous change for Thai society. Simultaneously, all sorts of modernities were introduced, from railways to postal services, but the crucial innovation was the establishment of centralized government. The new administrative system required modernly schooled people, and thus public instruction was introduced, while students were sent abroad to obtain the necessary skills and knowledge. They were supplemented by many foreign advisors. This rapid modernization served to prove to the western colonial powers that Siam had become a 'modern' and 'progressive' country.

The threat from Britain and France was real enough, and the king had to make many territorial concessions, but could preserve Siam's heartland. This was certainly facilitated by the fact that, in 1896, the two imperial powers had agreed to keep the country as a 'buffer zone'. And thus King Chulalongkorn kept Siam an independent, sovereign state, and strove to uphold Thai cultural, artistic and religious values, although its ruling class became partly westernized in outlook. Anyway, by the time he died, he had so many achievements to his credit that he is remembered as The Great Beloved King until this day.

The son who succeeded him was the first king to have been educated abroad. He was an outstanding author, and the first person to try to instil a western-style nationalistic fervour in his subjects; to this purpose he also founded his own paramilitary 'Wild Tiger Corps'. He was determined to uphold traditional Thai values, yet to modernize Siam. He legislated that people use family names, and thus be no different from the western nations. He introduced compulsory primary education, and established the first western-style university. His joining the Allies in the First World War earned the country praise and recognition from the international community.

He was succeeded by his younger brother who came to the throne in a period of economic malaise; consequential budgetary cutbacks resulted in some discontent. He desired to establish Siam as a 'modern' and 'liberal' country with a constitutional system of government. Before he could push his proposals through, matters were taken out of his hand by the putsch of the People's Party in 1932. This latter group was, in the main, composed of men who had been educated abroad; they were supported in establishing their ideas – a formal constitution and a national assembly – by the dissatisfaction caused by the recession.

From 1932 onwards, we witness a contest between the new democratic ideals and the pragmatism of power. Playing with democracy was basically an experiment in which the two groups that held real power, namely, the military and the civilian bureaucratic elite, alternated. Because of its organizational strength, the army held a decisive advantage. So, while Dr Pridi Phanomyong held various offices, he was definitely surpassed by the single-minded nationalist officer Phibun Songkhram when the latter assumed the prime-ministership in 1938. Because of his collaboration with the Japanese, he had to give way to a civilian government, in which Dr Pridi played his part again, in 1944. The unexpected death of the young king turned the tide in favour of Field Marshal Phibun once more.

Under his leadership, parliamentary democracy was established, and students emerged as a powerful political force, contributing to the overthrow of the field marshal, in 1957, by Field Marshal Sarit Thanarat who decidedly initiated the policies of economic development and national security that were continued by his successor, Field Marshal Thanom Kittikachorn. 'In response to unprecedented political confusion caused by the student uprising in 1973, Field Marshal Thanom relinquished the premiership'. All successive prime ministers are then named, yet, political stability, and thus a favourable investment climate, only returned in 1977. In the following years, the problem of insurgency was overcome, and when an elected premier came to office in 1988, Thailand was well on its way to become a NIC (Newly Industrialized Country).

Other developments in the period since the Pacific War are the country's joining the United Nations and its subsequent participation in the Korean War; the assimilation of the Chinese and the diversification of rural and urban economic life; the establishment of the Association of Southeast Asian Nations (ASEAN); and the recent active relations with the countries of Indochina.

The modern monarchy

This chapter not only describes the evolution of kingship to its present, modern shape, but also aims to explain to outsiders why the institution is so important and powerful. It provides a unifying element for the country, and gives all people an intense awareness of being Thai. This has at once much to do with the modern style of leadership of the present king, and with the respect monarchs deserved since the earliest days of Thailand as a nation.

The king is introduced as a man of many talents who was faced by the challenge of how to fashion a concept of kingship that meets the needs of a rapidly changing society. His decision to bring the monarchy into direct contact with the provincial population was a felicitous one, because these people often felt ignored by those in power. And so, since 1955, the king has been on the road, in that way becoming a father-like figure to millions of his subjects, also through providing advice and assistance in solving problems. Especially 'royally-suggested' projects of crop substitution, in the lowlands and in the hills, have proven to be so effective as to result in a Magsaysay Award in 1988. Other successful projects concern the provision of water, reforestation, inland fisheries, and rain-making. In the process, the king has become 'a trusted ally working closely with them in the ancient struggle for a better life', who is revered and the object of deep affection.

The weight of the king's moral leadership is such that it could end political strife and re-establish stability on various occasions. To end the communist insurgency, he was able to inspire confidence in the government. As the patron of religion, he promoted understanding among Muslims and the majority of Thais. The king's compassion contributed to allow sanctuary to the refugees from the Indochinese conflicts. Being a devout Buddhist, the king was ordained a monk in 1956. He presides over the graduation ceremonies at the major universities. Thus, when the population celebrates its king and sings the words of the royal anthem, these are not uttered automatically – such as with other anthems whose lyrics are often archaic or obsolete – but accurately mirror the sentiments of heartfelt veneration the king inspires in his people.

The other members of the royal family also work with unceasing devotion towards the common welfare. The queen travels as much as her husband, and takes a special interest in the welfare of rural women. Her efficacious projects brought her several international awards. She also introduced handicraft training in the camps for Indochinese refugees, and takes a strong interest in the preservation of the natural environment. 'Despite her deep involvement, royal ceremonies, and serving as Colonel-in-Chief, Her Majesty has also found the time to be an attentive mother, passing on to her children the same dedication to public service that has characterized the reign'.

This is followed by a brief portrayal of the crown prince and two princesses. In 1972, the prince was invested to succeed his father. In 1977, he married his royal consort who gave birth to their majesties' first grandchild the next year. In contrast to their brother, the princesses – born in 1955 and 1957 – received their entire education in Thailand, the elder sister receiving a Bachelor's degree from Chulalongkorn University, a Master's from Silpakorn University, and a doctorate from Srinakharinwirot University. In 1978, she 'was bestowed with the new style of title of *Somdech Phra Debharatanarajsuda Chao Fa Maha Chakri Sirindhorn Rathasimagunakornpiyajat Sayamboromrajakumari* in recognition of her services to the throne and to the nation'.

The younger princess 'graduated with a B.Sc. degree from Kasetsart University. A gifted scientist who was awarded the coveted Einstein Gold Medal in 1986, she also has a doctorate in Organic Chemistry from Mahidol University'. All the royal children 'have travelled abroad frequently to represent their country at a variety of ceremonies'. In brief, they 'have always carried out their duties with great efficiency and dedication, lending valuable support to His Majesty in his many tasks of national development'.

There still follows some information about the king's mother and sister, the royal residences, and the royal regalia, among which the 'white' elephants are of particular interest. 'The discovery of a white elephant is considered an auspicious omen, the animals being presented to the monarch so that his reign may prosper. Regarded as an honorary human being, each "significantly auspicious elephant" is awarded a lordly title and thereafter leads a correspondingly lordly life. King Bhumibol Adulyadej has had seventeen white elephants (eleven still living), the most any Thai king has ever owned, which is regarded as an extremely auspicious sign for the success of his reign'.

But more than to anything else, 'this success is due to the dedication and personal example of the ninth Chakri ruler, who in 1987 was popularly acclaimed as a "Maharaj", or King Bhumibol Adulyadej "the Great", by his loyal and loving subjects'. The last page of this chapter shows a picture of their majesties that is approximately a quarter century out of date.

The land and its people

On the verso of that page we find a picture of a new official centre, probably at the edge of a reservoir and having something to do with irrigation, set in rather arid surroundings, although with a good deal of low trees. It could possibly be on the west end of the Ubolrat reservoir. It is subtitled 'A typical village, with easy access to a waterway, near a cool grove of trees surrounded by green rice fields'. As observed before, accuracy is not a hallmark of the publication. On the recto the narrative begins with geographical information, and the enigmatic caption 'Traditional [whatever that means] and modern edifices coexist harmoniously in today's Bangkok'. The country is then presented as a land of plenty with abundant resources, inhabited by a people who regard themselves, whatever their ethnic origins, as Thai, culturally as well as by nationality. An exception to this statement is formed by the Muslims in the south and the hill tribes in the far north.

This information is followed by a lengthy exposition explaining the Thai way of life which has the – usually extended – family at its centre. Growing up in an environment that allows for little privacy, the communal style of life instils a strong sense of social harmony, thus fostering tact, compromise and tolerance. Respect for elders is inculcated at an early age, and soon a child is aware of its role, position and duties in the family hierarchy. This consciousness of relative position also informs the relationships in wider society, and explains the reluctance of young Thais to oppose seniors during their careers in business or government. This means that they find satisfaction in fulfilling the duties and role expectations inherent in their position; in the family setting this includes the responsibility of taking care of the parents in their old age. This is not seen as an onerous duty, because elders are honoured for their wisdom and are the moral teachers of their children's offspring.

Most Thais live in villages. There life centres on the institutions of headmanship, the temple, and the school. The elected headman or -woman preserves the social harmony valued so highly by all Thais, ensuring that nobody will feel cheated or lose face. The temple is the focal point of the village and acts as a major unifying element. Its abbot often enjoys more prestige than the village head, and his advice may be eagerly sought after. Besides, every young man, before he starts his own family, will spend a period of study and reflection in the *wat*; if not, he may have difficulty in finding a marriage partner. The school represents the nation.

Buddhist teachings inspire Thai values, such as consideration, compassion, and the spirit of sacrifice. They are also behind the attitude of peacefully submitting to forces beyond one's control (*mai pen, rai*). Although highly individualistic and resisting regimentation, inner freedom is best maintained by avoiding unnecessary friction; this is expressed in the feeling of *kre:ngcai*, which means an extreme reluctance to impose on or disturb others. In a similar vein, outward expressions of anger, despair, and even enthusiasm are frowned upon. Conversely, serene indifference (*choei*) is considered an important virtue. In this frame of mind, politeness toward outsiders is the norm, while deep friendships are sought among men; such bonds are worth sacrificing for.

Follows a description of the life cycle in the countryside in which words such as gentle, carefree, and responsibilities draw attention, next to the importance of merit making, male-female complementarity, and progeny. Then the seasonal cycle is described, obviously by somebody whose knowledge about the growing season of rice is firmly urban. Emphasis is on Buddhist celebrations, rain-retreat ordinations, merit making, and the solemnity and noisy cheerfulness that accompany all of these. Before the harvest, Loy Krathong is still celebrated in honour of the Goddess of Water. At the end of the cycle, and the beginning of the new, Thai New Year or *Songkra:n* is celebrated, which is again a time of pleasure and merit making.

Fun and natural gregariousness combine in the famed penchant for *sanuk*: the rural Thais are pleasure-seeking. They like to go on a trip, to drink moonshine, to sing and court, to watch performances, and to gamble. Spectacular are the skyrocket festivals, kickball games, kite flying, and Thai boxing in which almost everything is allowed to savage each other. Of all these descriptions of the pleasures of life, most love has been invested in presenting the thrills and wonders of the Thai cuisine – a bias that everybody familiar with Thai food will appreciate. This brings us to the city, and thus, Bangkok. The description would fit any metropolis, from the slums to luxury living, too many cars to overcentralization, urban problems to a cosmopolitan population, cultural manifestations to fast food, stress to the quest for fun.

The section about the city becomes more interesting when it is stated that, also there, Buddhism remains at the centre of the world view and moulds people's attitudes. Yet, 'the stress of Bangkok's fastpaced urban life style' causes alterations. For instance, the temple – where 'monks continue to practise their meditation, apparently undisturbed by the bustling life outside' – is now inaccessible because of the jammed traffic. For this reason, it has been replaced by a room set aside for family Buddha images and a small altar. There people pray and meditate in the morning and evening. Next to these ritual practices, Brahmanic taboos still hold some importance, while astrology and the quest for auspicious days remain as popular as ever. Yet, the importance of family ties weakens when the nuclear household becomes the norm. And because many young women appreciate a job in a factory, domestics become scarce which, in its turn, stimulates the sale of labour-saving appliances that would be considered wasteful only a few years ago. Despite all these apparent changes, traditional [?] Thai values are still strong, indicating the potent strength of the cultural heritage.

Religion, education, and the arts

The short chapter about religion highlights religious diversity, tolerance, and freedom of worship. After all, the king is the upholder of all religions followed by the people. Religion as such is an essential pillar of society: it is the moral force of the Thai family and community. Then, with reference to Buddhism, it is stated that it contributed to the moulding of this freedom-loving, individualistic, and tolerant people. This presumed connexion is repeated in the summary description of the Buddhist teachings.

The observations about education are technical, specifying the types of schools available, administrative structure, and suchlike. The very rapid expansion of the school system and the consequent difficulty to maintain quality education is obvious. In the same vein, the possibility to study for advanced degrees is still limited, with only ten out of seventy-eight universities and colleges offering Master's level courses (1990). Anyway, confirming what we have found about teaching in elementary school, formal education has always been considered as a key to national integrity, development and prosperity.

Arts and crafts are reviewed in a rapid fashion in which the frequent use of the words classical and traditional confuses. Since it also introduces the subject in a comparative perspective – 'not expected to be original or inventive, such as in the West'; 'western style mixed with Thai tradition' – the gist of the Thai genius is not really revealed. The chapter details information about manual arts, painting, sculpture, various crafts, music, theatre, architecture, literature, film making, publishing, the modern media, and so forth. Interesting is that the importance of Chinese potters (Sukhothai), professor Silpa Bhirasri (modern sculpture), and Jim Thompson (reviving the silk industry) are acknowledged next to the stimulating role of the queen in preserving and developing Thai crafts.

The variety of the information is dazzling, and ranges from pop concerts to the highly formalized performances of the Ramayana in which the masks 'perfectly portray the protagonists' personalities'. *Lakhon cha:tri:* is often seen 'at popular shrines where dancers are hired by supplicants whose wishes have been granted to perform for the shrine deity'. The comic folk opera offers social satire, and 'is freighted with outrageous puns and double entendres'. Older Thai architecture combined 'flamboyancy and serenity, perfectly mirroring the Thai soul'. It strives for ornamental decoration and gleaming elegance that are yet joined to a harmonious, polychromatic effect, of which the Temple of the Emerald Buddha is an outstanding example. It embodies the Thai ideal of a skillfully arranged complex imparting reverence and serenity. However, 'traditional Thai architecture declined around 1900 when buildings were increasingly in European styles', and by now buildings resemble those that can be seen in any large city of the world.

The modern literature discussed gives honour of place to the country's social-critical writers, even mentioning the case of an award-winning poet who once fled to the jungle following the violent revolution of October 1976. This contrasts with the sensational tone of the popular press. It reflects a taste in which a newspaper is as much a form of entertainment as it is a vehicle for information. Radio programming is heavily commercialized, although all the 480 stations must transmit the official local and international news. TV fare reflects a fully internationalized style of broadcasting. The great majority of Thai films 'are unashamedly made for entertainment purposes', too. Movies attempting to convey a social message have not been very sucessful.

Government, politics, and international relations

The two short chapters devoted to government, politics and international relations repeat the historical information given in the first to a considerable degree. They also add the idea that the Ratanakosin kingdom was established in Bangkok in 1767. The post-1932 period is the time of the democratic experiment and is witness to a lengthy series of constitutions. Continuous, however, are the stipulation that the king is sacred; the awareness that popularly elected government cannot be established overnight; and the idea many Thais hold that the prime minister is a 'protective figure, possibly due to their tendency to extend family structure into the sphere of government'. This is followed by short descriptions of the branches of government.

It is explained that, whatever the government in the capital, the lives of ordinary people were not affected by the successive shifts in power, and that the idea of constitutional democracy remained alien to the majority. As a result, democracy was in need of reconceptualization in order to adapt it to Thai circumstances. For this reason, the National Peace-Keeping Council (NPKC) took over the administration of the country, in order to strengthen the democratic processes through a revised constitution [the NPKC was in power when the book appeared]. 'Instead of retaining power in their (military) hands, as may occur in other countries', the subsequent government was headed by a civilian and staffed by 'experienced technocrats well-known for their liberal thinking and belief in democracy'.

It is then observed that Thailand's statesmanship has always defied outsiders' predictions. Never colonized, the country was once dubbed 'the next domino to fall'; instead, Thailand has emerged stronger and more prosperous than ever. This capacity to get out of harm's way can largely be attributed to its flexible, dynamic and pragmatic foreign policy. This is illustrated by familiar historical data, and by the post-war period in which the Southeast Asian nations came together, and in which Thailand had to respond with flexibility and purpose to the crises and tensions of its Indochinese neighbours. In spite of these, Thailand, and with it the ASEAN countries, as a high-growth area, has often been cited as a model of economic progress through free enterprise and market-oriented policies.

The economy

As mentioned in passing, forty percent of the book's space has been given to a description of the economy. It is the familiar success story of high growth rates, abundant resources, comparative advantages, and the impressive diversification of productive activities. Expansion in virtually all sectors brings its own problems too though, such as income disparity, the need for conservation of natural resources, the uncertainty of export markets, and insufficient administrative efficiency. Rice cultivation should be modernized, and forest depletion needs to be brought under control, as well as the problem of overfishing. Developing from its agricultural base, the economy's main engine is the manufacturing sector now. Besides, the prospects for industrial exports appear bright, because of the economy's strong and flexible agricultural foundation; close contact with world markets; low-cost skilled labour; the dynamism of the region; the freedom from high levels of protection or rapid inflation. Next to these, the state takes its role in public sector investment very seriously. And so Thailand has emerged from the 1980s as the most promising developing nation of the world, thriving, not only on its exports, tourism, and foreign investment, but also on strong domestic demand and capital outlay. A series of six chapters then describes the various sectors of the economy, detailing their problems and prospects. As can be expected, the subject has been presented in a manner that may stimulate foreign interest to participate in the Thai economic success.

The image

A self-presentation directed at outsiders is, naturally, selective. Moreover, what can be shown is necessarily incomplete. Add to this the expectations and understandings of the one who presents, and those of the audience. All these vicissitudes colour the outcome, and may turn the mix dull or exciting, distorted or blatantly biased.

The book at hand does not resolve such problems. It paints an official image, both with purpose and naivety, that, upon scrutiny, raises many questions. The basic picture is one of a nation united by an old history, presided over by kings who have always been devout Buddhists. These rulers have been revered and, during the present dynasty, have guided the country into modernity. Nowadays, progress is accelerating, and with an expanding and diversifying economy the country may be expected to become part of industrial modernity soon; nevertheless, the agricultural component of the economy is to remain important for a long time to come.

The countryside still inspires the Thai way of life, its values and attitudes. As a result, tradition and religion are alive and well, and form the foundation of life, even in the urban setting of Bangkok. Thus, in spite of apparent westernization, Thai culture is pervaded by its historical continuity. This is borne out by the persistence of basic family values, such as respect for seniors; hierarchy and its related roles and duties; harmony and the avoidance of conflict; and ordination as a monk. This family ethos is projected into wider society, not only in regard to the king as a paternal ruler through whom the Thais experience their unity and identity, but also to the prime minister. This may partially explain the sluggish development of democracy, although the hope is expressed that the current military junta can put it on the right track by rewriting the constitution.

Comments

The primary purpose of the book is to give basic information, and often it achieves this in a fashion that is superior to what we find in the schoolbooks. It is school wisdom, but presented in a more straightforward way that undercuts excessive ideological content. Yet, many idiosyncrasies instilled in the early days surface, simply because they have been taken for granted. As a result, the explanatory value of the book – aiming to introduce *Thailand in the 1990s* – is rather small. For instance, and while I positively appreciate the manner of presentation, the way history is told offers the reader a clear line until the period when planned national development sets in. Then, as happens in the teaching of history at school, the narrative gets flurried and fuzzy. This seems to be the case because the history of the present has not been sufficiently connected to economic development and growth. As a result, the momentous shifts in the national balance of power, and its effects on government, are neglected. This means that no basis is laid on which to build an understanding of the time immediately ahead.

Thailand has experienced distinctive displacements in its political centre of gravity. The palace dominated until 1932; since then, the bureaucracy and the military became the main – often contending – foci of power. This much the text explains. The subsequent ascendency of business, as of the 1960s, and the rise of an increasingly influential Sino-Thai class of economic bosses and managers – a class meanwhile fully integrated in national life – remains totally unexposed. The comeback of the palace as an important player in national affairs is, again, clear enough, but the role of the economy is not – and yet it seems that attracting interest and investment from abroad is among the very aims of the publication. Even at the time of its writing, it must have been apparent that, in spite of the NPKC, the importance of the part the military plays was waning. The bureaucracy too, though powerful, was not the real leader any more. Of course, the 'bureaucratic polity' has not been dismantled, but its sway over a 'pariah' business class is a thing of the past.[1] Chatichai's cabinet brought the economic establishment to the fore and clarified the pattern of present power relationships. Thus, while the temporary rise of the NPKC may be seen as an attempt to discipline the forces nurtured and released by the boom, it remains a flaw that the book neglects the political dimensions of the current developments.

In other aspects as well the text seems to dwell in the past rather than to inaugurate the 1990s. Thailand is presented as a mainly an agricultural country firmly based in village culture. While there is no disputing that over sixty percent of the people still work in the primary sector, time in the countryside has not been frozen. Spectacular developments in that sector illustrate the economic side of this. Such changes, though, together with the intensification of communications and administrative penetration deeply affect the countryside. Migration, often seasonal, leaves villages deserted but for the elderly and the very young. Dependency on the urban and international economy changes all expectations. Examples from the city – also spread by formal education – 'urbanize' village culture. These, and many other developments – the rape of the countryside for the benefit of the capital for one – totally invalidate the picture of the village way of life presented.

On the one hand, it seems as if the authors read too much Bang Chan-inspired literature. The strange mix of Buddhism, individualism, consideration, and indifference that that generation of anthropologists concocted in their speculations about life in that particular village on the outskirts of Bangkok in convenient

---

[1]   The related ideas of bureaucratic polity and pariah entrepreneurs refer to Fred W. Riggs's theory, elaborated in *Thailand: The Modernization of a Bureaucratic Polity.* Honolulu: East-West Center Press, 1966.

commuting distance from the Erawan Hotel,[2] has found its way straight into the book's narrative. According to the authors, the mix has much to do with Buddhism, even to the extent that saying 'never mind' is attributed to religion. Besides, religious practice also inspires life in town where monks meditate in temples and the laity in a special room at home. In this way, family values remain as taught in school; other 'values' are brought in line with an idealized practice of Buddhism; and life on the ground simply disappears. This obscuring of everyday existence by the blinders of Buddhism and idealization make the book – in places – read more like a tourist brochure than as a serious introduction to things Thai.

It is facile to state that Buddhism pervades all aspects of Thai life. The reverse of this statement is equally true. It may be taken as a matter of course, but what does it explain? Institutional Thai Buddhism is omnipresent indeed. Why is that so? What do the Thais have their religion for? Going over the various observations with a fine-tooth comb, a well-informed reader may find a few clues, but the book has not been written for somebody who knows Thailand already. The self-presentation it contains is addressed to outsiders, and thus kings are devout; religion must be kept in orderly condition; merit making is important; images are venerated; more and more temples are built; horoscopes are cast; the sacredness of rulers inspires awe and respect; royal ritual predicts the harvest. Is this so because all Thais share a deeply religious nature? As far as the authors go, the answer is apparently positive.

In the chapter about elementary school we also found a careful editing of religious information. The most common practices went unmentioned. Here, at least, shrine deities answer the vows of supplicants; sacredness seems to be tangibly embodied; astrology leads to auspicious dates. But then it stops. No word has been

---

[2] The study by Herbert P. Phillips contains the finest representation of this line of thinking. See his *Thai Peasant Personality. The Patterning of Interpersonal Behavior in the Village of Bang Chan.* Berkeley and Los Angeles: University of California Press, 1965.

spent on the omnipresent guardian spirits, or on the new Buddhist sects; the currently popular cult of King Chulalongkorn has not been mentioned; charismatic monks and their amulets do not exist. Yet, a cursory look at such things may reveal us something about the importance and use of religion in Thailand. Why is the king worshipped in a religious sense? Why is his predecessor, the fifth king, so popular now? Some hold the latter to be the incorporation of the *Saya:mthe:wa:thira:t*, that is, the tutelary spirit of the royal house and realm.

What should have been explained to the foreign audience is the importance of founding fathers as such. Their merit not only concerns the fact of initiating, but as parents they continue their care. Their merit remains as a protective force that can be activated; it translates as sacredness. In other words, ancestors should not only be worshipped and gratefully remembered, they also have the ability to protect. They act as tutelary spirits whose power can be invoked. As the father of the modern Siam that was to become Thailand, the invocation of the fifth king as a protector in these times of accelerated and confusing 'modernization' is only logical. Perhaps it comes so 'naturally' that the authors fail to explain such basics and take it for granted that others share in this thinking. After all, the merit, the *bunkhun* of seniors is the very gist of early socialization, and this doctrine is expanded to the highest person of the realm who so becomes the *mingkhwan*, the spiritual protector of it, incorporating a mother-like sacredness that should be revered above all else.[3]

These attributes of parenthood and kingship should have been explained in some depth and, as observed in passing, the coexistence of Buddhist and Brahmanic concepts of rulership would have offered a rewarding starting-point for such a discussion. It would have strengthened the other information given

---

[3] For theorizing that it is the mother who, because of her sacrifice, is the very symbolic representation of protective goodness, also because fathers, and other males, are too closely associated with amoral power, see Mulder, *Inside Thai Society*, chapters 2, 4 and 5.

about the monarchy. This hints, perhaps, at the general weakness the Thais have in elucidating things Thai. In the exposition of the so-called Buddhism-inspired values we almost seem to be reading the – foreign researched and written – anthropological literature of the 1950s and early 1960s. The Brahmanism-inspired – or are they just Thai? – values of hierarchy, ethics of place, and patronage have been mentioned, but their pervasiveness, and 'opposition' to the so-called Buddhist ones, receive scant attention other than the observation that juniors are very reluctant to contradict seniors. The other illustrative comment on patronage, namely, that the way the prime minister is seen as a patron shows the 'extending of family stucture into the sphere of government', may also be interpreted as a clever euphemism to describe the practice of blatant godfatherism.

Religion is conspicuously paraded through the book's noneconomic chapters, but it is taken as a matter of course, and sometimes confused with idealized Buddhism. From olden times onwards kings are said to be devout and to promote religion. Why is that so? What does 'devotion' mean? It transpires, in the description of the first reign, that religion is an instrument of statecraft, yet, the overall presentation is such as to suggest that it equates with ethics. This fully neglects the central fact of all religion, namely, that it is a relationship with power: with the power to bless, to protect, and to win wars. It is the source of potency of kings, of the realm, of monks, and even of ordinary people. And thus the one-sided interpretation leads astray, at the same time that the secularization of current life is covered up by the information that people meditate and pray at home. The last observation is another slip of the Thai mind. Most readers of English who have an inkling of Buddhism think to know that there is nothing to pray for and nobody to pray to in the Buddhist religion; so, how come Thais pray? To whom and for what reason? To shrine deities, or the Goddess of Water? Further questions are raised by the summary explanation of Buddhism itself, in which a person is said to persist through many lives, until reaching perfection when, through Nirvana, 'a person simply is, yet is

completely at one with his surroundings'. As is often the case, it is
to be preferred to have no knowledge at all than to have too little
of it.

Another thing that has to be taken at its face value is the idea
of the ancestral heritage. Buddhism, Brahmanism, and so on, are
said to be important elements of Thai culture, together with the
original Thai heritage. As with comparable statements found in the
schoolbooks, one would like to know what is meant here.
Although I, as an anthropologist, have speculated about these
things,[4] and even would defend that such a heritage pervades all
aspects of Buddhism in Thailand, I still hope that Thais will learn
to explain themselves to themselves by reflecting upon and
researching themselves. Just mobilizing 'hierarchy' and 'patronage'
as explain-alls – such as we found among the reasons presented
for the vicissitudes of democratic development – is not enough.
Such facts of life, and the practical and psychological dependency
they often seem to imply – rather contrary to self-confident
individualism – need extensive elaboration. Unfortunately, serious
reflection is not popular, and most people are just content to hide
reality behind appearances. And thus the National Identity Office
creates a pleasant appearance, its plausibility, or lack thereof,
notwithstanding.

An interesting aspect of 'pleasant appearances' is to label them
'traditional'. Throughout the book, the word has been used
umpteen times in connexion with an equally vast array of
phenomena. For instance, 'the traditional dress has been adopted
as the unofficial national costume'. Then, for women, the
boromphima:n style of dress is described, while the accompanying
pictures show the *cakri:* variant. These very successful innovations,
promoted by the queen, antedate the 'traditional dress for men',
that is, 'the shirt given by the king'-style that enjoyed some
popularity in the 1980s. Floats with many beautiful women are also
said to be traditional, while 'the most glorious battles in traditional

---

[4]   Mulder, *Inside Thai*, chapters 2-9.

wars took place on elephant back'. 'Traditional commercial interaction relied mainly on water', and even the nineteenth century administrative bodies, en vogue before the western-style ministries were created, are said to be traditional. Besides, all kings, from the fourth of the current dynasty onwards, are said to have upheld traditional Thai values. Again, some reflection and illustrations could have clarified much; now information is rarefied instead by using a senseless epithet. Ancestors and Thai traditions need explanation; these are not matters of course.

A last, and delightfully Thai idiosyncracy, is the statement about the masks that 'perfectly portray the protagonists' personalities'. This – for the western reader – baffling piece of information highlights the Thai tendency to take presentation very seriously, the well-trained person demonstrating his *bukkhalikapha:p* by his demeanour and graceful comportment. As we have noted, the school is expected to contribute to this, to make people move elegantly and to be in control of their physical selves. That is *bukkhalikapha:p*, the mastery of self that is taught under hygiene and physical education. The point is thus that this type of mastery of self, of presenting one's social mask, is far from what a westerner, familiar as he is with popular psychology, would call personality. Perhaps the mask merely portrays the protagonist's role, in the same way as a temporary ordainant should present himself as a genuine monk.

Chapter 8

CONSTRUCTING
THE PUBLIC WORLD:
THE DISCOURSE OF THE 1990S

The modern public world arises when it has been animated by
the opinions of people who press for having a say in public affairs.
In this sense, the modern Thai public world emerged only
recently: it first came to the fore in 1932. The people who
appropriated the public world at that time, who filled it with their
discourse, had been nurtured by the state; they had been trained
to staff the bureaucracy and the military. Meanwhile, we have
come a long way in the further development of the public world,
very much so because of the expansion and diversification of the
economy; the arising of a Sino-Thai class of businesspeople and
professionals fully integrated in urban life; the explosion of
education; and the spread of the media. Besides, the global flow of
ideas exerts a powerful influence on public discourse. Even so, the
very recentness of the modern public world in Thailand
inadvertently causes its discourse to still be strongly informed by
lifeworld reasoning; such can only be expected. The familial view
is promoted and reinforced by the state through its influence over
the primary and junior high school curricula, and by the
patronage-promoting political process.

The input from the lifeworld

While the experience of being born and early nurture may be rather similar for small children the world over, early socialization is not. What is similar concerns the experience of dependency on grown-up people who are literally big in relation to the child. One could say that in one's early years hierarchy comes naturally. The interpretation of this situation is different among cultures, however. In the Thai setting, being born means the gift of life, and dependency means the gift of nurture, and thus the arising of debts of gratitude. This gives a strong moral flavour to hierarchy. Inequality is not only natural; it is moral too. This type of thinking is subsequently applied to all sorts of relationships, at least as long as they are personalized. After all, one can only be put under a debt of gratitude by receiving a benefit from somebody; at that point, one has been obliged to that person.

In the family, and later at school, this reasoning is drilled in. In the hierarchical setting of its experience, the child knows that it will receive, and that it has to reciprocate. In line with the fact of inequality, the resulting give-and-take will consist of unequal exchanges. Nurture is reciprocated by honour, teaching by tractability. All of these constitute obligations, of givers and receivers, that are inherent in their relative positions and roles. It places seniors in positions of honour, and juniors under the obligation to respect these. This also entails that there is a strong tendency to equate persons with their relative position, and a strong sense of the role and obligations that belong to it.

We have noted the heavy emphasis primary school teaching puts on all this, and further how social studies at the junior secondary level keep personalizing the world the child lives in, through a certain interpretation of national history and the patrimonial state, and by collapsing the ideas of the nation and wider society. All the king's subjects, at basis, constitute a family. Its hierarchical order, and the consciousness of role and duty, are a safeguard against conflict. To put it otherwise, if everybody behaves according to his position, society will be in harmony; it will be family-like.

These interpretations have their effect on the ideas of personhood and ethics. The person is first and foremost seen as a member of a family, of a group that spells identity and that defines the relative position and all that follows from it. The reputation of the group is a person's reputation, which thus needs to be jealously guarded. A good means to do so is to be conscious of role and duties, of appearance and presentation. Therefore, persons need to be filled with such consciousness. They need the social rules and the religious precepts in order to be fully human, to be cultured persons as opposed to being part of the jungle. Socialization and formal education aim at handing down the rules by which to go; they offer the individual the opportunity to appropriate them. Apparently, ethics lie outside the person, and need to be learned together with the way in which persons should present themselves. As a result, elementary education places a heavy emphasis on the teaching of moral rules and physical presentation.

As long as individuals are enclosed in the hierarchically structured group, they are tractable. As soon as they break free, they become a danger to 'harmony'. Driven by egoistic motives, their personal sense of direction cannot be trusted. They need to be kept in place by *The Treasure of the Gentleman*,[1] that is, the ethical rules they have appropriated. Somehow, individuals are not thought of as capable of being their own guide, of taking their own moral decisions and, when out of sight, their respect for the laws of the land must be doubted. Besides, what is the relationship of the latter – abstract as they are – to a life imagined in the personalized terms of a communal setting?

This lifeworldly conceptualization is emphasized throughout the school career. It results in the perception of society as a moral construct, and thus in the view of the individual as being

---

[1]   This is a reference to *Sombat khô:ng phu:di:*, the classical primer on good manners that Thais, until twenty years ago, were brought up with.

encompassed by and subordinated to family, group, community, nation, state, society, all of which are thought to equate with and to substitute for each other. The subordination is substantiated by the roles and duties that follow from the relative position and the demand to recognize one's debts of gratitude. This moral thinking implies hierarchical order, and in such a structure all signs of 'individualism' are suspect.

In a small, surveyable setting, this type of moralism probably makes sense. Yet, Thai society is not quite surveyable these days. That does not preclude the moral model from being the measure of all things. Thus, in the current public discourse we hear the voices of many respected luminaries who propagate moral solutions to social ills. Often they idealize the past, or life in the countryside. They speak a language most Thais understand 'intuitively'. Yet, as soon as the moralistic drum is beaten, its dissonance with the conditions of wider society stands out, not only because person-centred moral measures are imposed on society-in-the-abstract, but also because of a serious source of abuse that is rooted in the same lifeworld construction, namely, hierarchy and the privileges inherent in inequality. Interestingly, the moralists severely criticize the abuse of power to promote individual ends at the expense of the public interest, but they fail to see that the remedies they advocate belong to the private world and rely on seeing the country as one big family.

These days the lifeworlds of all the people in the kingdom are deeply affected by forces beyond their control. The great players in this encompassing social system are the state and the economy, two abstract fields of power whose institutions affect each and every denizen of the country. Besides, work, the sale of produce, the pursuit of advanced education, travel, and so on, also make people operate in the sphere of society. There they are anonymous to each other, and because of it, everybody pursues his own interests. Anonymity also results in equality and, in the abuse of power. The experience of society individualizes, sets people free from the moral constraints of the lifeworld. This, in turn, problematizes a person's identity, as we shall see later.

In brief, it seems that lifeworld reasoning plays an important role in the perception of society, at the same time that it is a bad guide through the – urban – experience of anonymity and self-centred pragmatism. Its popularity in the public discourse founds on the fact that it provides the only native moral model available, and that other ways of reasoning about wider society, for instance, in terms of legality and the moral equality of citizens, are very foreign indeed. This is not to say that the latter do not play their part in the public discourse. We found that they figure prominently in the print media, and they were even alluded to at school. Yet, such ideas are not widely shared, let alone well understood by the Thai public. We have noted already that the teaching of the foreign concepts concerned is very defective. Yet, the state was doing something about that – so, let us scrutinize what.

Input from the state and politics

Politics and the state are the subjects par excellence of the public debate; they also provide many of the important inputs. They are keen on influencing public opinion; they need a measure of legitimation and acceptance. Because of their power, they also have the means to do so, yet they fall far short of being able to cover up all that is rotten in the realm. The interplay of power and morality causes confusion and contradictions everywhere, also in Thailand.

This is apparent in current educational practice. Through its school system, the state has the means to exert a powerful hold on the minds of the young. As observed, the school is there to produce moral people (*khon di:*), 'people the nation desires'. To do this, it propagates the moral model that founds on the family, and projects it into the wider society which, in Thailand, is easy to do because of the monarchy. By promoting it as the moral heart of the country, the idea of nation as a family under fatherly guidance acquires a compelling logic.

311

From the first to the ninth grade, the model remains intact. Then, in senior high school, variations are introduced, but they fail in their confrontation with the moral paradigm. Democracy, constitutional rights, the rule of law, such cannot be explained, or be brought in harmony with the ideal lifeworld construction taught, because they are based on premises that are alien to it. Besides, what democracy is for, what it is meant to achieve, cannot be fitted into the prevailing social imagination. This may also clarify why the so-called scientific explanations in the higher social studies course are so awkward and devoid of theoretical consistency. This field of problems needs some elaboration.

As we argued, the moral ideas Thais are intimate with revolve around the axis of hierarchy. Respect for seniority, gratefulness for benefits, and recognition of obligation are its cardinal values. These contrast starkly with doctrines that hold that all men are born equal, have rights vested in their being human, and should be judged according to the same standards. Such ideas of moral equality and the rights they entail – balanced by the idea of citizen's reponsibility for the public interest – are extremely difficult to imagine on the basis of Thai experience. Besides, the way society is understood, is personal, and thus experiential, taking the ideal of the family as its model. As a result, it is very hard to imagine society-in-the-abstract; school even impairs the possibility to do so. Democracy then becomes a way to rule the family, which is rather preposterous, even in the modern West. In Thailand this is institutionalized in the mantra-like expression 'the system of democratic government which has the king as its head'.

The country is seen as family, as nation, as a social unit that is functionally integrated, and in which differences are merely complementary. Conversely, democracy has been designed to deal with the fact that people, individually and as social categories, have conflicting ideas and interests. As contending partners for the resources of their shared common weal, they have to come to terms with each other on the basis of the idea that all are invested with the same rights and meet as equal partners.

Put in another way, the manner in which most Thais want to see their social surroundings – personally and functionally – prevents them from taking a distanced, a scientific perspective that reasons in abstract relationships, institutions, and social forces. Such sociological reasoning has slowly become part of western culture, at least since the Enlightenment; it exists in juxtaposition with the familial, and hierarchical, moral model that applies to the private world in the West too. The public world, however, must be seen in abstract terms, and given moral content by the practice of democracy and the majesty of the law. So far, the Thai experiment with British-style democracy has not resulted in making it imaginable in these original terms. As a godfather and money democracy, it remains anchored in hierarchy and patronage; its most salient feature is the fierce competition for power and resources that it has difficulty to regulate.

These qualities of practical Thai statecraft pervade the modern public world in which economic forces seem to prevail. Although the school does not really train its students to come to intellectual grips with this vast realm surrounding private experience, it does prepare them – inadvertently? – to join the rat race that moves the outer world. The school is not just a moral backwater filled with mantra-like knowledge, but also reflects social reality in that it is a highly competitive social environment that goads its students into passing first on their exams. In doing this, it stimulates the behaviour sociologists expect to find in anonymous society: at school, students will primarily take care of their own interests.

As a result, the experience of schooling itself already invalidates the moral model school propagates. It equips students with a set of admonitions that may be useful in their private worlds, but that leaves them without good ideas about how to comprehend society and operate in it. By the very idea that nation equates with family, the school trains for subjectship rather than citizenship. It does not prepare for moral autonomy, social responsibility, and independent decision making. As a result, the students are morally abandoned in the public world, and quite a few get lost. Whether they will all go the way of 'Botan's victims is to be doubted. Thanks goodness, many people survive the restrictions of formal education without losing themselves; that they will open out like *Stunted's* Chom can only be hoped for.

It is not only through the school that the state sends its messages. It uses its influence over the broadcast media to propagate its image of the nation. Yet, the same media, and the press, also send messages about practical politics with which every adult is familiar. They show the pragmatism of power, the expediency of political decision making, the manipulation of the law, and suchlike, and the resulting image is a far cry from the moral nation. The state is clearly double-faced, and its most blatant expressions sprout from the popularly elected politicians. Next to these, many of the instruments of state have an unenviable reputation: the police is seen as corrupt and arrogant; the land department connives with land grabbers; the forestry department squanders the wealth of the nation; there is no end to such practices, and everybody knows. Practical politics is now mostly in the hands of those in business suit, although the boys in uniform still play their part. After all, they command a lot of force.

The flavour of politics is personal, not programmatic. It is commanded by godfathers, no matter from what sphere, whether business, the military, or the bureaucracy. These people run their fiefs with impunity. The fun is to see them clash. Their direct input in the public discourse is, expectably, their rhetoric and their off-the-cuff remarks. The first gives rise to a pervading sense of cynicism regarding politics, while the latter merely confirm that politics is a power struggle that no moral arguments can cover up. Still, there is a moral instance, the very symbol of the state and high above the partiality of everyday politics that may arguably provide some extra room for politicians to do as they please. Only on the rarest occasions will they be admonished by the king.

If the palace once was the incorporation of the state, it now is at once its symbol and one of the important players. It reinforces the moral element in the public discourse, and lends convincing legitimacy to the edifice of state. So, while it may be argued that the performance of the actual politicians does not lead to their moral legitimacy, they can somehow operate under the cover of the most legitimate symbol of the nation. It gives them breathing space and elbow room, because part of the public gaze is deflected by the high hope it cherishes: as long as the king is there, we are protected; with his presence, nothing can really go wrong.

Associated with the state of old, and part of the art of government, we find institutional religion. It is needed for blessing, ritual, and ceremony; it has a powerful symbolic value: to make things Thai, merit making and the blessing of monks are necessary. This is so at the level of the state, and in everyday life. They are at the heart of what is called 'our beautiful and good customs, traditions, and culture'. Yet, omnipresent as it is, the institutional religious contributions to the public discourse are negligible. The establishment is ornamental to Thai life, and when it presents itself as less decorous, it causes irritation because religion is being defiled. When such happenings are publicized, some people are quick to accuse the newspapers of damaging Buddhism. In other words, institutional religion remains a taboo; it does not invite debate.

This is not to say that there is no religious input in the public discourse. There is, but it does not originate from the state and its establishments. The religious contributions to the social debate come from civil society itself, from new urban middle-class people in search of a moral format, for identity in the city's rat race, for consolation, security and new sources of blessing. Of course, in everybody's quest for playing it safe, the old religious establishment remains the overwhelmingly important source of auspiciousness, and many prominent people publicly seek the blessing of reputed monks. They, and many other people, make lavish contributions to the well-being of institutional religion, and this merit making visibly extends the current building boom into the temple compounds. Particularly interesting are the new dwellings and offices of famed abbots and other charismatic advisors. Their air-conditioned luxury reflects the prosperity of the new middle and upper classes. Thus, routine religious practice remains ornamental, and the quest for blessing and advice is still going strong. Yet, that is it. The inputs into the public discourse tend to come from certain outstanding monks, representing themselves, and from the laity. We therefore had better discuss the latter when we turn to civil society.

The state preaches moralism, practises the pragmatism of power, and promotes national development. While it controls a vast apparatus to diffuse its moral messages, discussion about the exercise of power is shared among the instruments of state, elected politicians, and the general public. The origin of the modern Thai state is located in the fact of centralization; in the concentration of power in the capital at the expense of the relative autonomy of the provinces. Since all resources seem to be sucked to or dominated by the centre, provincial interests increasingly demand a voice in the debates. They express frustration with their colonial status *vis-à-vis* the powers that be, and press for a say over what they consider their affairs. Well, democracy has not advanced far enough that influential politicians in the capital are impressed by such demands. In their minds, centralization comes 'naturally'. Consideration of these topics steadily surfaces in parliament and in the press, in proposals for constitutional amendments, and in the platform of the Phalang Tham political party. The very constitution of the state is an important point of public debate.

The state means power, and the scramble for its exercise in an open system is intense. Much of that power is vested in the bureaucracy, other segments of it are in the hands of the military, and these days the political cum business establishment seems to hold the state hostage. That power corrupts is a truism familiar to the Thais, yet, in their cultural milieu it is not only expected, but power, arguably, also gives rights, or privileges at least. And if power is protective, it even deserves to be rewarded. Needless to say – the exchanges in the newspapers are clear enough – this is an endless subject of debate. To clarify it, the book *Corruption and Democracy in Thailand* [2] has been written. This study is

---

[2]   Pasuk and Sungsidh, *Corruption.*

fascinating, because it must oscillate between the extreme positions of might is right – such as the provincial grandees of yore collecting taxes as they saw fit – and rigid moralism that disallows for any material reward for services rendered. This last position is untenable in the Thai setting that places so much weight on *bunkhun*, gratitude, and the obligation to reciprocate. On the other hand, the exercise of power sheerly to rob the other blind is not quite acceptable either.

According to the study referred to, corruption has – in relative terms – not increased since the regimes of the marshals. On the contrary, the authors estimate that the military loot was considerably more than the percentage flowing into private pockets these days. I do not know how to judge the subject. The practice needs to be extended by the state-engendered idea of development as desirable, and the political power to award cronies rents that are in fact public resources. This exercise of power, namely, privatizing what belongs to the country, can also be seen as a corrupt practice, yet it is glossed over as contributing to development. In brief, the culturally acceptable compounds with ideas of privilege and right; the unconditional acceptance of development as desirable; and rent-seeking. All of these fuel what is modernly known as *khô:rapchan*. It promises to be a hot topic – and a political weapon – that will move public opinion for a long time to come.

Input from the economy

The above discussion demonstrates some aspects of the interface of the state and the economy. The practice of state-stimulated development has given rise to new middle classes, to the phenomenal expansion of formal education, to a new urban environment, to the very existence of a modern public world and the discourse that fills it. During the recent boom years, however, it seems as if the economy has taken over the role of prime mover of things.[3] It is the expediency of business that fuels politics, and businessmen-politicians direct the state to an important degree. They stand in no contradiction to the country's profesional bureau- and technocrats who revel in Thailand's winning of NIC status, and who sometimes handsomely profit by this. In this evolution, people, culture, and society have changed. Thailand not only became an urban-centred polity, but urban culture imposed itself on the country as well. The rustic rural and stately royal images the country once had have been thoroughly invalidated; they have become legendry propagated by the National Identity Office, and are still regularly celebrated as identity-confirming ritual.

The predominance of economic considerations, and the subjugation of the rural and national hinterland to urban interests has called forth a good deal of reaction. Farmers try to protest, all the way up to the prime minister's doorstep; they are supported by students and other social activists. A lively NGO scene has grown. Calls for administrative decentralization and local autonomy have become louder. Human-rights advocacy has become respectable. The prestige of government per se has been slipping. Criticism of politicians, the police, the judiciary, corruption, and bureaucratic complacency, has been on the increase. In brief, there is no shortage of topics to fill the pages and the public mind. It is not all neatly classified, but how could that be in the disorderly, hectic, and often stressful environment of the metropolis?

It is a fact, though, that economic growth has resulted in many issues worth worrying about. Income distribution has become extremely skewed. The rape of the environment goes on unabated. Pollution caused by the building boom, the traffic, and industrial waste has assumed staggering proportions. Yet, the protection of people and environment is neglected. Often it is legislated. Laws by themselves, though, do not compel. If they are not enforced, nobody is protected. Priority is given to economic growth, to an elite which grows richer – and more powerful. Their might spells

---

3   Pasuk Phongpaichit and Chris Baker, *Thailand's Boom!* Chiang Mai: Silkworm Books, 1996.

their right. Their patronage means protection. To sail in their wake is the way up for the new middle classes. The protestations at the fate of those left behind, of those suffering and exploited, are weak, not well organized, only occasionally successful. So, while it cannot be denied that all the problems resulting from rapid economic growth are talked about, that they have a place in the public discourse, there are also many other topics in urban culture that deflect attention away from them. Besides, paying lip service to problems, initiating legislation, publicizing concern – all of these show that one is worldly, that one has a heart, that one is sensible and, that one trims one's sails according to the wind. After such demonstrations, most people will go on with the business at hand. Is it indifference, or the deep-seated conviction that opposing superior power is senseless anyway? Apart from this, the seats of power have become conveniently abstract, are hard to pinpoint personally, as they appear as companies, as growth, as desirable development. To oppose the economic juggernaut may even be seen as unpatriotic.

All these things are pointed out in the public discourse, and some people strongly champion the cause of the law. Yet, how to practically apply the law to a society organized on the principles of hierarchy, privilege, and patronage? Does it make any sense to accuse the police of neglect of duty? Other voices in the discourse appeal to morality, or advocate retreating from the madness of modernity. They want to reinstate community where it has gone lost in the process of becoming society. Sociologically seen, anonymous society has expanded very rapidly, throwing individuals back upon themselves, while overwhelming – and invalidating – the still prevailing, community-based social imagination. Even at school it is not realized that the coming into existence of society necessitates a new social imagination if it is to be mastered. Social reality has simply outgrown the way people are taught to think. This is also reflected in the public discourse in which only a few intellectuals represent 'sociological' positions, that is, identify the social forces at work and mull over their effects on individuals and society.

319

We noted in passing that such luminaries do not think highly of the so-called Asian values and the enlightened patrimonial semi-dictatorship they imply. While it comes close to what the school teaches, they – and with them, most Thais – are realistic enough to know that it does not work so pleasantly, and their historical experience of statute labour and slavery can only confirm this. Hierarchy is motivated to maintain itself and its inherent privileges. It seeks power, and finds it in the economy. It defends itself against all comers. So much is abundantly clear. Yet, when the same modern intellectuals then pontificate on the rule of law, the implementation of human rights, the marvels of Westminster-style democracy, and suchlike, in order to bring society under control, they basically advocate things that run counter to the short history of modern Thai society.

The idealistic arguments basically belong to an earlier period when the country was run either by the palace, or by the bureaucracy and the military. These arguments relate to the desire to be emancipated from paternalistic tutelage, and recognize a measure of individual autonomy and responsibility. These reflect a certain spirit of optimism: individuals have the potential to grow into responsible citizens; together, these can make society a better place. What was first expected of budding citizens and a programmatic, constructive way of dealing with society – expectations that fuelled the democratic period of 1973-76 – is now expected to be accomplished by the economic machine. If the economy is good, so will society be. In the process, it also frees the individual, perhaps not totally from paternalistic tutelage – after all, society remains a structure of unequal relationships – but at least from much social control and, because of money and urban anonymity, from an overdose of inequality.

'Breathing urban air sets free' or so the European expression runs, and whether that is applied to the medieval municipality where one was free from the impositions of the nobility or the modern metropolis, the idea seems to hold its truth. The modern Thai city, though, is not the product of emancipation and the evolution towards citizenship. It rather is the creation of a modern economy that was originally the exclusive preserve of outsiders to society at large, to wit, the nobility, western enterprises, and the Chinese. Its subsequent recent whirlwind growth to an economy-driven free-for-all has set individuals free indeed: urban anonymity equalizes, and money gives one the possibility to do as one pleases. In Thailand freedom has come as a consequence of urbanization and economic expansion.

This growing economy is the dominant factor in the explanation of current cultural developments. It stimulates the criticism and the moralism we found in the public discourse. It also drives people to be consumers and to assert their individuality in a wide variety of ways. Let us concentrate for a few moments on the first, on consuming. In the Introduction we noted Habermas's opposition between citizens who are critically participating in, and the modern public which merely consumes, its culture. In scrutinizing the newspaper and the university curriculum, we also found that there are people who critically reflect. This should not blind us to the fact, however, that the latter are a small minority, and that the modern public is primarily made up of consumers; they even consume the public discourse as a form of entertainment.

In the Introduction it was suggested that with so many people consuming modernity, they were doing little to invigorate the public debate. Possibly true, but there is more to say about this. For one, the discourse draws in the messages of the globalized media; the messages of advertizing; the discussion of national and international sports; the gossip about the latest episodes of the popular soaps; the comments on the exploits of singers and stars; the evaluation of cars and other gadgets. The importance of these preoccupations on which a whole lifestyle industry thrives, such as the cursory inspection of any news-stand shows, distracts from the more high-minded messages about the condition of Thai society. The latter are noted, but do not sink in. They somehow become part and parcel of the fleeting fads and fancies that fill the public world, and that do not stimulate reflection, let alone sincere involvement or commitment to a cause. In other words, the current fascination with consumption, with the celebration of individual economic success, with the shaping of modernity may dull the public discourse, may marginalize it because these motivations lead, on the one hand, to social inattentiveness and political indifference, and, on the other, to a preoccupation with the own particular affairs. As long as the economy produces purchasing power, it is self-legitimizing, and with it, politics will just remain a spectator sport.

This, in turn, results in a largely unrestricted free space for politicians and businessmen to operate in. Their expedient decisions become 'policy', their prosperity the measure of national success. In short, the economy impels Thai society into the future, and such a development is hardly hemmed in by legal restrictions, and considerations of social justice and income distribution. As Pasuk and Baker suggest, the boom seems to be out of control; in order to sustain it, it may need disciplining.[4] This is possibly the greatest problem Thailand faces right now. It surfaces in the social discourse as issues concerning the environment, the deprivation of the livelihood of villagers, the arrogance of power, the self-centredness of business, the problems of crime, poor living conditions and health, and further worthy causes. These are aspects and effects of the boom. To address the boom itself as the problem is probably more than can be hoped for right now.

Civil society

While the state could possibly once impose its legitimacy by presenting itself as the embodiment of moral order, it now needs to work on its legitimation by producing a steady stream of propaganda and by covering up the more unsavoury aspects of the exercise of power. Yet, it cannot fool all people all the time, and so it has to play an active role in the public discourse. The economy contrasts with the state. It does not promote moral

---

4   Pasuk, *Boom!*: 241.

causes. As the engine of modern society it legitimizes itself through its success, through the idea of progress. It imposes such ideas on the discourse, and needs to actively agitate to keep people believing in its supreme importance. And, as people know of old, when money speaks, morality and wisdom keep silent.

Attempts at legitimation, from the state, the economy, or wherever, become necessary when a critical public arises. As an active component of civil society, this public has its doubts, wants to know, wants questions answered. Its members do not take school knowledge for granted; they apply the moral measures the state proposes to the working of the state itself; they are equivocal about the blessings of progress; they propose laws and regulations. In brief, they voice criticism, dissect certain pieces of propaganda and, above all, they analyse and comment upon politics. It is civil society creating public opinion, evaluating the social condition, introducing new ideas into the debates. The question is, how much weight does it carry? Does it influence the course of the nation? Is it going to make Thailand a more pleasant, a more liveable place than it has come to be?

Civil society arose in pace with the urban modernity some of its members question and confront. They fill the public discourse with their opinions, and it is the debates they engender that animate the modern public world. For many, though, that world is lively enough as long as it is filled with consumer-oriented messages and pastimes, with the fashions and fads of modernity. The latter do not struggle with the realities of their society; they just live them. Sometimes they feel addressed by political issues, may even attend a demonstration, then go home. They want to send their children through school; they complain about doctor's fees; they inveigh against the traffic conditions; they get irate about enrolment tea money; they feel stressed because of the demands of urban living. Finally, they take it all in stride. Such is life, what can be done? They are thrown back upon themselves, upon their families, upon their small groups. There they should find comfort and solace. To confront the madness of 'the system' cannot possibly lead to a better life.

By its very nature, urban society tends to separate people, to set them apart from each other and, in the absence of ideologies that fit with the special conditions of the diverse collectivities, there is little that can bring people together as protestors, debaters, and action groups. The national ideology – which has been accepted, it seems, by most – homogenizes: it is thought to unite all the Thais, and therefore it does not offer any type of specific platform. To be openly critical of it is unwise and may have nasty consequences. But however much it may unite people and cancel their differences, for most it offers too little in terms of a personal identity. As a shared identity, it is fine; as a particular one, it is far too little.

Yet, identity, the quest for it, and the shaping of it, are important enough in individualizing urban anonymity, and people are offered quite a range of options. The most conspicuous is to choose befitting status symbols and lifestyles. The supply of these is virtually unlimited and yet, what people choose is often remarkably similar. With the vogue of the tie and the business suit, leisure wear has acquired a new importance, even if the lines department stores have on offer are almost identical with those in such venues the world over. And so it goes for all the gadgets money can buy. In short, consumer-oriented urban modernity supplies the articles with which a person can purchase himself a public identity that, most of the time, tells others rather precisely where to situate him or her in social space. Those in the bureaucracy and the army still have their uniforms and decorations with which to distinguish themselves. For many of them, as representatives of the royal polity, these differentiating and identity-affirming markers remain very important, and often Thailand still strikes the visitor as a nation in uniform. Yet, there are clear tendencies to finding more individual expressions of identity, away from the formal position a person holds. Thus, while older people feel comfortable in being their rank – *acharya*; doctor; elder sister – many among the young are shopping for the diverse symbols of youth culture in order to set themselves apart. They, and those yuppies eager for distinctive lifestyles, have tired of the formerly pervasive formalism. For those with spending money, the world has opened out widely.

Not everybody is satisfied with shaping their identity with the products on offer in a highly diversified global consumer market. They look for ethical and religious identities to fill the moral vacuity of economy-driven urban life. Some are attracted to the Santi Asoke sect. It emphasizes a 'Buddhist' style of life characterized by austerity, discipline, and a strong moral awareness. Such ideas, reminding of the so-called protestant ethic, fit with the entrepreneurial ethos of the ambitious members of the middle classes from which the sect appears to draw most of its adherents. Yet, its emphasis on frugality and strict ethical practice do not make it a mass movement. It found massive support, though, for its political expression, the Phalang Tham: The Force of Righteousness. This party was successful in drawing in the middle-class vote, representing all those aspiring to more transparency and honesty in politics. While this party is still partly identified with its moral platform, the pragmatism of business has taken over since; its constituency has diminished accordingly. Its evolution, though, highlights two things: the quest for a moral format in the alienating metropolitan environment, and the hope that there are moral solutions to worldly ills.

In terms of membership, the Thammakai sect is doing much better. It draws its members from all segments of the middle classes, and recruits particularly successfully among students. It distinguishes itself by its unusual temple compound to the north of Bangkok, its very disciplined rituals and appearances and, above all, its meditational practice that is thought to bring the dharmic inner body of the person to life. In this sense it combines discipline with a certain esoterism and exclusiveness: elements that define its very existence as sectarian.[5]

---

[5] About these developments in urban Buddhist expression, see Apinya Fuengfusakul, 'Empire of Crystal and Utopian Commune: Two Types of Contemporary Theravada Reform in Thailand'. *Sojourn* 8/1 (1993):153-83, and Peter A. Jackson, *Buddhism, Legitimation, and Conflict: The political functions of urban Thai Buddhism.* Singapore: Institute of Southeast Asian Studies, 1989.

Other people set on one charismatic monk or another, a *luang phô:* reputed for his preaching, meditation, age, sacred power, and most often, his talismans. These followers do not combine into organized groups, but are individually attracted, and feel that a touch of religion is helpful to sustain themselves through life. This *luang phô:* phenomenon, and the cult of amulets, have grown spectacularly since the late sixties, and highlight the continual importance of sources of sacred *saksit* power in Thai life. People seem to need it when surrounded by uncertainties, whether the old contingencies of nature or the modern uncertainties of a rapidly changing social order. It is not just the aged monks who attract the devotion of many. Compelling charisma may also be vested in relatively young preachers, such as *phra* Yantra, and the founders of the main reformist movements were all young when they started to attract attention. The field has not been well surveyed, but already in 1985, the Religious Affairs Department announced that the number of unauthorized religious centres had increased to 4,900,[6] which may be a good indicator of the viability of the religious phenomenon in a period of transformation.

Some people seem to seek a protective, prosperity-enhancing father figure, which they find in the worship of King Chulalongkorn. Others look for a benign mother whom they find in the Chinese boddhisatva-goddess Kuan Im (Kuan Yin). Both cults have been growing explosively in recent years, and many of the adepts report subsequent success in business. So, while Santi Asoke or Thammakai membership may be interpreted as a quest for moral identity in urban life, other people who put their trust in charismatic monks and other revived cult figures, may be differently motivated. What it all hints at, though, are individual-centred quests for moral stature, esoteric power, and protection that are devoid of social messages or programmes. Similar to consumer culture, current religious practices too seem to lead away from political and social issues. They emphasize moral or even crude particularism in facing an unsurveyable world.

---

6   Jackson, *Buddhism*: 180

This tendency away from active concern with the public interest weakens the vitality of the public discourse, marginalizes it in the teeth of economic growth and a technocratic, developmentalist state. The requirements of the latter fire the rat race, the scramble for diplomas, and the cult of money. These, in turn, individualize but do not furnish the individual with much moral guidance. In certain people this inspires some form of religious participation, but for the majority religious expressions are merely luck-enhancing. There is much colour in Thai life that derives from institutional Buddhism; its practice, though, has little to do with ultimate ends, and far more with success in the here and now.

It seems that the various factors that create and affect civil society combine into a middle-class culture that is in the main self-centred and rather apolitical. Urban individualism – everybody caring for his own affairs – overpowers tendencies to social reponsibility and commitment. The latter often surface in newspaper columns that take them as measuring rods to demonstrate that they are most often absent. While eulogizing occasional social activists – killed, or intimidated by the police – they observe the power of 'the system' that is driven by political expediency and the forces of the market. In other words, the state and the economy are not going to be overwhelmed by an assertive civil society anytime soon. In their interchanges, the three of them create a public discourse that opens vistas on the public world, and in the past few years, the paradigms proposed to dissect it have become more to the point than the steady stream of moralism that accompanies them. Yet, the fact that there is critical analysis – and that certain newspapers have begun to publish a fair amount of it – is not a good indicator of the influence of civil society. In parliamentary debate, one hears little of it. There politicians are critical of each other, and not constructive of society. There governmental desires for centralization still predominate the demands for democratization from below. Therefore, civil society seems to carry little weight in the places where it really matters, the state and politicians jealously controlling what they see as their empires.

Thus, if one would conclude from what one learns from the public discourse that politics is low in legitimacy in spite of the electoral process, one is definitely right. The instruments of state do not score high either, but they are accepted as unavoidable. This situation seems to stimulate resignation rather than activism, 'individualism' rather than social commitment, cynicism rather than optimism. The very rapid growth of educated middle classes has created people who have no tradition, no culture to fill their new social space. They are not familiar with the great social vistas of political ideologies, and these are largely absent from the current debates. They would need so much explaining as to pre-empt the possibility that they be understood and motivate. It is more attractive to stuff modern 'urbanity' with consumer culture, the quest for money and, for some, with sectarianism and cults. So, while a public discourse is undeniably there, public opinion still carries little political weight, and those who are keen and critical, such as the monk-scholar Prayut Payutto, 'Botan', Wimon Sainimnuan, academic and newspaper luminaries, do not really point a way out.

The changing tone of the public discourse

To begin the story of Thai public discourse in 1932 is arbitrary, and not even justifiable. Early in this century we find a well-publicized case of lèse-majesté that clearly indicates that ordinary people had begun to think publicly about their own, and the social, condition. In 1911, a coup had been planned by a military faction opposed to the near total concentration of power in the palace. In the tens and twenties, strikes were organized protesting the exploitation of labour. And even the sixth king himself tried to engender debate by way of a steady stream of publicly accessible comments on the issues of the day. What the coming to power of the People's Party indicates is, therefore, that an opinion producing civil society had come into existence which was influential enough to impose its will upon the ancien régime, to replace the old order.

Still, 1932 is an attractive date, because, apart from the coup, it is also the year in which Buddhadasa Bhikkhu founded his forest retreat at Chaiya. The ideals that motivated the emancipating civilians have been incisively described by Sri Burapha in his *Look Forward*. These ideas were cultivated and debated – then as now – as the symbol of the intellectual emancipation of the commoners, that is, at Thammasat University that was founded soon after the coming to power of the People's Party's dispensation. From then we can draw a direct line to Thammasat 1973, when the Tyrannical Trio was driven into exile, and Thammasat 1976, when reactionary forces came to power through massacring the students there.

In spite of the mostly army-dominated governments in the period running from 1932 into the seventies, military repression and state-sponsored nationalism could not prevent the continual arising of progressive opinion with which the marshals and their policies were measured. That opinion, like the democratic ideals that fired the People's Party's revolution, were basically optimistic. Society could be improved, it could be made a better place. Such ideas were not the monopoly of aspiring civilian politicians, such as Dr Pridi Phanomyong, but also motivated the actions of Marshals Phibun Songkram and Sarit Thanarat. Apart from the policy of state-run enterprises of the first, he also wanted to civilize Thai society by enforcing his cultural mandates.[7] Marshal Sarit was strongly convinced that Thailand needed to, and could, evolve into a modern, economically developed nation; he stimulated the country accordingly.

Whereas the marshals set on state-led change, in no contradiction with the early ideas of Dr Pridi, there was another current of equally optimistic ideas, to the effect that individuals could open out and develop themselves into self-responsible and socially committed people. This individual-centred message is, of course, at the heart of Buddhadasa Bhikkhu's rational Buddhism, and also surfaces in the social-critical novels of Sri Burapha and

---

7   Kobkua Suwannathat-Pian, *Thailand's Durable Premier: Phibun through Three Decades, 1932-1957*. Kuala Lumpur: Oxford University Press, 1995.

Seni Sawwaphong. Both of them wrote early works, set in Australia and France respectively, that are very much individual-centred. Persons can become aware of themselves and their place in society. When their self-awareness matures, they cannot but be motivated to help their fellow men. Needless to observe that these writings are coloured by a good deal of moralism, yet the emphasis on social commitment is what stands out, and what has motivated journalists and activists in the fifties. It landed many of them in jail or drove them into exile.

This progressive discourse is also reflected in the two great novels of those days. Sri Burapha's *Look Forward* took a historical perspective, tracing the ideas, the deceptions and disappointments in the discourse of the previous twenty years. In Seni Sawwaphong's *Evil Spirit*, the time frame has been less precisely set. Both novels deal, to an extent, with the position of the underdogs in Thai society, with the obstacles confronting them in their quest for a better life, such as the highly hierarchical organi-zation of society. Yet, both of their main protagonists profit from the patronage that this organization also entails. In that way, their heroes receive the education that frees them from poverty and that opens the possibility not only to advance themselves, but also to act as protectors of those they left behind in the countryside. Their message seems to be twofold: hierarchy compartmentalizes society, separating classes and alienating citizens from each other. If people only had equal chances for education, society would be-come morally enlightened and whole. It is the hero embodying the 'evil spirit' of change – as seen from the point of view of the upper class – who bridges the gaps between the groups, who breaches the lines of separation. He can do so because of his academic training and strong moral, idealistic consciousness.

These ideas clearly played their part, first, among the students of the 1950s, and flourished most openly during the years of open society, 1973-76. Then the books referred to were repeatedly printed. Buddhadasa-inspired ideas made the students organize a seminar, 'Operating on the Buddhist Religion', in which they, in parellel with the Young Monks Movement, targeted the fossilized, state-serving hierarchy of the Brotherhood of Buddhist Monks (*Sangha*). Society should be reformed, too, and socialist ideas inspired the analysis. The students went out into the countryside, preaching their messages of democracy and resistance to a bewildered rural audience. Their band, Caravan, with its 'songs for life', entertained themselves and elevated their public.

Irrespective of the reactions against dictatorship and an overdose of freedom that characterized the period, other things had been in the making, and began to foreshadow the public discourse we find today. Bangkok's skyline was notably rising from year to year. Apparently, economic development was having its effects, and not on the material environment only. It required lots and lots of trained and schooled people who were produced accordingly. These new people were not high on idealism and did not have clear political ideas. If anything at all, they believed in conservative moralism and the benefits of an expanding economy. Thus, they measured morally, and hoped for a career. Money, the possibility of having it, the mobility and individual freedom it provides, had begun to motivate people in town and countryside. Besides, money does not ask moral questions.

There was a clear turn in the tide of idealism. New religious alternatives presented themselves next to Buddhadasa's rationality. Both the Santi Asoke and the Thammakai movements began to emerge in the early 1970s. They are not modernist in the sense of believing in progress through intellectual effort but emphasize ethical conduct and esoteric meditation respectively. They retreat from the world as it is, whether in Santi Asoke's Buddha Land where they practise biological agriculture, or in the thirty-two hectares of the Thammakai temple compound – surrounded by a further three hundred hectares of real estate – where they celebrate their fellowship. They fit in with the times and the development of urban society; they make the individual important, while providing a collective yet exclusive identity that highlights morality and discipline.

The most successful author of the 1970s also reflects the spirit of the times. On the one hand, Bunchoke Ciamwiriya is as much a moralist as Sri Burapha, but on the other, he seems to be devoid of the social constructivist ideals that inspired the earlier authors. In his *The Revolutionary District Officer*, he describes the tribulations of a D.O. who has the interest of the people he has come to administer at heart. Apart from this noble motivation, he wants to be honest and straightforward too. Needless to say that such an official merely creates trouble for himself, and for his bosses, the mafia of the Interior Ministry in Bangkok. Persevering in his righteousness, the revolutionary D.O. finally leaves the civil service in disgust. It is of interest to note that this autobiographical novel has been the most successful piece of Thai fiction ever, and was sold in unprecedented editions. Obviously, it struck a chord among the public aware of living in a rotten, corrupt environment in which self-respect can only be maintained by personal moral integrity. This theme was further elaborated in the book's sequel, *Black Sky*, and the monumental *The Human Element*. The last title exposes the urban condition. People profit from each other, exploit each other, and just care for themselves regardless of the consequences for others. In brief, it describes life in the urban jungle, and does not offer a way out.

To be lived by the conditions of the city and the dictates of the economy grows to be the dominant experience of life from the late 1960s onwards, and has definitely matured during the 1980s. The economy spurs society ahead, and people enjoy their money. If they reflect on the urban experience, they may feel fine by expounding on the benefits of righteousness, and there is no shortage of recommendations to instate the American-style middle-class 'family values' as a solution to all sorts of ills and, of course, to fight AIDS. 'Tonight, go home early – be an exemplary father – the envy of the neighbours'. Yet, will such slogans have much effect? There is, of necessity, a new middle-class culture in the making – after all, these people are themselves new in their new positions, and although the western ideal of monogamy does not quite connect with older Thai ideas, it may well be that it is in line with the emerging situation in which people live in nuclear households. But whether such ideas will change practice?

Besides, how can one be an exemplary father if – even without a stop at the brothel – traffic conditions keep you on the road until bedtime? 'Botan' painted a glaring example of the vicissitudes of contemporary family life. The sacrifice of the parents notwithstanding, everything went awry. The author merely recorded this, and did not volunteer any solution. Yes, we need modern, self-responsible citizens. Where to find them? The urban jungle reproduces its own conditions, and the family is not going to benefit from them. The current urban divorce rate has already climbed to twenty-four out of every hundred. This 'modern' condition was also diagnosed by Wimon Sainimnuan, an exercise which he commended as a means to keep his own sanity in the madness of a society that has gone off the rails, that is beyond control and volition.

What we see at present is stock-taking and coping. Authors record the conditions they see, but have little to recommend in the way of improvements. At some universities, sociological analysis is coming of age. Again, the people concerned research and record, but have few recommendations. Some have concluded that the very boom is the problem, a position that in a way tallies with Wimon's view that so-called development forever keeps creating new problems. The solution to one question automatically raises the next; we keep running in a treadmill: everything moves fast, yet we are stuck in nowhere. Anyway, the new generation of critical minds – most of them well under the age of fifty – is coming to grips with the ways the country and society move. They are not blinkered by the moralism and nostalgia that hold the minds of most of the older generation – of social scientists as well – hostage. What we have arrived at is a rather businesslike analysis of a businesslike situation in which people are particularly critical of the practice of politics, yet also aware that the combination of power and greed defies the wisdom of morality. What needs to grow is the rationality that has begun to surface in the public discourse.

CONCLUSIONS

This study is about the modern Thai culture of the public world, and was guided by the question of how people – in the main a diversity of members of the ruling and middle classes – learn to think and actually debate about it. To answer our question, we surveyed the school curriculum concerning social studies; critical academic opinion; the reporting in the press; a few incisive novels; and an official introduction to Thai culture, society and economy. We looked at these sources in three ways: what did they say; what did they suppress or evade; and how did they do this: what was the tone of their presentations? In doing all this, we uncovered much information and many ideas that may be deemed peripheral to our main quest for the culture of the public world, but that yet presented us with a wealth of insights. What we excluded from our considerations, in spite of their prominence in dressing up the public world, were the consumption-oriented pursuits that colour modern life, such as sports, television, foods, fashions, museums, video and film, just to mention a few. We concentrated on opinion making, on the public discourse, in their stead.

Opinion about public education, the school system, its accessibility, may be expected to be an important subject of debate everywhere. It is one of the tasks taken out of the hands of parents who naturally worry about their wards, and their subsequent school careers. At the hands of the state, formal education has become an ever-expanding enterprise that involves a considerable proportion of the population at any moment. In this study we traced part of the school trajectory children are to follow, and came to certain conclusions that sometimes play their part in the exchanges about education, but that are definitely not prominent. As long as the elite can send their offspring to special schools, the subject of the quality of education does not stand out in the debates. Still, it may be important to make a few observations about it.

Going by the newspaper, the discussion focuses on the accessibility of schools. This means three things: enrolment fees, entrance examinations, and distance, or travel time. Schools that suddenly threaten to close, the tea money to get admitted, teachers' salaries, and other financial issues involved – after all, the provision of education is also business – often stand out in the discussions. This is not so because the giving of tea money is illegal. Money freely given to enhance the quality of the school or just to support it, similar to indulgences given out of compassion to helpful civil servants, are perfectly above the board. But sometimes money has been invested, and yet the child is not admitted, or the school closes, or more money is demanded and then, of course, the parents raise the hue and cry. In terms of examinations, we may note occasional commentary on the excessive pressures placed on school children; especially in the aftermath of a spectacular suicide, such comments keep recurring. Distance and travel time, as much as the traffic itself, and zoning measures to reduce the distances students travel, constitute evergreen topics too.

The observations about the quality of school education are most often alluded to by bold negative statements, and the comforting information that the department concerned is drafting plans. The ministry recognizes that there is need for change. In the press, I have seen little more than good intentions, and since the curriculum we reviewed has been revised recently, I doubt the boldness of any changes that will be introduced in the near future. Formal education goes its own soporific way, and particularly social studies are far from inspiring. Yet, as we have seen, seventy-five percent of elementary school time is devoted to social subjects. It teaches moralism, manners and nationalism, next to some handiwork, cooking and first-aid skills, high level physics, gymnastics, dancing, and suchlike, or rather, such unlike. That it is a highly original mix, nobody will dispute. But what does it lead to? Is the time well spent?

Elementary school teaches how to be a good subject, 'a child the nation desires'. This means that it suppresses initiative, self-responsibility, and individual maturation. I fear that 'Botan' is right: it stunts personal growth. The stress is on rote learning, drilled in through repetition; on discipline, and thus obedience; on cramming, not on understanding. I think such teaching kills curiosity and initiative. Thailand, Thai history, being Thai, they become lists of overrepeated points of information that suffocate historical consciousness, interest in public affairs, and the social imagination. The senses are dulled rather than activated. Again, it is just my opinion, but I think that such teaching is a waste of time, that it does not train for life in urban modernity, and that it is years and years out of date. The teaching of subjectship, morals and manners, and the like, should require some ten percent of the hours available; then, the rest of the time could be spent in a more stimulating manner. Yet, to implement such a vision, even if the responsible bureau would conceive of it, will immediately reveal some serious bottlenecks. It is not just a matter of curriculum and textbooks. The very rapid expansion of education has resulted in the hasty training of rather poorly qualified teachers; in very crowded classrooms (fifty to sixty pupils); in authoritarian school leadership that suppresses the initiatives of teachers; in cramming and the quest for diplomas, rather than in the opening out of individual students.

One could, therefore, surmise that there is enough to opine about, and that there are plenty of problems awaiting a solution. Yet, these subjects do not seem to strike a chord with the public in general that still needs to wake up to the dysfunctionality of current educational practice. Expanding the years of compulsory education from six to nine does, in itself, not solve any problem, as long as elementary is so wasteful of the talents of its students. To a large extent, such an expansion merely means more of the same, at least as far as the social subjects and the exercise of curiosity and initiative go. It results in a general sphere of intellectual placidity, in taking things for granted that had better be taken for urgent problems. It contributes to the often noted absence of critical self-knowledge, privately and nationally.

It is of interest to digress on this subject while, at the same time, still trying to integrate it with the confusing treatment of the social subject matter students are exposed to at high school. The continual emphasis on morality results in an antisociology; it highlights individual role and obligations, thus setting individuals apart from each other while treating their value-oriented, or value-driven actions as causes of social order – or disorder. Poor people are poor because they hold the wrong values; diligence will overcome all obstacles; yet, socially beneficial action is contingent on education. If the poor would be educated, they would know how to act righteously, and all social problems will vanish.

What such a moralistic view does not bring into focus is the very substance of the social sciences. These are about people living together, the basic unit of interest thus becoming relationships. Relationship, like society or economy, is, of course, highly abstract: one can think it, but can't actually see it. You can draw inferences from observable behaviour about the quality of relationships, but you cannot just evaluate them as 'good' or 'not good', as it is done with individual action. Relationships are about interaction, ranging from intimate face-to-face transactions to those that are as distant as writing a cheque to a foundation for the blind. Anyway, the individual-centred ethical view does not bring such relationships into focus, and thus does not qualify as a social-scientific approach to society.

The persistent moral evaluation of things social hides the socio-cultural process, and results in simplistic blether. At school, society is seen as a community that equates with nation and state, stressing 'harmony' and 'adaptation' while never mentioning conflicting interests. The idea of culture is always substantiated as beautiful customs-culture-and-traditions, and thus Loy Krathong is in, visiting brothels – not beautiful – out. Religion is about ethics, and not a reflection of the quest for power, protection, and blessing. Politics cum government – and law – serve an orderly, peaceful, and contented society, and not the competition for authority, prestige, privilege, and economic or natural resources. Monks provide the field-of-merit, not the amulets, predictions and scandals.

Such one-sidedness makes it very difficult to obtain a good focus on things Thai, and although most people will realize that an analysis like Wimon Sainimnuan's is possible, being recognizable, they will shy away from declaring such a reality to be eminently Thai, an outcome of the rapid transition from 'community' to 'society' that yet remains informed by many basics that are firmly rooted in a former Thai situation. Perhaps that people find the quest for roots in an urban environment that hurries towards the future, irrelevant. Why would the Sino-Thai population of the metropolis be interested in their Thainess? Still, it is exponents of that group who tend to be the most serious in questing for the – often idealized – meaning of being Thai, or Buddhist, at the same time that they acknowledge that curiosity and intellectual vigour is not a shared tradition.

Common are authoritarian and bureaucratic ways; an admiration for western civilization; an insularity that is not accustomed to compare oneself to 'the other'; the ideology of the Three Institutions that freezes thought about the social edifice; the newness of the urban way of life and the absence of older middle-class lifestyles to pattern the own existence; and, importantly, the underdevelopment of the public discourse. If the latter would start to flourish in the years to come, self-knowledge and a linking of the future to the past might become possible. Who knows?

Listening to the critical voices in the public discourse – novelists, academics, editors – we cannot escape from a prevailing atmosphere of unsatisfactoriness. Is Thai society on the right track? Is it developing in a desirable direction? This is not the place to summarize social problems or to make an inventory of obstacles. These things have been presented unequivocably in the main body of the text. What is relevant to this conclusion, though, is to briefly reflect upon the basic problem that seems to underlie questions about Thailand's course. It is the problem of the legitimacy of power, or rather, its exercise. Are the people who take decisions representative of anybody except for their faction, their clique, or themselves? What sort of responsibility do they carry for the public interest? And then, what is the public interest?

In the Thai polity, we found a two-tiered system of power. The power of the king is sacred and inviolable, and so it should be in a benevolent constitutional democracy of which the king is the head. We argued that this widely accepted royal power takes the spotlight off the civilian politicians and the instruments of state. This enhances the freedom of movement of the latter two. Yet, they cannot escape from the scrutiny of the public, and the legitimacy of their exercise of power is increasingly questioned. This is an inherent part of the struggle with democracy. Officially the politicians derive their mandate from 'the people' whose votes brought them to power – but do they represent their constituencies in any way? Provincial representatives may channel pork barrel funds to their districts, but there it seems to stop. To be a member of parliament, and even more, to be in the cabinet seems to entitle one to privileges first of all, which set these honourable gentlemen very much apart from 'the people'. They may – and do – act as patrons to some, and further exploit their power by seeking personal benefit. In the discourse, they are frequently presented as the new khunna:ng, the new grandees who use their position 'to squeeze the people while hiding this practice from the king'. The monarch, being above it all, is seen as moral; his henchmen are seen as ruthless, authoritarian and arbitrary. It is they who define the public interest. They call it national development.

This situation is reflected in parliamentary representation, and in the underdevelopment of the public discourse. The interests of groups of people at large are not represented. While two thirds of the people depend on agriculture and dwell in the countryside, the

MPs they vote into Bangkok do not represent farmers' interests. They are businesspeople and entrepreneurs representing themselves. If the voice of villagers is heard, it is normally through people who worry in town and who project themselves as their spokesmen. Similar observations can be made about the absence of labour interests from the debates, or of women, minority groups, and so on. Occasional champions of the supposed causes make themselves heard in the public discussion, but is such advocacy representative? Let alone, do the people concerned represent themselves?

The public discourse far from articulates the diversity of the voices of the public at large. The public world is still the domain of a small minority of educated and/or influential people. Participation in it is limited. Besides, a vast part of it is dominated by the culture of consumption, leisure time activities, lifestyles, and other preoccupations that have grown in pace with urbanization. While highly informed and informative debate is going on in the public world, it really occupies a small segment only. Its political relevance is small, although it turns some politicians defensive and authoritarian.

The state still holds the advantage in the production of images in the minds of people. The intrusion of the economy, by way of commercialism, careerism, and the fascination with filthy lucre, may crowd out the moralistic images the state propagates, and replace them by the imagery of a business and market-oriented society. In such a society, folklorized identity images, such as school and the National Identity Office produce, certainly have their place: these are commodities, like any other, with some symbolic value and no moral or intellectual content. Still, if compared with a mainly state-dominated, almost premodern public world, such as in Burma or Indonesia, the growth of the social discourse in Thailand has been vigorous and astonishing to somebody who knows the country since the mid-sixties when marshals, Americans, and anti-communism held their sway. As the discourse matures, it is to be hoped that more and more people want, and get the chance, to participate in it. At this moment such participatory interest is still too much the affair of some highly educated people in critical discussion with representatives of the dominant interests of the economy and state. What is needed is the growth of a more diversified, actively committed civil society if the country is not just to be run by its versatile economy.

REFERENCES

Books in English

Bourdieu, P. and J. C. Passeron, *Reproduction in Education, Society and Culture*. London, etc.: Sage Publications, 1977.

Habermas, Jürgen, *The Structural Transformation of the Public Sphere: An Inquiry into a Category of Bourgeois Society*. Cambridge, Mass.: MIT Press, 1989 (German original 1962).

Haas, Mary R. *Thai-English Student's Dictionary*. London: Oxford University Press, 1964.

Geertz, Clifford, *Negara: The Theatre State in Nineteenth-century Bali*. Princeton: Princeton University Press, 1980.

Girling, John L.S., *Thailand: Society and Politics*. Ithaca: Cornell University Press, 1981.

Jackson, Peter A. *Buddhism, Legitimation, and Conflict: The Political Functions of Urban Thai Buddhism*. Singapore: Institute of Southeast Asian Studies, 1989.

Kobkua Suwannathat-Pian, *Thailand's Durable Premier: Phibun through Three Decades, 1932-1957*. Kuala Lumpur: Oxford University Press, 1995.

Mulder, Niels. *Inside Thai Society: Interpretations of Everyday Life*. Bangkok: Editions Duang Kamol, 1994 (4th revised edition). Amsterdam: The Pepin Press, 1996 (5th revised and updated edition).

Mulder, Niels. *Inside Southeast Asia: Religion. Everyday Life. Cultural Change*. Amsterdam: The Pepin Press, 1996 (second revised and expanded edition).

National Identity Office of the Prime Minister, *Thailand in the 90s*. Bangkok: 1991.

Pasuk Phongpaichit and Sungsidh Piriyarangsan, *Corruption and Democracy in Thailand*, Bangkok: The Political Economy Centre of the Faculty of Economics of Chulalongkorn University, 1994. Chiang Mai: Silkworm Books, 1997.

342

Pasuk Phongpaichit and Chris Baker, *Thailand's Boom!* Chiang Mai: Silkworm Books, 1996.

Phillips, Herbert P. *Thai Peasant Personality: The Patterning of Interpersonal Behavior in the Village of Bang Chan.* Berkeley and Los Angeles: University of California Press, 1965.

Riggs, Fred W. *Thailand: The Modernization of a Bureaucratic Polity.* Honolulu: East-West Center Press, 1966.

Thak Chaloemtiarana, *Thailand: The Politics of Despotic Paternalism.* Bangkok: Thai Khadi Institute, 1979.

Thongchai Winichakul, *Siam Mapped.* Honolulu: University Press of Hawaii, 1994. Chiang Mai: Silkworm Books, 1995.

Books in Thai

'Botan', *Maidat (Stunted).* Bangkok: Chomromdek Publishing House, 1990.

'Botan', *Yüa (Victims).* Bangkok: Chomromdek Publishing House, 1991.

Buddhadasa Bhikkhu, *Khwa:mlongphit khô:ng sangkhom nai rüang ka:nthambun (The Misguidedness of the People Concerning Merit Making).* Bangkok: Organization for the Revival of the Buddhist Religion, 1973.

Bunsong Cirawut *et al., Cariyasüksa: (Ethics).* Bangkok: Watthana Phanich (Book 5 (1991)).

Duean Khamdee, Nuek Thongmeephet, *Sô: 606 Sangkhomsüksa: (Social Studies 606).* Bangkok: Watthana Panich, 1993.

Educational Technique Bureau, Department of Education, *Nangsü:rian sa:ngsoem prasopka:nchi:wit (Studybook Preparing for the Experience of Life).* Bangkok: Book Development Centre of the Educational Technique Bureau of the Department of Education. (Books *1* (1991), *2* (1991), *3* (1991), *4* (1978), *5* (1978)).

Educational Technique Bureau, Department of Education, *Nangsü:rian sa:ngsoem prasopka:nchi:wit (Studybook Preparing for the Experience of Life).* Bangkok: Sales Organization of the Khurusapha. (Books 6. *Muat sukkhapha:p ka:i lae cit (Section Physical and Mental Health*, 1992), 6. *Muat manut kap singwae:tlô:m (Section People and Environment*, 1992), 6. *Muat ba:nmüang khô:ng raw lae prathe:tphüanba:n (Section Our Country and Its Neighbours*, 1991), 6. *Muat setthakit lae ka:nthamma:ha:kin (Section Economy and Work*, 1993).

Educational Technique Department, Ministry of Education, *Nangsü:rian sangkhomsüksa: prathe:t khô:ng raw (Social Studies Textbook Our Country)* 1, 2, 3, 4. Bangkok: Khurusapha. Books *101* (1992), *102* (1992), *204* (1992), *306* (1993).

Kanika Lekbunyasin (ed), *Bot a:n wicha: sangkhom lae: watthanatham thai (Reader on the Subject of Thai Society and Culture)*. Chiangmai University: Faculty of Humanities, 1991.

Saci Suthat na Ayutthaya *et al.*, *Klum ka:nnga:n lae phü:ntha:n a:chi:p (Grouping Concerning the Basics of Work and Profession)*. Bangkok: Khurusapha. (Book 4 (1991), 6 (1991)).

Sanguan Ongsikun *et al.*, *Klum ka:nnga:n lae phü:ntha:n a:chi:p (Grouping Concerning the Basics of Work and Profession)*. Bangkok: Khurusapha. (Book 2 (1990)).

Sukhum Nualsakul, Dr Preecha Suwannathat, *Sô: 402 Sangkhomsüksa: (Social Studies 402)*. Bangkok: Watthana Panich, 1991.

Thaemsuk Numnont *et al.*, *Sô: 605 Sangkhomsüksa: (Social Studies 605)*. Bangkok: Watthana Panich, 1993.

Watchara Khlainathorn, Phenkhae Kittisak, Tueanchai Ketusa, *Sô: 401 Sangkhomsüksa: (Social Studies 401)*. Bangkok: Watthana Panich, 1991.

Wô: Winitchaikun, *Se:thi: mai (The Upstart)*. Bangkok: Watsatree, 1990.

Wimon Sainimnuan, *Kho:kphrana:ng (The Subdistrict)*. Bangkok: Tonôô Co. Ltd., 1990.

Wimon Sainimnuan, *Khon song caw (The Medium)*. Bangkok: Tonôô Co. Ltd., 1988.

Articles in English

Anderson, Benedict R. O'G., "Studies of the Thai State: The State of Thai Studies". In Eliezer B. Ayal (ed), *The Study of Thailand*. Athens, Ohio: Ohio University, Center for International Studies, 1978, pp. 193-247.

Apinya Fuengfusakul, 'Empire of Crystal and Utopian Commune: Two Types of Contemporary Theravada Reform in Thailand'. *Sojourn* 8/1 (1993):153-83.

Appadurai, Arjun and Carol A. Breckenridge, "Public Modernity in India". In Breckenridge, Carol A. (ed), *Consuming Modernity: Public Culture in a South Asian World*. Minneapolis/London: University of Minnesota Press, 1995, pp. 1-20.

Interview

Interview with Phrathammapidok (Pô:ô: Payutto), The Light of Wisdom ... Prayut Payutto. *Dô:kbia ka:nmüang (The Politics Interest)* 242 (January 7-13, 2539): 4-12.

INDEX OF NAMES

SUBJECT INDEX

GLOSSARY OF TERMS OF ADDRESS

acharya   pronounced as *a:ca:n*. Term of address for headmasters, high school and university teachers, and possibly for anybody else who is thought to hold some special knowledge.

bhikkhu   a priest, a monk. (N.B. Members of the *Sangha*, the Buddhist Brotherhood of 'Monks', can neither be classified as 'priests' nor as 'monks' in the western sense.)

caw mae: 'ruler-mother' = female spirit/seat of power.

caw phô: 'ruler-father' = male spirit/seat of power.

farang   term referring to white-skinned foreigner; Westerner.

khun   polite term of address; Mr., Ms, or Mrs.

luang phô: 'venerable father' = elder priest/monk credited with charisma. Normally these *ô:ng*, holy objects or subjects, spent their whole adult life in the monkhood.

maha: priest/monk holding a degree of learning in Pali, the sacred language of Theravada Buddhism.

352

phra priest/monk; king; holy object.

phu:yai 'big person' = superior; leader; influential person. Also: adult.

thawkae: a rich Chinese; the owner, the boss.